The Nick of Time

By George Alec Effinger

DEATH IN FLORENCE (Utopia 3)
DIRTY TRICKS
FELICIA
HEROICS
IDLE PLEASURES
IRRATIONAL NUMBERS
MIXED FEELINGS
THE NICK OF TIME
NIGHTMARE BLUE (with Gardner Dozois)
RELATIVES
THOSE GENTLE VOICES
WHAT ENTROPY MEANS TO ME
THE WOLVES OF MEMORY

The Nick of Time

GEORGE ALEC EFFINGER

DOUBLEDAY & COMPANY, INC.

GARDEN CITY, NEW YORK

1985

Part One, "The World of Pez Pavilion: Preliminary to the Groundbreaking Ceremony,"
first appeared in *The Magazine of Fantasy and Science Fiction,* copyright © 1983 by Mercury Publications.

Library of Congress Cataloging in Publication Data

Effinger, George Alec.
The nick of time.

I. Title.
PS3555.F4N5   1985   813'.54
ISBN: 0-385-19641-5
Library of Congress Catalog Card Number

First Edition

For Debbie

Things are more like they are now than they ever were before.
DWIGHT D. EISENHOWER

Time is an illusion perpetrated by the manufacturers of space.
NOBODY

Book One

The World of Pez Pavilion: Preliminary to the Groundbreaking Ceremony

Day One

Just at noon on the seventeenth of February, 1996, Frank Mihalik became the first person to travel backward through time. He looked like an explorer and he spoke like a pioneer. He was tall and broad-shouldered and well-muscled, with a deep chest covered with the right amount of dark hair—virile but not atavistic—with large strong hands but the gentle manner of a man who has made a gracious peace with the powerful body nature had given him. He had short dark hair and bright unyielding eyes. His face was rugged and handsome, but not pretty and definitely not cute. He spoke in a low earnest voice and smiled often. He was intelligent but not tedious, a good friend in times of happiness or sorrow, a joy to his aging mother, a solid citizen, and a good credit risk. He had been chosen to make the first trip into the past because Cheryl, his girl friend, had roomed at college with a woman who was now a talent coordinator on a popular late-night holovision talk show. Such a woman had a lot of influence in the last years of the twentieth century.

The journey—or, at least, Mihalik's departure—was broadcast live all over the world. People in every nation on Earth saw Mihalik step from the silver van where he'd eaten breakfast and gone through his final briefing. Accompanied by the brooding brilliant director of the project, Dr. Bertram Waters, Cheryl, and Ray, Mihalik's backup man, the volunteer walked the last fifty yards to the embarkation stage. At the foot of the steps leading up to the stage itself, Mihalik shook hands with Dr. Waters and Ray. He hugged Cheryl and kissed her, fondly but not passionately; this was a moment for emotional control and steadiness. Mihalik went up the steps and sat in the folding chair that had been placed at the target point. He waited while the voice of the project's control counted down the seconds. At T minus zero there was a flicker of amber light, a sizzle, a snap, and a moderate clap of thunder. Mihalik was gone. He had plummeted into the past.

He was now sitting in a darkened room. He knew immediately that it was no longer 1996. He wondered where he was—rather, *when* he was. He would still be in New York City, of course. He stood up, a crooked smile on his handsome face. He ran a hand through his mildly rumpled hair, made sure his fly was zipped, and felt his way across the room toward a door that leaked a thin line of light at the bottom.

Outside it was summer. In 1996 it had been February, cold and bleak; here it was warm and bright, the sky partly cloudy, the temperature in the mid-eighties, the humidity somewhere around 40 percent. There was a large crowd of people outside, and they were wandering from one building to another; it seemed to Mihalik that he was in some kind of exhibition. The people carried maps, and the parents among them struggled to control their small children, all of whom wanted to run off in directions other than straight ahead. Mihalik walked close to a young couple with a baby in a stroller. He looked at the book the man was carrying: *Official Guide Book—New York World's Fair 1939, For Peace and Freedom.*

The building Mihalik came out of was the Hall of Industry and Metals. He walked along the avenue, marveling at the past and the peace and quiet and brotherhood and Christian fellowship everyone showed toward his or her neighbors. There were no fights on the sidewalk. There were no vagrants, no troublemakers, no drug dealers or prostitutes. There were only happy families and corporate exhibits. This was the golden past, an era of innocent bliss, of concern for the rights of individuals and respect for private property. Mihalik was grateful for the opportunity to escape the mad world of 1996 to spend a little time in this more humane place. He would return to the present refreshed, and he would be able to help his own world identify the essential problems that created jealousy and mistrust among people. Mihalik was not unaware of the weight of responsibility he carried; he had been charged with the duty of returning to 1996 with some token of what society had lost in the intervening sixty years.

Mihalik walked toward a great white needle and a great white globe. He had seen pictures of these structures: the Trylon and Perisphere. They were located at the Fair's Theme Center, and Mihalik had a feeling they represented something important. His first task, as he began to orient himself in the world of 1939, was to find out just what these two imposing symbols meant to the people of his grandparents' generation. He stopped a young woman and spoke to her; she looked at his unusual costume—he was wearing the thin, olive green one-piece garment of 1996 —and assumed he was one of the Fair's employees. "What do these marvelous buildings mean to you?" he asked.

"The Trylon?" she said. "The Trylon is a symbol of man's upward yearnings, pointing into the sky where dwell all hope and ambitions."

"That's just what I was thinking," said Mihalik.

"And the Perisphere, well, the Perisphere is the promise of Democracity, you know."

"Democracity?" asked Mihalik.

"You walk into that big bowl and spread out before you is a model of the city of the future. Have you ever seen a city of the future?"

"Yes," said Mihalik, "on numerous occasions."

"Most cities of the future are too conservative, I feel," said the young woman. "We need monorails. We need aerial bridges linking cloud-piercing office buildings and apartment towers. We need parks where slums now blight the boroughs. We need fourteen-lane highways that parallel new sparkling waterways. We need shopping and recreation centers where citizens may spend their newly won leisure and newly earned wealth. We need bright, airy schools where young minds may learn to value the gift of life that has been given them. All this lies within the Perisphere—a dream of times to come, a vision of the New York City that will exist in our childrens' lifetime in this place. The Perisphere is a ringing challenge, a concretalization of our hope and ambitions as symbolized by the Trylon, drawn down to earth and made manifest for our inspection. It is a kind of miracle."

"I can't wait to see it," said Mihalik.

"Yeah, but there's this huge line all the time," she said. "You got to be ready to wait. I hate lines, don't you? You'd be better off seeing something else."

"What would you suggest?"

The young woman thought for a moment. "Have you seen the Monkey Mountain in Frank Buck's Jungleland?"

"No," said Mihalik, "I just got here."

"I love to watch monkeys," said the young woman. "Well, enjoy yourself." She waved goodbye.

"Thank you," he said. He decided to see Democracity another time. He wanted to look at the other buildings, the exhibitions, and the beautiful, quaint Art Deco architecture of this harmless island in the past. The buildings themselves reminded him of something: their graceful curved lines where, in 1996, they would instead have had sharp forbidding edges; their naive pride in proclaiming which company or nation had erected them; their clean accents in glass, brick, and stainless steel. After a moment he knew what they made him think of—it was the colors, the pastel pinks and pale greens. They were the same colors as the little candy hearts he used to see on Valentine's Day, the ones with the clever little slogans. *Oh Baby* and *Kiss Me* and *You Doll* and *2 Much.* The candy colors contributed to the feeling of childlike innocence Mihalik felt. It made no difference that the buildings celebrated the very things that turned this wonderful world into the anxiety-ridden bankrupt ruin of 1996.

He walked toward the Lagoon of Nations. It was heartwarming to see

families enjoying their outing together. That sort of thing was rare in
Mihalik's time. Here in 1939, mothers and fathers still protected their
children from the evils of the world, instead of just throwing up their
hands in futile despair. Here there were parents who wanted the best for
the young ones, who still thought it was valuable to show the children
new things, educational things, sights and sounds and experiences that let
the boys and girls grow up feeling that they participated in an exciting,
vibrant world. Mihalik wished that his parents had been more like that.
He wondered, then, where his parents were; in 1939, he realized, his
mother had not even been born. His father was a boy of two, running
around in a darling little sailor suit somewhere in Elkhart, Indiana.
Mihalik was sorry that he had only a few hours to spend in the past; he
would have been curious to visit his grandparents. That was only one of
the interesting things he could do in 1939.

Adventures in Yesterdayland

Mihalik looked at his watch; it was eleven o'clock. He sat on a bench
along Constitution Mall, under the cold stone eyes of the giant statue of
George Washington. There was a newspaper on the bench. Mihalik paged
through the paper happily, laughing aloud at the simple views people had
of the world in this day. He expected to be astounded by the prices in the
advertisements, and he was: linen suits went for $8.25 or two for $16, a
beef roast was $0.17 a pound. They didn't have linen suits or beef roasts
in 1996. But Mihalik had been prepared for this. He had been briefed, he
had been carefully indoctrinated by technicians and specialists so that
whatever era he ended up in, he wouldn't be stunned into inactivity by
such things as the price of a beef roast. So Mihalik was not paralyzed by
temporal shock. He found that he could still turn the pages of the newspaper. On the sports page he read that both the Dodgers and the Giants
had lost, but that the Yankees had crushed the Browns 14–1 on Bill
Dickey's three home runs. He didn't have any idea what any of that
meant.

"Hello," said a man in a tan suit. He looked like he never got any sun;
Mihalik thought the man's face was the unhealthy color of white chocolate Easter bunnies. The man took a seat on the bench.

"Hello," said Mihalik.

"I'm from out of town. I'm from South Bend, Indiana." Mihalik recalled that Indiana had been one of the fifty-two "states" that had once
composed the United States. "You're probably wondering why I'm not
over at the Court of Sport," said the resident of 1939.

"Yes," said Mihalik, "that's just what I was thinking."

"Because they're raising the blue and gold standard of the University of Notre Dame over there, right this minute. But I said to myself, 'Roman,' I said, 'why travel all this way by train and come to this wonderful Fair, just to see them raise a flag and give some speeches?' "

"I know exactly what you mean. I came a long way, too, and I'm trying to decide what to see first."

"I'm looking forward to seeing the girls in the Aquacade."

Mihalik looked at his watch. He didn't know how long he would have in the past, and he thought he could spend the time more profitably examining all the fascinating little things that contributed to the peace and plenty and harmony he saw all about him. "Someone recommended the monkeys in Frank Buck's Jungleland," he said.

The man from Indiana seemed angry. "I didn't come all this way to see monkeys," he said. He stood up and walked away.

"No," thought Mihalik, "you came all this way to see shameless women." He glanced through the newspaper a little further. In the comics, Dixie Dugan was wondering about a handsome stranger who was coming into the Wishing Well Tea Shoppe every day. An article informed him that in Berlin the Germans were having practice air raid drills because, as a German spokesman said, the fact is that air attack in modern times is not beyond the range of possibility. Mihalik recalled that the Second World War was due to start any time now, so the Germans were laughing up their sleeves at the rest of the world. And the United States had revoked its trade agreement with Japan because of Japan's conduct in China, and in a few months there would be an embargo on raw materials.

Yet all around him, Mihalik saw happy people enjoying the summer morning, crushing the carnations along Constitution Mall, dropping paper cups on the sidewalk, littering George Washington's feet with mustard-covered paper napkins. Could they not see how international events were building toward the great cataclysm that would lead inexorably to the terrifying world of 1996? Would he have to grab them all, one by one, and scream into their faces, "Behold, how the world rushes headlong to its doom!" Would they listen? No, admitted Mihalik, not with the Yankees so comfortably in first place. To these people, everything was right with the world. Everything seemed normal. They had no idea that they were the architects of the future, each of them individually, and that their attendance here at the World's Fair was part of the reason their descendants fifty-seven years hence were suffering. "Enjoy it while you can," murmured Mihalik bitterly.

Further up Constitution Mall were four statues, four white figures in the overstated, heroic manner that Mihalik always associated with totalitarian governments. "I must be wrong," he thought. "These statues were put here to celebrate the best aspects of the American Way, as it was understood decades before my birth, during one of the great ages of the ascendancy of the United States." The statues represented the Four Freedoms. There was a half-naked woman looking up, depicting Freedom of Religion. There was a half-naked woman gesturing vaguely, illustrating Freedom of Assembly. A third half-naked woman with a pencil and notepad took care of Freedom of the Press. And a partially draped man with his hand upraised somehow conveyed the notion of Freedom of Speech. The statues were white; everything along Constitution Mall was white: the Trylon and Perisphere, the flowers, the statues, all the way to the Lagoon of Nations. Things in other areas were color-coded: each building in a particular section of the Fair was the same color, but the farther away from the Theme Center it was, the deeper the shade. It was not long before Mihalik learned to find his way around the complex of streets and walkways.

About noon he realized that he was very hungry. "They ought to have sent some provisions with me," he thought. For the first time, he felt that the scientists who planned his journey into the past had overlooked some important details. They had failed to foresee all the difficulties he might encounter. For instance, he had no money. There were hamburgers and popcorn and cotton candy and Cokes all around him, but Mihalik was helpless to get anything to eat. He watched sadly as little children dropped large globs of ice cream on the sidewalk. "What a waste," he said to himself. "That could feed a family of six Dutch refugees in 1996." It also could have fed him. He sat on another bench and tried to devise a way of getting something to eat. He didn't know if he would have to spend an hour in the past or a day or a week. He had had a good breakfast in the silver van, but now it was lunchtime.

"Tired?" said a man who sat next to him on the bench. Mihalik made a mental note to report on the friendliness of the people of the past. They all seemed eager to share his views and listen to his opinions. That was very rare in 1996.

"Yes," said Mihalik. "I've been walking all morning, and I've just discovered that I have no money."

"You've been robbed? A pickpocket?" The man seemed outraged.

"I guess so," said Mihalik.

The man looked at Mihalik's green jumpsuit. "Where did you keep your wallet?" he asked.

"My wallet?"

"You don't have any pockets."

"Well," said Mihalik lamely, "I carried my money in my hand."

"Uh huh," said the man dubiously. "Do you still have the stub from your ticket?"

"Yeah," said Mihalik, "it's right here. Oh, my God! The thief must have stolen that, too!"

"Sure, pal. I'm a detective, and I think I ought to take you—"

Mihalik got up and ran. He didn't look back; he was big and strong and fast, and he knew that he could outdistance the detective. Mihalik ran to the right, into the Heinz Dome. He looked around briefly, but what interested him the most were the samples of all the Heinz products they were giving away free. He went back to each again and again until the employees of the Dome began whispering among themselves. Mihalik took that as a cue to leave, and he walked out of the building. Several spoonsful of relish and catsup had done little for his hunger, but he did have a nice plastic souvenir, a pin in the shape of a pickle. On the top of the Dome was a statue of the Goddess of Perfection. Mihalik was not aware that there *was* a goddess of perfection, in anyone's pantheon; it was just something else that had been forgotten on the way to the end of the century.

He checked his watch again, and he found that it had stopped at 1:07. The sky was becoming darker; the newspaper had mentioned a great drought the city had suffered for more than a month. It looked like this afternoon there would be some relief. "Just my kind of luck," he thought. But there would be plenty of interesting things he could see while he waited for the rain to pass.

The first heavy drops fell just as he left the Washington State Exhibit. The rain fell with flat spatting sounds on the concrete paths. Mihalik looked around quickly, then ducked into the Belgian Pavilion. He saw more films and exhibits of things that would soon become extinct. He wondered how horrified these people would be if they knew how tenuous their existence was, how little time was left for their world, for the things they so took for granted. A Belgian girl was working away in poor light, making lace. What place was there in 1996 for lace, or for Belgian girls either, for that matter? Both had virtually ceased to exist. Yet Mihalik dared not pass that information on to these people: they very definitely were not world leaders, not even stars of stage and screen who would have some influence over world opinion.

In one part of the Belgian Pavilion there were diamonds from the Congo, which at this time was still a Belgian colony. There was a copy of a statue of King Albert made of diamonds. It looked foolish to Mihalik, but the diamonds made him think of rock candy, the kind he used to eat when he was young, with the little piece of string inside that always stuck between his teeth. There were many diamonds and other precious gems; Mihalik wished that he had just one to buy a hot dog with.

The day passed quickly. Mihalik wondered what he ought to do. He knew that it was very expensive to keep him in the past; he was surprised that he hadn't been brought back already. He didn't think he could learn much more at the Fair: the really interesting exhibits charged admission, and he didn't have a single penny. And he might as well not even bother going over to the amusement section. It didn't make any difference where he was when the technicians recalled him; he didn't have to be in the same place he started from. But he hadn't completely answered the questions the great thinkers of the future wanted solved. "I've been here since about ten o'clock this morning," he thought. "It's now after nine o'clock. Maybe they're going to go for a full twelve hours." Mihalik shrugged; in that case, the best thing to do was stay at the Fair. At ten o'clock there was going to be an invasion from Mars, and he kind of wanted to see it.

At quarter of ten he started walking toward Fountain Lake, where the 212th Coast Artillery had set up. Mars was as close to Earth as it had been in fifteen years, closer than it would be for another seventeen. The management of the Fair had taken the opportunity to show what would happen if Martians took it into their pointy little green heads to attack the 1939 New York World's Fair. Airplanes flew by overhead. There was a complete blackout around Fountain Lake, and instead of the usual nightly spectacular, there were flares and fireworks and antiaircraft bursts and machine-gun fire, all for Peace and Freedom, and then the fountains themselves began dancing and throwing their red, green, blue, and yellow streams at the invisible, cowardly invaders. In a few minutes it was all over, and the public began walking slowly toward the Fair's exits. It was time to go home, time to digest the marvelous holiday, time to tuck in Junior and Sis and thank God and Mayor LaGuardia for the swell day at the Fair and the victory over the Martians. It was time for Mom and Dad to count their blessings and hug each other and realize just how lucky they were to be living in the World of Tomorrow. It was time for Frank Mihalik to figure out what he was going to do next. He obviously wasn't flashing back yet to 1996, and he wasn't welcome any longer on the Fairgrounds, not until nine o'clock the next morning. This was something he hadn't considered: he had no money and nowhere to go.

He walked with the crowd through the exit and into the subway. Even though he didn't have the fare, he was able to slip on a train in the middle of the throng. He stood in the crowded subway car, trying to keep his balance and at the same time avoiding shameless body contact. He wondered if there could be any rides in the amusement section of the Fair that were as frightening and revolting as the subway; he doubted it because anything so terrible would have made its mark on civilization, and would have been known to the historians of 1996. "We're jammed in here like a boxful of Milk Duds all crushed together," he thought. He rode for a long time, through the borough of Queens and into Manhattan. He was tempted to get off and walk around the famous places that had once existed in New York: Broadway, Times Square, Fifth Avenue. But he didn't think he would be so lucky later, trying to get back on the subway without money. He decided to spend the whole night on the train.

There were fewer and fewer people on the train as time passed. He looked at his watch: it was almost midnight. The train was pulling into a large, noisy underground station. He waited for the doors to open. There was a flicker of amber light, a sizzle, a snap, and a moderate clap of thunder. Then everything went dark. "Thank God!" said Mihalik aloud. He knew he was back home. Very soon he would see Cheryl, his girl friend, and Ray, his backup. Ray would be sorry he missed the Fair. At least Mihalik had brought back a pickle pin for Cheryl. He got up and tried to feel his way in the dark. He wondered where he had materialized. He found a door after a few moments and walked through.

A Necessary and Fundamental Change in Game-Plan

Outside it was bright daylight. "That isn't right," thought Mihalik. The time in 1996 was two hours ahead of 1939; he had left at noon and arrived at ten in the morning. He had last looked at his wristwatch just before midnight; it ought to be 2 A.M. "I'll bet I know what it is," thought Mihalik, a wide smile appearing on his face, "I'll bet there's this time-dilation principle. Maybe twelve hours in 1996 translate to more or less than that in 1939. So I really wasn't kept in the past as long as I thought. I just got the benefit of the Mihalik Effect." He liked the sound of that a lot.

He was less happy when he left the building. It turned out to be the Hall of Industry and Metals. "My God," he thought, "they brought the whole building back with me." All around him he saw laughing, happy people enjoying what was clearly the 1939 New York World's Fair. Mihalik was sturdy and he was almost fearless, but he had a tough time handling disappointment. Sometimes he chose the most incredible theories rather than face up to the truth. "They brought the whole damn Fair back!" he cried. "Well, at least they'll be able to study this period at their leisure." Privately Mihalik thought it was an extravagant waste of time, energy, and research bucks.

In lighthearted moments, Mihalik had tried to imagine his welcome back in the gritty, weary world of 1996. He had pictured plenty of blue and yellow bunting hanging from buildings, political figures on hand to share his glory, beautiful San Diego screen stars with orphans for him to kiss, bands, cheering, free beer. He saw none of that. It was all very disillusioning to him. There *was* a band, he had to admit that, but it was the Saskatoon, Saskatchewan, Girls' Pipe Band, and they had played at the Fair yesterday and had somehow been snatched into the future along with the rest of the World of Tomorrow.

He saw a young couple wheeling a stroller. They looked familiar; it took a moment, but Mihalik recalled them. They had been the couple whose copy of the guidebook yesterday let him know where he had arrived. And evidently, they had returned to the Fair for a second day, only to be whisked through time along with the Saskatoon Girls' Pipe Band. He felt he owed them some sort of apology.

He found a bench and sat down to wait. Someone would come to get him soon, he knew. He needed to be debriefed. He needed to be debriefed and fed. He hoped the scientists and technicians had a hearty meal waiting for him, and a warm bath, and a nice bed, because he didn't feel that he could face world leaders and San Diego screen stars in his present condition. He would be ashamed to spend another hour in the same green jumpsuit.

There was a newspaper on the bench. Mihalik picked it up and read it for a moment before he realized that it was from the day before. That made him wrinkle his brow; he was sure, from all that he had seen, that the Fair's sanitation employees wouldn't have left the newspaper on the bench all day and all night. But there were the same stories: the air raid drills in Berlin, the revocation of the Japanese trade pact, Dixie Dugan and her handsome stranger, Bill Dickey and his three home runs. He took the paper with him, intending to throw it in a trash container. He had always been civic-minded.

"Hello," said a man.

"Hello," said Mihalik.

"I'm from out of town. I'm from South Bend, Indiana. You're probably wondering why I'm not over in the Court of Sport."

Mihalik studied this joker. He was wearing a suit the color of Bit-O-Honey. Why had all these people come back for another day, and why were they all wasting their time going back to the same places he had seen them at yesterday? Didn't they realize it was 1996 beyond the Fair's gates now, no longer their comfortable, secure 1939? Well, he didn't want to be the one to tell them. Let them find out on their own. There was no real way to prepare them for it, anyway. "I'll bet I know," said Mihalik. "I'll bet you said to yourself, 'Roman, why travel all this way by train

and come to this wonderful Fair, just to see them raise a flag and give
some speeches?' "

The man stared at Mihalik. "How did you know I was going to say
that? How did you know my name was Roman?"

"Did I guess right?" asked Mihalik.

"Right as rain. Both times."

"I'm an amusement attraction. You owe me twenty-five cents."

"Gee," said Roman, still astonished, digging out a quarter from a little
change purse, "they don't have anybody like you in South Bend."

Mihalik nodded wisely. "You got to come to New York for that," he
said. "This is the big city. You be careful now, you hear?"

"Gee," said the man again. He walked away, shaking his head.

"You came to see the girls in the Aquacade, right?" Mihalik called
after him. The man's mouth dropped open. "Don't worry, that one's on
the house. Have a good time!" Mihalik wished that the designer of the
official time-travel project's suit had foreseen a need for pockets. It meant
that he had to carry the quarter in his hand until he decided how to
spend it. He walked around the Fair, noticing many other people he had
seen the day before. He found that increasingly odd.

As he was sitting on another bench, a man came up to him. "Tired?"
the man asked.

"Yes," said Mihalik. "It's tough, guessing people's occupations, you
know. I bet I can guess yours, easy. For a dollar."

"Concessions like that are all over in Carnivaland," said the man.
"And don't none of them cost a dollar."

"You're scared to try," said Mihalik.

"You're a liar," said the man. "All right, go ahead. What am I?"

"You're a detective."

"Naw."

"Yeah, you're a detective. You've got a badge in a black wallet in the
inside pocket of your jacket."

"Do I look like a detective to you?" said the man grimly.

"You want me to fish the goddamn badge out for you?" asked Mihalik.

"Sure, pal, you just try. Say, I ought to—"

"Never mind, keep your dollar. I must have been out of my mind."

The man studied Mihalik closely. "How'd you know I was a dick?"

"Your intelligent face," said Mihalik.

"Look, pal, I think I'm going to take you—"

Mihalik got up and ran. He thought while he ran, something he had
learned to do while still in his teens. He realized that he was faced with
two mutually exclusive explanations for the day's events. The first was
that the whole Fair had been picked up bodily from Flushing Meadows

in 1939 and transported to 1996, and the people who had done the moving were taking their time about announcing themselves. The second was that, in some weird and super-science way, he was living Thursday, July 27, 1939, all over again. He had reached no conclusions when he came to the Heinz Dome; neither of the choices were particularly attractive.

The matter was decided not long after. While he wandered into a part of the Fair he had not seen the day before, he casually looked at his watch. It had stopped at 1:07, the same time it had before. "Hmm," said Mihalik. He knew significance when he encountered it. Evidence was piling up in favor of the second explanation.

He passed by some more things he either had already seen or wasn't interested in. It seemed that he might be forced to spend longer in 1939 than anyone had anticipated. "Maybe this is all a dream," he told himself. "Maybe yesterday was all a dream, and this is it coming true. Maybe yesterday was real and I'm dreaming about it now." For a few minutes those thoughts were more entertaining than the film he was watching in the Science and Education Building. It was called *Trees and Men*. He was sitting through it because he wanted to see the one that came after, *Dawn of Iran*. He was curious to find out what an "iran" was.

He saw more people he recognized, and turned his early twenty-five-cent victory into a tidy four and a half dollars, which he spent on a Maryland soft-shell crab at one place and some strawberries in Moselle wine at the Luxembourg Exhibit in the Hall of Nations. Individually the items were spectacular. Together they were lousy; but Mihalik had little experience in dining so extravagantly. Real strawberries surprised him. They tasted nothing like the Lifesavers and Turkish Taffy that presented themselves as strawberry-flavored.

The rain started right on time. Mihalik smiled and went into the Petroleum Industries Building and watched another terrible film, *Pete Roleum and His Cousins*, a puppet animation. In 1996 there was a worldwide ban that prohibited puppet animations; now Mihalik understood why.

It rained on the twilight concert of the Manhattan Music School Chorus and on the Reverend Carleton F. Hubbard of the Ocean Parkway Methodist Church, who gave an address few people listened to. Mihalik was getting very tired. He had been robbed of his entire night and had not slept now in—how long? He'd lost track. He wondered where he could go to spend his second night in the romantic past. He looked around the Fair, at the people who were still having a terrific time. "Personally," he thought, "I've had just about enough." Finally he decided to do just what he had done the night before. He watched the obsolete airplanes fly to victory over the no-show Martians—interplanetary combat decided by default. Mihalik shook his head ruefully—if only the real thing had been so easy in 1992.

He got on the subway and was again disgusted by the crowded conditions. It was only natural that he'd feel the same; these were the same people. He was getting weary of the beauties and quaintness of this bygone age. He was sick to death of Thursday, July 27.

Just at midnight there was a flicker of amber light, a sizzle, a snap, and a moderate clap of thunder. Then everything went dark.

A Sign from the Future or God or Something

Mihalik sat on the chair in the lightless room. "I've been here before," he thought. He was exhausted, hungry, and thirsty, yet his curiosity urged him to ignore all that and run to the door. There were two possibilities: either he had returned to the future, to his home in 1996; or he had cycled around once again, locked into Thursday as if on an endless tape loop of the hours between 10 A.M. and midnight. Neither logic nor the way these things work out in stories permitted anything else. Suddenly despairing, Mihalik was in no hurry to learn the truth. He stretched himself out on the floor and slept until his spent energies had restored themselves. Only then did he rise and feel his way to the exit. He grasped the doorknob, took a deep breath, and went through.

He was still at the Fair. Mihalik accepted his fate quietly: he was stranded in the past, marooned upon the reefs of time, lost possibly forever on this same long-dead day. He maintained some hope because he had faith in the science of tomorrow and the dedication of everyone involved in the time-travel project. He realized that his fate included an unusual inconvenience: he would have to adjust to a fourteen-hour day.

He made the unused room in the Hall of Industries and Metals his home, his fortress. "I must begin to provide for myself," he thought. It was seven o'clock in the evening. He wandered through the Fair in the slackening rain, and he saw that fortunately everything he required for a good life was available here. There were food and shelter, clothing and companionship, candy and balloons. He looked at his watch, which had again stopped at 1:07 during his nap. It was a symbol to him of his isolation. It also suggested that if he relied on his intelligence and wits, he would suffer little in a material way. He could do nothing, however, about the essential loneliness of the shipwrecked traveler. The world he came from could not be reached on a handmade raft of logs.

The days passed, all of them basically identical. Mihalik amused himself by learning the movements of the people and things he saw during the day. After a while he began to win money by betting with visitors.

"See that woman in the white hat?" he would ask. He pointed to a woman with a hat decorated with many white balls, like a chocolate nonpareil covered with round white sprinkles.

"What of it?"

"I'll bet you a buck that she stops by that bench, bends down, and takes off her shoe."

"You're crazy."

And soon Mihalik had the price of a dinner of hot dogs and a soft drink. It didn't take long before he knew who would accept a bet and how much he could raise the stake. He even began calling the people by their names, like old friends, startling them or fooling them into believing he had strange mental powers. It made no difference: after midnight, when it all began again, they always forgot what happened on the previous version of the day.

But in a similar and more ominous fashion, Mihalik lost everything he gained during the day. He tried to build up a supply of food, but it disappeared at midnight. A pillow and a blanket that he moved into his secret home vanished during the night as well. Every mark he made upon this world of the past evaporated with the rising of the sun at 10 A.M. Mihalik was forced to go out each day and begin all over again. He could not save against hard times. He could not afford to be sick or to take a holiday. His life became a daily struggle to hunt for or gather food.

The man from 1996 avoided thinking about the ramifications of that fact. He had been given, in effect, a license to perform the most hideous crimes—whatever catastrophes and personal tragedies he created would all be made better at midnight. Whatever the police did to him, wherever they took him, at midnight he would be back in the dark room in the Hall of Industries and Metals. On a few occasions, in unsettled moments, he allowed himself to behave without conscience, knowing that no genuine damage could be done. He robbed, he assaulted, and once he beat a man severely beneath the granite gaze of Freedom of Assembly. He was frightened by the fear and frustration that were unleashed; he didn't know such horrible things were pent up inside him, and he vowed to stand guard against being taken over by them.

"A man in my situation will descend into madness," he thought. "It is the natural and expected course to follow." Mihalik decided to forego the years of slow deterioration and fall apart in one quick plunge. That was the way things were done where he came from.

Although he knew it was a pointless thing to do, he began a journal. "This Fair has become a Carnival of Despair," he wrote. He rather liked that line; he thought it showed a certain style. "I am alone here, among a crowd of 101,220 (71,491 paid; Fair Total to Date: 15,562,809). Everyone

I knew is dead to me, or might as well be—Cheryl, my beloved; Ray, the greatest old backup a man could want; all the guys in the long white lab coats; every friend and relative and enemy and total stranger I ever saw. In these last few days I have railed against the fate that brought me here. That was a fruitless exercise. I have cursed the gods for singling me out for this punishment. That, too, brought me no nearer a solution. I perceived at first that I had no chance of relief: I had neither food, house, clothes, nor weapon on which to rely. There was nothing but death before me. Is this the way it would end for Frank Mihalik, Chronologic Trailblazer? Devoured in the past? Murdered by savages in a savage time, starved to death in the midst of plenty? As night approached I again fought off these phantoms and determined to sleep soundly, and to take appropriate measures in the morning.

"This I attempted to do. In the light of the new day I saw, to my great surprise, that upon the shores of time's great ocean, upon which I had been cast up by the inscrutable Governor of the universe, there were also such things as I needed for my livelihood, if not my complete happiness. I tried to build a little store of things, a gathering of provisions won by cleverness, stealth, and yes, occasional violence. But these provisions disappeared at midnight, like the magical accoutrements of Cinderella, and I was left each morning with only those things I had brought with me through the corridors of time—myself, my clothing, and my wristwatch." Mihalik abandoned his attempt to record his trials when he realized that the journal, as well, would disappear at midnight, and that he could never keep track of anything from one day to the next. A calendar was impossible; even scratches made on the wall or slashes carved into a wooden pole would vanish with the day. It was just as well, he told himself; the journal had started to go off the deep end before it was a page old.

Mihalik was troubled by the notion that his imprisonment was, in fact, a form of punishment, something that had been planned and implemented by unknown forces in his own time, something kept secret from him but set up specifically to torment Frank Mihalik. He didn't understand why; he had always been a model citizen. His only flaw, or, at least, all that he could recall anyway, was that he coveted his neighbor's ass. But there was a lot of that in 1996; he thought it was unfair that he had been singled out for such monstrous treatment. He wanted everyone to know he was heartily sorry. But that didn't seem to be enough.

One day Mihalik rose from his sleep sometime after noon—his watch had stopped as it did every day, at 1:07—and went forth to have fun and find entertainment among the people. The newspaper was where it always was, on the bench. Mihalik read it once again, paying attention this time to articles he had only glanced at before. He thought he might go into Manhattan one evening to see a movie; the scientists in 1996 would want to know about popular entertainments. He considered seeing *Naughty But Nice,* with Ann Sheridan, the Oomph Girl. There was a serious lack of "Oomph" in Mihalik's world of the future. He would be doing everyone a great service by returning with his impressions of the real thing.

But there were a lot of exciting shows to choose from. There were funny little items in the news, too, and he wished that he could talk about them with Cheryl, his girl friend. He missed her and her simple, guileless approach to life.

One article caught Mihalik's eye. He had read it before, but had paid little attention to it—it had been just an amusing example of how foolish these people could be when they took themselves too seriously. The story described how some scientists at a major university had unlocked the secret of atomic structure. "Within the heart of the atom," claimed Dr. Z. Marquand, "is a solid little nucleus, shaped like a football. Tiny things called electrons whip around the nucleus, and that's about all there is to it."

"This will make an entertaining diversion," thought Mihalik. He went to a public telephone, dropped in a nickel, and had the operator connect him with Dr. Marquand's office at the university.

"Hello," said a gruff no-nonsense voice at the other end, "this is Zach Marquand."

"Hello, sir. My name is unimportant. I am calling in reference to your announcement concerning the nature of the atom."

"Yes, indeed. A major leap forward in our understanding of the world around us, if I do say so myself."

Mihalik withheld his laughter. "Tell me, Dr. Marquand," he said, "what is the little football nucleus made of?"

There was a long silence on the line. Finally Marquand spoke up. "I was afraid someone would ask me that. Who is this? Is this Niels Bohr? Is that you, Niels?"

"Dr. Marquand, I am a traveler from the future. I come from the year 1996. In my time we know quite a bit more about the mysteries of the universe, and I can tell you candidly that the nucleus is not football-shaped. It looks like a little root beer barrel. And it's made up of protons and neutrons, which are in turn made up of smaller things, which in turn are made up of even tinier things. There doesn't seem to be an end to it."

"I knew that already," said Marquand. "We just made that announcement to throw the Germans off the track. Say, are you really from the future?"

"Sure," said Mihalik, "why would I lie?"

"Then you could tell me marvelous things. Would you answer one question for me? It would mean a great deal."

Mihalik hesitated, but then he recalled that this conversation was not really taking place, that at midnight Dr. Marquand would forget all about it. "Ask anything you like," he said.

"Will skirts ever get any shorter?" asked the scientist.

Marquand hung up the telephone; so much for the day's fun. Now it was time to find lunch. He looked around the Fair. A seagull flew by overhead, the same seagull that flew by every day at precisely 4:25:18. That meant that he could meet a man named Eddie Rosen from Paramus, New Jersey and win a dollar from him. That would buy a pleasant meal and leave him enough change to go into the General Motors Futurama, which was his favorite exhibit.

The afternoon rain fell, but Mihalik ignored it. He saw Eddie Rosen walking toward him, just as he did every afternoon, but something new had been added: with a shock, the time traveler saw five children holding the strings of helium-filled balloons. He had never seen the children before. "How can that be?" he thought. He felt a chill of apprehension. He had adjusted marvelously to being marooned; but if now the universe had decided to play impish tricks on him by changing the natural way of things, Mihalik realized he was in serious danger. There was something about the balloons the children carried, something tantalizingly familiar. . . .

Red, yellow, black, orange, green.

He knew that sequence. It represented something to him.

Red, yellow, black—a black balloon? Mihalik had never seen a child with a black balloon before. Now he was sure it was some sort of signal. But from whom? And what did it mean?

Friday, at Last

At 10:15, the forces of Earth began their defense of the home world once again. Mihalik watched it all wearily. He had twenty-two dollars in his pocket, and in one hour and forty-five minutes it would all melt away. He considered taking a taxi into Manhattan and getting blitzed in some dismal nightclub; he wouldn't need to worry about getting home, of course. That was a function of the universe. All around him antiaircraft guns blasted, flames danced, fountains sprayed, and colored lights flashed. But somehow it was different. Mihalik came quickly to attention: *somehow it was different.* There was a rhythm and a pattern to the colored lights as they played upon the fountains. Blink, blink, blink,

blink, blink. Instead of smoothly shifting melodies of color, the lights changed in regular, staccato order. Two colors, then a beat of darkness, then two more colors; the sequence repeated itself exactly, over and over. It had never done that on any of the previous Thursday evenings.

Red, yellow, darkness, orange, green.

It was the same sequence as the colors of the children's balloons.

Mihalik was a good man, a kind man, who would someday make a wonderful husband and father. Everyone liked him in 1996, and he felt certain that some of the folks in 1939 enjoyed talking with him, too; they might have become friends, if they didn't forget all about him each night at twelve o'clock. It caused the young man a great deal of mental anguish that some great cosmic force was toying with him, teasing him and torturing him, for unknown reasons. How could he hope to fight the power of natural law? It was a hopeless struggle; Mihalik had always avoided hopeless struggles before because they looked bad on his resumé, but there seemed to be no escape from this one. He left the Martian invasion and went into the amusement area, Carnivaland. He thought the pure lunacy of the rides might distract his mind.

He rode the Dodg'em for fifteen cents and smashed into a car driven by a little old lady with blue hair; it didn't make him feel any better. He shattered china dishes with wooden balls. He rode through the Laff in the Dark and didn't laff. He dropped two hundred fifty feet on the Parachute Jump, yet the mystery still waited for him on the ground. He watched motorcycle riders challenge the Wall of Death but nobody crashed and it was almost midnight.

Then, like a wallop from Elektro, the Moto-Man, the significance of the balloons and lights hit him. Red, yellow, black, orange, green: that was the color sequence in a package of Chuckles. Mihalik was overcome with elation. It couldn't be coincidence; taking ten possible color choices, the number of permutations taken five at a time is given by the formula $M = n (n - 1) (n - 2). \ldots (n - p + 1)$. Mihalik substituted 10 for n and 5 for p, multiplied it out, and arrived at the conclusion that the odds of the balloons appearing in just that sequence were 1 in 30,240; the odds of both the balloons and the colored lights repeating the sequence were therefore 1 in $(30,240)^2$. Did they have Chuckles in this primitive time? It made no difference—it could mean but one thing: the scientists of 1996 had not abandoned him. They were even now working feverishly to spring him from the temporal slammer. He hurried to gobble down the rest of a hamburger; it would vanish in less than fifteen seconds. As the second hand of his watch approached twelve, a voice called to him over the loudspeakers: "Mr. Frank Mihalik, please report—"

There was a flicker of amber light and all the rest of it.

"Ouch! Damn it!" said someone in the dark.

It hadn't been Mihalik's voice. "Who is it?" he asked.

"I can't see a damn thing," said the voice.

"Wait a minute, I know where the door is." Mihalik walked quickly to the exit and opened it; light flooded into the room.

There was another chair near his own. His girl friend, Cheryl, was sitting in it.

"Cheryl!" he cried. "What are you doing here?"

"They sent me back, Frank, to let you know they're having a little trouble." She joined him by the door. He touched her long auburn hair and thrilled again to the vivacity in her green eyes. Her luscious gams were hidden by her green jumpsuit, but his memory of them was impeccable. She was some dish. He put his arms around her and held her for a moment. Then he gazed deeply into her eyes and kissed her. It was an emotional moment.

"Oh, Cheryl," he said, "I've missed you so."

"I've missed you, Frank."

"How's Ray?"

"Ray's fine, he sends his regards."

Sadness filled Mihalik as he realized how Cheryl had sacrificed herself to bring a message that was rather self-evident. "We may never go home," he said. "You may be trapped here with me forever."

"It makes no difference to me where we are, Frank, so long as I'm with you. What is this place?"

Mihalik led her out into the morning sunshine. He put his arm around her shoulders and let her drink in the spectacle. "This," he announced grandly, "is the New York World's Fair of 1939!"

"Oh," she said, sighing.

"You sound disappointed."

She shrugged and smiled. "It's nothing," said Cheryl. "I was just hoping for something really exciting, like the Italian Renaissance."

"But this *is* really exciting! I have so much to show you. Wait until you see the thrills and wonders they've collected here."

They walked along Constitution Mall. Cheryl exclaimed over such things as the quaint clothing and odd architecture. "The buildings are so strange," she said. "They're built in laminated layers, like licorice of all sorts. They pile horizontal planes or stick them on end beside one another, and then round off all the edges."

"Yes," said Mihalik, "this is a safety-conscious age. These people are the sowers of the seeds of our world. These are our ancestors, Cheryl. Everything we are, we owe to them. Think of it: the Mediterranean still exists in this time. The Antarctic Inflow hasn't been discovered yet.

There is no space travel, and people still haven't learned the terrible truth about vitamins."

"What a brave old world it is," said Cheryl. "I'm hungry."

Mihalik led her to the bench near the Washington statue, the one with the newspaper. They sat down; he held her hands in his strong grasp. "Cheryl," he said, "let me tell you of the nature of our imprisonment." And he sketched for her the immutable laws under which they had to live.

"Why, that's not so awful," she cried. "We can make a wonderful life together. We can overcome anything, so long as we have each other."

"But we can't build anything. At midnight, everything we've accomplished is destroyed, leaving us with nothing. We return to the same point in time and space, and have to begin again."

Cheryl was not distressed. "I have confidence in you, Frank," she said. "Your mother told me what a clever little boy you were. She told me all about the summer you were a camp counselor and the time you found that lost little kid in the woods. I'll put my well-being in your hands and trust to Providence that we'll be happy and healthy and everything. We'll earn money during the morning and spend it at night. Then we'll get plenty of rest, maintain a regimen of good grooming habits, and get married somehow. It will be swell, Frank, don't you see? How many people get the opportunity to honeymoon in the past?"

Mihalik said nothing for a few seconds. "We don't have any identification, Cheryl," he said. "We don't have our birth certificates or our nucleotide registers."

"What does that matter? We're young and we're in love, and this is the romantic past. These people of 1939 will move mountains to see that we're happy, just like in all those musical comedies."

"We'll see." Actually, Mihalik was touched by her faith. He didn't explain to her his theory that they had been trapped as a punishment for tampering with the mechanisms of time. He had come to believe that there were certain things that should not be messed with by the hands of men. He was sure that he was being punished, but he didn't know by whom—people of the far future? Nature? God? The Hershey Chocolate Company?

Cheryl was enthralled by the possibilities. "We have the chance to influence our own world, Frank," she said, indicating that she hadn't been paying close attention. "We can create an atmosphere of harmony and understanding, and steer the world away from the terrible course it will take without our guidance. We can start right here, right in this Fair. We can give them a new path to follow that will alter the future. Can't you see it, Frank? Right over there, among those statues, there will rise a tall, sharp, clean building that will teach these primitives what they must learn if they are to avoid their fatal errors. I can see it as plain as day: a spacious central court decorated with cement swans, artistic but disciplined exhibition areas on both sides, every surface a different material, everything in cool pastel colors, a tribute to the after-dinner mint and Necco Wafers and—"

Mihalik slapped her face, hard; she stopped rambling. "I'm sorry," he said. "But if we're going to live in this place, we have to keep a deadly realistic outlook."

"Yes, dear, I understand," she said. "Maybe we should just forget about the Necco Wafers."

"I have been thinking about leaving notes for people in the future to discover. They buried a time capsule in the Westinghouse Building. It will be opened in the year 6939."

Cheryl felt her jaw; nothing seemed broken. "6939? But we'll be dead by then, Frank," she said.

Mihalik nodded grimly. "I know that. But no doubt they will have perfected time travel, and they will be able to zip back here and rescue us, then drop us off in 1996 on the way back to their own era."

"If that were true, they would have done it already. The fact that they haven't rescued us means that they won't rescue us."

Mihalik considered her objection. "But we haven't left the note yet," he said.

Cheryl explained it to him slowly, as if he were just another dim bulb from the past. "It's all the same whether we leave the note today or tomorrow or ten years from now. The note will get to 6939 at the same time, whenever we put it into the capsule, see?"

Mihalik squinted his eyes and tried to focus on her meaning. "Let's suppose I plan to put the note there this afternoon."

"Okay."

"At the moment I'm walking toward the time capsule, up there in the future it's already 6939."

"That's right."

"And the note is already there."

"Uh huh."

"Then why do I have to bother putting the note in the capsule?"

Cheryl chewed her lip thoughtfully. She had been an adhesives major in college and it hadn't prepared her for this sort of reasoning. "Because," she said, "if you look at it that way, the note was in 6939 even before you came back here. The note has always been in 6939, but it hasn't always been here. So you have to put the note in the capsule here before they can come get us."

Mihalik pretended that her explanation made sense. "But at midnight everything we do disappears. The note would disappear, too."

"Maybe it wouldn't," said Cheryl. "Maybe it would be safe in the time capsule."

"How are we going to get it into the time capsule?" asked Mihalik.

She looked exasperated. "I don't know," she snapped. "Why do *I* have to think of everything? *You're* the big hotshot explorer. *You* think of something for a change."

"Here comes Roman," he said. "I'll get us money for lunch."

The World of Tomorrow Delivers the Goods

There was no way for Mihalik to know how long he had been trapped in Thursday, July 27, 1939. It had been many months, but whether they totaled a year he did not know. Cheryl had been with him for at least six weeks, and she had adjusted to the routine of life. Indeed, she seemed to have a quicker grasp of the possibilities than he did. It was her suggestion that prompted him to give Dr. Zach Marquand another call.

And so, at quarter past twelve on the afternoon of July 27, Mihalik, Cheryl, and Dr. Marquand rode the subway out to the Fair—to Mañana Meadow, as it was called, to view A Happier Way of American Living Through a Recognition of the Interdependence of Men and the Building of a Better World of Tomorrow with the Tools of Today. They had virtually kidnapped the scientist, bribing him with bits of information, luring him with hints of the future. He hadn't visited the Fair yet, anyway, and like the hayseed from Indiana, he had heard all about the attractions that featured swell dames.

They got off the train and paid their way into the Fairgrounds. "Now watch closely," said Mihalik. "Do you see that man over there? In about five seconds he's going to take off his suit coat and a wallet will fall on the ground."

Dr. Marquand said nothing. In a few seconds, just as Mihalik described, the coat came off and the wallet fell. "How did you know that?" asked Marquand.

Mihalik shrugged. "I've seen it happen again and again, every day at just this hour. I've lived through this day hundreds of times. I know exactly what is going to happen. Look, quickly, over there. That kid with the candy cigarette in his mouth is going to lose his balloon. See? And in about ten seconds a band will start playing some march."

" 'The Thunderer,' " said Cheryl.

"Great Caesar's Ghost!" cried Dr. Marquand when the band started playing. "You've persuaded me. You are indeed travelers from the future. But how can I help you?"

They walked slowly along the avenue, past the statues of the Four Freedoms. "The crew in our time gave me a message," said Cheryl. "They haven't been able to return Frank and me to our own era because they can't overcome something they call temporal inertia. No matter how much energy they pump into their apparatus, they can't budge us from the past. That has to be done from this side. What you have to do is find some way of giving us just a tiny shove, and then the people in 1996 will be able to recover us easily."

Dr. Marquand stared at a young woman straightening the seams of her silk stockings. "Then what we need is a source of great energy," he said, "enough energy to topple you out of the space-time trap. Too bad we don't have that cobalt bomb you told me about."

Mihalik stopped to win a dollar from a young married couple he had come to know and like. He told them their names, their address, the names of their parents, the years they graduated from high school, whom they voted for in the last election, where they had spent their honeymoon, and the location of a strawberry birthmark on the young woman's body. He came back and gave the dollar to the scientist. "Does it have to be something like an explosion?" he asked. "Maybe they could drop us off a building or something."

"I'd rather be blown up all at once," said Cheryl.

"I suspect," said Dr. Marquand, "that there's something here at the Fair that would serve us. Let me think. . . . I've seen pictures in the newspaper—I know! The General Electric Building! Let's go."

Cheryl wanted to pick up a souvenir for Ray, who would be disappointed if they returned without bringing him anything. She chose a pickle pin from the Heinz Dome. "He'll like this," she said. For herself, she found a pin in the General Motors Futurama that said *I Have Seen the Future*. It was poignantly appropriate.

"He'll get a kick out of the pickle pin," said Mihalik.

The two chronoventurers walked hand in hand. Mihalik took the opportunity to say goodbye to all the people he'd come to know here on Day One; of course, none of them knew who he was, but they all acted polite, if uncomfortable.

"What a sweet age this is," murmured Cheryl. "How they slumber unaware. There are no monostellaphenazide leaks, no Chou-Tsien plague, no tickworms in the Midwest, no signals from Sirius to worry about."

"It isn't *all* wonderful," said Marquand. "We have our share of worries, too."

Mihalik paused to take a last look around the Fair. "It's been wonderful," he said, "but I kind of look forward to not knowing what's going to happen next. Dr. Marquand, do you want us to tell you what is going to happen in your world?"

The scientist thought for a moment. "It would give me a peculiar responsibility," he said. "It could be a terrible secret to know ahead of time, a fearful curse. But why not? What the hell, go ahead. Tell me."

Mihalik and Cheryl took turns filling in the history of the world, as much as they could recall, from 1939 to 1980. Mihalik was able to remember some of the winners of certain sporting events as well as financial trends during those decades. "In 1980, the presidential election will be won by Ronald Rea—"

"Who cares?" said Marquand. "I'll probably be dead by then. Here we are, the General Electric exhibit."

They went in. Dr. Marquand's reputation allowed them to examine the machinery used in the demonstrations of artificial lightning—really just a static electricity generator that produced dramatic displays of metal-vaporizing and timber-shattering. The centerpiece of the demonstration was an arc of ten million volts that leaped thirty feet from one pole to another. "Gee," murmured Cheryl.

"Yes," said Dr. Marquand soberly, "science is our friend; but we must be careful, for without a sense of responsibility the playthings we create may become our deadliest enemies."

"Like nuclear energy, for instance," said Mihalik.

"Well," said the physicist, "I was thinking of the martini and the gimlet, myself. There won't be another exhibition here for almost fifteen minutes. Let's position you on that target pole and whip a couple of bolts at you. That ought to do the trick."

Cheryl slipped her hand into Mihalik's. "Are you afraid?" she whispered.

"Not at all," said Mihalik. He laughed in the face of death.

"If this doesn't work," said Dr. Marquand respectfully, "it will char you into a little pile of black powder. You're a very brave man."

Mihalik laughed again. "We'll try anything, sir," he said. "We're from the future."

"Yes, I keep forgetting. Okay, hold still. I'm all ready here. Before you go, however, there's something I want to ask you. Do you know which of all the different versions of today will be the real one? The one everyone will remember?"

Mihalik shook his head. Cheryl had no answer, either.

"Another thing," asked Marquand. "Why do sweets play such an important part in your lives? Is there some situation in the future that makes candy more valuable than it is today?"

Mihalik looked at Cheryl. "Dr. Marquand," he said, "we can't answer that, either. All we know is that over the years the manufacturers have become immensely powerful. It began during the Second World War, I think. We don't know how or why, but something started civilization on the road to what, in 1996, amounts to a virtual sucrocracy. It is a mystery that baffles our historians."

"Thank you," said Marquand. "I will watch the trend carefully. Knowing about it will guarantee me security in my old age. Now hold very still—"

The technology of the past exploded upon Mihalik and Cheryl; ten million volts of blazing lightning smote them, but all they experienced was a flicker of amber light. . . .

With an echo of thunder in their ears, they fell to the floor. Both were dazed and groggy. They opened their eyes. They were no longer in the General Electric Building. They were now in a small room that appeared to be someone's office. There was a desk and a filing cabinet, a telephone, a typewriter on a small stand, and a framed picture of the Man from Mars—the chairman of the candy company who had become boss of the world years ago. "We're back," whispered Mihalik. "Such a miracle as this is evidence of the secret hand of Providence governing the world, that the eye of an infinite power searches into the remotest corner of space and time, and sends help to the miserable whenever it pleases."

"Well," said Cheryl, "I give a lot of credit to Dr. Marquand, too."

"Or else it was all just a lucky accident. I wonder whatever happened to Marquand, that primitive genius. We will have to find out. But for now it's enough just to rejoin our world and our own time. Ray will be glad to see us; I have to admit that I've missed his ugly mug. Say, did those pins come with you through time?"

Cheryl opened her hand; the souvenirs were gone. "He'll understand," she said sadly. "Maybe I dropped them."

"Tough break, kid."

"I wonder about something, Frank. Do you suppose that our telling Dr. Marquand about candy could be what actually began the trend? That somehow we influenced our own present by going into the past?"

"You mean that if we hadn't told him about it, when we came back here it would all be some other way?"

Cheryl nodded.

"What difference does it make?" he asked. "If it hadn't been candy, it would have been something else. Something worse, like green vegetables or fossil fuels."

"You're right, Frank. I'm lucky to be your girl friend."

Mihalik smiled.

They went to the door of the office. He put his hand on the knob. "We've left the sepia-tinted days of yesteryear," he said. "It was fun and it was terrifying, but now we're safely home. Once we step through this door, we'll be back in our very own dull, drab, nougat-centered, cavity-prone World of Tomorrow."

"Can't you wait just a moment?" asked Cheryl. She pressed her warm, moist lips against his in a lingering kiss.

Mihalik pulled away. "No," he said decisively, "I'd like to stay here with you, but I have a duty to the project. I'm crazy about you, Cheryl, but you must respect my moral obligation."

"I do, Frank, really. I'm sorry for acting so foolish."

So together they left the office and walked into the uncertainty of the rest of their lives. That, in the final analysis, is the great adventure in which each of us takes part: what more courageous thing is there, after all, than facing the unknown we all share, the danger and joy that await us in the unread pages of the Book of the Future. . . .

Book Two

1361 A.D. *Considered as a Row of Tenements*

A Slight Miscalculation?

When they walked through the door, the returning time travelers were greeted by a roomful of people. Colorful streamers hung from the glowing panels overhead; blue and white crepe paper decorated the edges of a row of tables, on which lay trays of hors d'oeuvres and bowls of punch; like tinted snow, handfuls of confetti drifted gaily down on the heroes' shoulders. It was a glorious moment, fit for song, laughter, and drunkenness; but there was also history to consider.

Frank Mihalik and Cheryl were entirely surprised and pleased by the reception. They stood like noble statues for a moment, poised, speechless; Mihalik was still considering history, and laboring mightily to come up with something memorable to say. The people in the room cheered and cheered. Cheryl tugged at Mihalik's sleeve and whispered, "Say something." Mihalik's mind was blank, a condition invariably induced in him by those two terrible words: *Say something!* He felt like an idiot, and he was glad that it was such a spectacular occasion, because no one would really notice how foolish he looked.

"Hi, everybody," he said. "It's nice to be back." At least six people scribbled down his exact words, for they would quickly be carved into the pediments of town halls and the cornerstones of libraries newly dedicated to the first volunteer to travel into the past and return.

His words, as simple and straightforward as the man himself, set off another round of cheering. By now Mihalik was beginning to get control of himself. He had always handled himself well in front of crowds; that had been part of his training after he had been selected as the first chrononaut. He had studied certain aspects of public relations: waving confidently to camera crews; flashing brief determined smiles that bespoke courage; suddenly becoming modest and even self-effacing on an instant's notice. All these things were the difficult part of his instruction. Traveling through time was the easy part; all he had to do was sit in a chair and be struck by some kind of ray.

Mihalik raised one hand, and the shouting died away. "Say," he said, smiling briefly, "can I get something to drink? A little gin, if you've got it. Beer, if you don't. Cheryl?"

She was still looking around the room with wide eyes. It hadn't occurred to her before that she was a hero, too. "Oh, just some soda water," she said. Neither she nor Mihalik was used to luxury, or even comfort. In their impoverished world of 1996, a bottle of beer was something to remember for days.

Yet both celebrities saw that there was a buffet spread for them more elaborate than anything they had ever seen. Mihalik looked past the appetizers and saw standing rib roasts and baked hams, huge turkeys stuffed and waiting for the carver's blade, pans of succulent vegetables keeping warm, all set for the preliminaries to end and the real festivities to begin. "Look," he murmured.

"Gee, I know," whispered Cheryl. "It's some layout."

"I wonder if they were expecting somebody else. Maybe we were supposed to bring somebody back with us from the past."

"You know that would have been impossible, Frank," she said. She clutched his arm more tightly. "All this is really for *us!*"

Mihalik was still dubious. "Cheryl," he said, "they don't even throw this kind of a clambake for the Heisman Trophy winner." Before his companion could reply, Mihalik noticed a large info set mounted on the wall nearby. Glowing figures said *February 18, 1996.* According to the calendar, they had been gone only a day—yet both he and Cheryl had spent weeks, months, perhaps a year stranded in the past. And yet it was only the eighteenth of February; they hadn't even managed to miss the end of winter. "Look at the date, Cheryl," he said.

She was as astonished as he had been. "But it can't be!" she said. While they watched, the clock changed from 12:59 to 13:00.

"Thirteen o'clock?" asked Mihalik. "That's strange."

A man came toward them with their drinks. He was wearing a military-style uniform of silver and blue. "This is a real privilege for me," he told them. "I'm General Vadín Ransom. I'd like to introduce you to a few important people. If you'll just come with me—"

"Certainly," said Mihalik, waving confidently to the camera crews.

Once again, Cheryl tugged at his sleeve. "Frank," she said in an urgent tone, "I'm sure there's something wrong."

He smiled down at her; how dear she was, how sweet, how wonderfully in need of protection. "You just have to get used to it, honey," he told her. "We're famous people now. We're going to get this kind of treatment for a while, and then, as quickly as it came, it will all go away again. It may be some time before we even get a little privacy. It's just another one of the sacrifices we knew we'd have to make."

"It's not *that,* Frank! Look around! Everything's *wrong!*"

Mihalik paused to sip from his glass. He wondered what Cheryl could possibly mean: everything seemed just swell to him, so far. The gin was okay. Then, slowly, he felt an uneasiness spread through him. Things that he had heard and seen since their arrival had, at last, become the basis of thoughts. He almost choked.

There were framed pictures on the wall. One of them was a familiar pose, a photograph of the Man from Mars, the titular head of the candy company and the actual ruler of the world—but the face in the photograph was wrong, different. The festive bunting should have been blue and yellow, not blue and white. The general was wearing a uniform Mihalik had never seen before in his life. And everyone else should have been wearing the uniform of 1996, olive green jumpsuits, like Mihalik, like Cheryl; but there wasn't another jumpsuit in the crowd. Attire ran more to casual slacks and sports coats for the men, with the women wearing knee-length plaid skirts and sweaters with circle pins. The most unusual feature of the room was the abundance of framed slogans everywhere:

LESS IS MORE

MARS IS EARTH

TOMORROW IS YESTERDAY

"Holy crow," said Mihalik in a hoarse voice, "what the hell *is* this?"

"Is something the matter?" asked General Ransom. "Did you pick up some disease in the past or something? What can we do for you?"

"I suppose," whispered Cheryl, "that we better talk to someone from the project, and quick."

"You'd think Dr. Waters would be here," said Mihalik. "You'd think that he'd be the first one to meet us."

"That's something else to wonder about," said Cheryl. "And where's Ray?"

Mihalik nodded, knowing that no force on Earth could have prevented Ray, the faithful backup man, from being there. "Don't worry, baby," said Mihalik, "I'll handle it." His bravery training took over, and for a few moments he would be able to function without regard for the unsettling things his mind was beginning to tell him. When he spoke, it was with a clear and manly voice. "General," he said, "we're quite healthy and in good spirits. However, there is one small matter of a highly scientific and technical nature that we must discuss immediately with one of the upper-level supervisors of the project. It is of the utmost urgency." And with that, his bravery slipped away; he seemed to wilt just a little as panic, confusion, disorientation, and mild nausea attacked him.

General Ransom hadn't worn a uniform for thirty years without learning when a situation was obviously out of his hands. "Right," he said briskly, and turned away to find someone to give an order to.

The Proof Is in the Eating

Cheryl led Mihalik toward the buffet tables. "I've never seen food like this before," she said. "I remember my parents talking about it some-times. Like they sort of missed it. Once my mother described to me something called a 'cutlet.' I was too young to understand, though."

"This is like the food we saw in the past," said Mihalik. "Real meat. Real vegetables. And lots of it all." A thin narrow-shouldered man was standing beside them, staring at them and munching on something on a cracker. Suddenly Mihalik turned to him and grabbed him by the shirt. "Hey!" Mihalik cried. "Where's all the candy?"

The man sprayed a cloud of cracker crumbs into the air and coughed. Cheryl took a quick glance up and down the tables; it was true—there wasn't a single bowl of M & Ms or sour balls or those awful orange peanut-shaped things that taste like bananas.

"Answer me!" Mihalik demanded. He had lifted the poor little man off his feet; dangling there, the fellow looked less like a human being than an accessory or attachment for someone Mihalik's size.

"Frank!" said Cheryl sharply. "Put him down!"

Mihalik looked at her, blinking, then slowly returned the small man to the floor. "Sorry," he muttered.

The man looked at Mihalik with a mixture of astonishment and fear. He plucked at his rumpled shirtfront, but he couldn't improve its appear-ance. "It's all right," he said when he'd regained his composure. "You've probably been through a lot. You were zipping through time there for a while, you're bound to be a little jittery. Forget it."

"Okay," said Mihalik. He held out his hand. "Frank Mihalik," he said.

The man shook hands. "Name's Smith," he said. He turned to Mihalik's girl friend. "You must be Cheryl. I saw you hurrying past my office last night. Before they shot you back through time."

Cheryl smiled pleasantly while she scooped potato salad onto a paper plate. "You may not believe this, but we spent a long time in the year 1939. Months went by. And now here we are, and it's only the day after we left."

Smith looked impressed. "No wonder you're jumpy. But it'll make a terrific story. I'll bet you'll be able to sell it to the movies for a fortune. They'll have famous San Diego film stars playing you, and when they finish with it, it won't be anything at all like the real truth."

"Probably not," said Cheryl. "Would you pile some of that ham and turkey and some of that roast beef on this plate, please?"

"Sure," said Smith. "I thought the tech boys had all the angles figured out."

"So did we," said Mihalik. "They drilled me on possible malfunctions for weeks. We went through every damn emergency procedure they could think of. So what happens?"

"A paradox," said Smith.

"A what?" asked Mihalik.

"A time-travel paradox," said the small man. "There wasn't any failure with the equipment. It wasn't the hardware. You just ran into one of the basic laws of the universe, something we don't know much about yet. Fortunately it was just a little paradox."

"*Little?*" cried Mihalik. "We were trapped back there on the very same day, Thursday, July 27, 1939. It kept repeating over and over, exactly the same way every time, for month after month. I was going crazy. I felt like the Robinson Crusoe of time, until Cheryl showed up. And you're saying that's a *little* paradox?"

"He means that it could have been a whole lot worse, Frank," said Cheryl.

"How the hell does he figure that?"

Smith looked around nervously. "Could you kind of keep your voice down?" he said. "They're looking."

"Let 'em look." Mihalik was starting to feel annoyed with Smith. He began piling food on his paper plate. He skipped the vegetables.

Smith picked up another hors d'oeuvre. "I meant that it could have been one of those cases where you go back in time and change some little, insignificant thing, and when you get back home, everything's different. It isn't the same present anymore."

Mihalik glanced at Cheryl over Smith's fair-haired head.

"Well," said Cheryl slowly, "you know, we *have* noticed just a teensy bit of that around here."

"You have?" asked Smith. He suddenly looked very frightened.

"Uh huh," said Mihalik. "Like, who's that guy in the picture?"

"That's the Man from Mars," said Smith. "You have to know who *he* is."

Mihalik's face suddenly bore a weary look. "I know all about the Man from Mars. But that joker isn't him."

Smith winced. "Yes, it is," he said. "He's the *new* man from Mars. He has been for the last twelve years."

Cheryl swallowed a forkful of candied yams. "When we left—yesterday—it was still the *old* Man from Mars. The first one. Where is he these days?"

Smith shrugged. "He just disappeared twelve years ago, and they had to name a successor. The company stopped making candy altogether back then. They have too much to do just governing everybody, I guess. That's why there isn't any candy here; it stopped being important twelve years ago. But you should know all of this."

"Look, pal," said Mihalik, poking a heavy forefinger into Smith's sunken chest, "we don't know any of that. That just isn't the way the world was when we left. So we're only a trifle upset to come home and find everything all screwed up like this. With no one from the project here to tell us what's going on. Isn't that just a little unlikely?"

Smith looked around the room at the other guests, who were lining up at the buffet tables and freshening their drinks. "This reception is strictly an Agency affair," he said. "The Agency gets to show you off before the scientists get their hands on you."

Mihalik closed his eyes and rubbed his forehead with one hand. Then he opened his eyes again and looked squarely at Smith. "What, if you don't mind my asking, in the name of Baby Ruth is the Agency?"

Smith dropped his cracker. He grabbed Mihalik's arm with one hand, and Cheryl's arm with the other. "You mean you don't know what the Agency is?" he whispered.

"There was no Agency where we came from," said Cheryl.

"Oops," said Smith. "We have to get out of here, and very fast. Just ease toward the door there. Pretend that you're browsing along, looking at the food. Smile at people. That's it."

"Where are we going?" asked Mihalik. He jerked his arm out of Smith's grasp.

"My apartment," said Smith.

"What for?"

"Trust me," said Smith. "You're in big trouble. And so am I, probably, for talking to you. The Second Squad will be here any minute. I'll bet you were never supposed to leave this room."

"I don't understand any of this, Cheryl," complained Mihalik. Smith urged them through the admiring people.

"Don't ask *me,*" said Cheryl.

"Are we going to trust this one lunatic, or wait until the normal, reliable official dignitaries show up?"

"They should have been here already, Frank," said Cheryl thoughtfully. "Maybe we don't *want* to know who's going to come. This situation is getting crazier by the minute."

They were almost to the door. Mihalik stopped suddenly. Smith turned to him, his mouth open to plead that they continue to hurry. Mihalik shut him up with one good authoritative frown. "One thing first, Smith," he said. "You got anything to eat at your place?"

Smith was surprised by the question. "Plenty," he said. "Everyone here *always* has plenty to eat."

"Well," said Mihalik, giving in at last, "that does it. That *proves* we're not home. Where we come from, the only place you can see stuffed turkeys is in the Smithsonian." Quietly, cautiously, the three slipped out of the room.

What a Difference a Day Makes

It was a cold, grim, gray afternoon. The wind lashed freezing rain in their faces as they hurried across a large marble-paved plaza and down a broad flight of marble stairs. Mihalik and Cheryl had spent the last year in summer, and neither had really given any thought to the fact that here it would be entirely different. The fierce weather was only the first in a series of shocks.

Mihalik grunted as the wet winter gusts bit through his thin garment. "I'm beginning to think we should have stayed in 1939," he said as they made their way toward a parking area.

"A lesser man might have chosen that, Frank," said Cheryl. "To stay there in that placid time, on that tranquil day. But you've explained to me too often about honor and duty and your responsibility to the project. That's one of the reasons I love you, Frank. Just as we faced the terrible fact of being marooned there, we'll face this trouble together, too. Whatever it is."

"Yeah," said Mihalik unhappily, "sure."

Smith led the way; his small automobile was parked somewhere in a vast many-storied garage that served the huge building they had just exited. This was another shock: in the 1996 that Mihalik knew, only top government officials and certain entertainment personalities were permitted to own cars. Here there were thousands of them; the garage rose level upon level into the sky. The cars were every color they could be, rather than the standard olive green. "This is mine," said Smith, looking for his keys. He'd stopped beside a grimy blue coupe.

"How do you remember where it is?" asked Cheryl. It wasn't a large car; it was built for economy rather than comfort. Even so, it was much more luxurious than the best model Cheryl had ever seen in her own world.

"We're assigned places. It's very organized. The Agency is very organized about everything." Smith unlocked the doors; all three sat squeezed together on the front seat.

On the street beyond the parking garage, Mihalik could study the Agency Building. It was a huge, cheerless edifice, all white marble more than a hundred stories tall. There were few other buildings anywhere around it. As Mihalik looked down the avenue, first in one direction, then in the other, it struck him that the street seemed only occasionally populated with any sort of structure at all. And there were very few people about. "This is creepy," he said. "Where *is* everybody?" He was from a New York City where buildings leaned against one another, crowding the narrow streets and taking up every available plot of ground. There were no open spaces in the New York of Mihalik's time. And he was used to sidewalks teeming endlessly with bustling pedestrians, day and night. They were always visible, always reminding you of how insignificant you were, and how powerless to alter your futile life or your dismal fate. That was why there was such a sensitivity to what people called "shameless body contact"; there was so little free space that one was always aware of the proximity of some stranger.

Here, though, things seemed to be different in that regard. For instance, the people at the party had mingled in an easy and relaxed manner, without the hostility and defensiveness that usually marked the group gatherings Mihalik was familiar with. He shook his head. He was feeling the very same sort of culture shock here, in what was supposed to be "home," that he had experienced when he first arrived in 1939. He shuddered.

"Look, Frank," said Cheryl, pointing to another large building several blocks away.

"That's the Ministry of Eternity," said Smith. "The Second Squad works out of there. Scary place. You don't want to go there. Minitern, we call it."

"Ministry?" said Mihalik. "What's a ministry?"

Smith turned his head and regarded the time traveler for a few seconds. "The government is divided up into bureaus; they're called ministries. The heads of the ministries advise the Man from Mars. Sometimes I think you just ask these things to make me think you don't really know the answers."

Mihalik felt himself getting angry. He would have liked to grab Smith's shirtfront again, and he would have if Smith hadn't been speeding along through traffic. Cheryl sensed the tension. "Where we come from, Mr. Smith, the government is divided up into departments," she said. "We have the State Department, the Defense Department, the Offense Department, and so on."

"Department, ministry, it probably doesn't matter very much," said Smith.

"It matters because it's not supposed to be this way," said Mihalik. "Any change is a frightening change. Even this city has me upset. There isn't the tiniest resemblance to the New York we grew up in."

"Well," said Smith with a sigh, "I can understand why you'd be upset."

"Yes," said Mihalik, "because somehow the entire world has been changed."

"Yes, of course, there's that," said Smith. "But I meant that this isn't New York, old boy. This is London."

There was a cold, sickening silence in the car for a long moment. "It couldn't be," said Cheryl at last.

Smith turned toward her and smiled. "Trust me," he said. He pointed across their bodies, out the right passenger window. "Do you know what that is?"

"Yeah," said Mihalik, "some bridge across a river."

"You don't have a bridge like that in New York, do you?"

"No," admitted Mihalik.

"But you've seen it before? Pictures of it, I mean? In books and movies?"

"I guess so."

"We're in London, Frank," said Cheryl gloomily. The time displacement was ugly and terrifying, but at least it was a part of their original situation: they had gone back in time, and something strange had happened; now they had gone forward in time, and something strange was happening. But the spatial aspect was more difficult to fathom. It was hard to see how they could have been transported neatly from one continent to another.

"I think I can explain that," said Smith. "Look, imagine that while you're in the process of moving through time, the Earth itself is also continuing to move. Rotate, revolve, you know. So between the instant that you left the past and the instant you appeared here, the Earth turned a bit. You started in New York City and landed, luckily enough, in London. You could have plopped down in some more unhealthy place."

"It didn't happen going the other way," objected Mihalik. "I left New York in 1996, and when I got to 1939 I was still in New York. The same was true for Cheryl."

"Aw, hell," said Smith, "what do you want from me? I don't have *all* the answers."

They were passing the Ministry of Eternity; an immense portrait of the

Man from Mars decorated one face of the stark building, and below it were the three slogans:

LESS IS MORE

MARS IS EARTH

TOMORROW IS YESTERDAY

Cheryl leaned closer to Mihalik's ear. "Look at that man's face, Frank," she whispered. "Doesn't he remind you of someone?"

Mihalik studied the billboard-sized poster as they drove by. "Uh huh," he said. "That guy who played the leader of the Danish Remnant in that holofilm we went to with Ray. The guy who tried to tunnel under the Copenhagen Wall."

"No, no! Look at him! Doesn't he look like your chief? There's a real resemblance there, Frank."

"Dr. Waters is a hell of a lot younger than that guy," said Mihalik.

"Then he looks like he could be Dr. Waters' big brother."

"Nah," said Mihalik.

The Golden Country

They drove for a long while, and Mihalik thought that if this was indeed London, then it was a strange and decimated version of the city that existed in the true world. Every section of the city, every neighborhood, was as sparsely built-up as it was near the Agency headquarters. The Londoners themselves must have been in hiding, because all the way from Hyde Park to Smith's residence in Stepney they saw no more than a dozen people about. "They're all at work," said Smith with a shrug. "You saw all the cars in the parking garage. I'd guess that a quarter of London's people are employed in the Agency Plaza. The rest work for the various ministries."

"What about the shopkeepers and merchants?" asked Cheryl. "What about the customers in those shops? We should have seen them."

"Oh," said Smith, growing tired of explaining things, "there isn't a great deal of shopkeeping these days. The Agency provides everything we need, and in abundance. It's considered almost unpatriotic to go into a shop and actually buy something."

"So what's the actual population of London, then?" asked Mihalik.

Smith thought for a moment. "Forty or fifty thousand, I'd say. But that's including all the suburbs and the outlying villages."

Mihalik shook his head. "Another thing, Smith—"

"Just a second, please. Let me just get this car up to the curb. I've never been very good at parallel parking. Well, this is my place. There are six apartments in the building. I'm on the first floor."

"That's something else I wanted to ask you about," Mihalik continued, as they got out of the car and back into the swirling blizzard. They moved as quickly as they could toward the shelter of the building's foyer. "Why don't you sound like an English guy? I mean, sometimes your accent's all right, but then you use words like 'apartment' instead of 'flat.' That kind of thing. I've been noticing it all afternoon."

"I honestly don't know what you mean," said Smith. "I speak the way I speak, the way everyone speaks. If you're suggesting the English we use here in London has become more like that in New York, blame modern communications. Having direct holovision broadcasts from around the world come right into your home has made everyone sound more or less alike. Didn't that happen in your world?" He glanced quickly into his mailbox, but there was nothing there. Mihalik looked at the card taped above the doorbell: *W. Smith. Rm. 101.*

"No," said Cheryl, "we don't have holovision in our homes. We're lucky if they print a newspaper twice a week."

"Sounds dreary," said Smith. "Come along, my place is just down here. It's not fancy, but it's home." He unlocked the door and gestured for them to enter.

It was a spacious, magnificent apartment. There was a large living room furnished with good taste and an eye for elegance. There was a lot of old dark paneling, polished to a rich glow; rare Oriental rugs lay upon a beautiful parquet floor; the furniture was likewise old and lovely and in excellent condition. A fire was already blazing in the hearth. Mihalik went over to it and warmed himself. "Nice place," he said.

"Thank you," said Smith, "I find it comfortable. Let me see what the cook's done up. You're welcome to share my little supper."

"Oh, no," said Cheryl, still thinking of her own 1996, where a person's supper might consist of only a rice ball or some marinated plant stems.

"I'm sure there's enough. The cook always prepares enough so that if I decide to entertain during the day, I needn't worry. I usually throw away more than I eat. As I said, the Agency provides in abundance."

Mihalik watched as Smith went out of the room; then he turned to Cheryl. "I don't know what to make of all this, honey," he said.

Her shoulders slumped. "I feel like we're getting farther and farther away from home the longer we're here."

Suddenly Mihalik knew that it was all up to him once more. He was going to have to be a hero all over again, even though he'd already done enough of that for one day. That morning, which had begun with the luring of the physicist, Marquand, to the World's Fair, seemed like a week ago. "I hope we did the right thing, coming to Smith's apartment," he said. "We still need to get some answers. We have to understand just what kind of world this is. Then we have to figure a way to get home."

"Maybe we should go back to 1939 again," said Cheryl. "Then we might try another method of finding our own 1996."

"Maybe," said Mihalik doubtfully.

"I think you'll enjoy this," said Smith, returning with a little card in one hand. "The cook has prepared *Foie gras en croûte,* accompanied by a rather fine Dom Pérignon 1991; *Poulets à la portugaise,* with a Château Margaux 1976; Saddle of lamb, with a Château Latour 1971; Mimosa salad; *Crêpes spécialité de la maison,* with a most remarkable Château d'Yquem of 1975; and, of course, *Café brûlot.* Come into the dining room with me. I'd hate for the pâté pastries to cool."

Mihalik waited for Cheryl to walk by him. "Do you know what all of that was?" he asked.

"I could understand the French words," said Cheryl, "but I find it very hard to believe that people in this world eat some of those things."

"Don't tell me about it," said Mihalik. They joined Smith in the dining room, which was just as elaborately furnished as the room they had left. There was a huge old oaken table; Smith took his seat at one end, and Mihalik and Cheryl sat to either side of him. They were served by a smiling young woman.

"Is she the cook?" asked Cheryl.

"Oh, Kalila? Yes, she is. She does quite a lot of things around here for me. She was provided by the Agency. The Agency provides—"

"Yes, so you keep saying," said Mihalik.

"I do think," said Smith, "that you can drop that tone of voice with me. Particularly here, at my table."

Mihalik once again felt like a fool. "I apologize again, Mr. Smith," he said. He looked down at the little pastry that had appeared before him. It was light and flaky and perfectly done. He wondered what he'd find inside it. Kalila smiled at him and filled his glass with champagne; Mihalik had become familiar with champagne in 1939, and he liked it. If nothing else in the meal proved edible, he was sure that he could fill up on Dom Pérignon. It would help to make this bizarre version of reality more acceptable.

He tasted the *foie gras* and rolled it around on his tongue, deciding if he liked it. He did, evidently, because he didn't have to force himself to take a second forkful.

"I understand, Mr. Mihalik," said Smith. "You're a rugged explorer.

You have a few rough edges. And you're a stranger to our world, our society. I suppose I'll have to be a little more tolerant, too. Are you enjoying your food?"

"Yes, indeed," said Cheryl. Kalila's dark eyes shined; she seemed very pleased, smiling even more broadly. But she still hadn't uttered a word.

One after the other, the courses followed, each accompanied by its appropriate wine. It was a rare treat in Mihalik's time to dine on two separate dishes. Here, at this banquet fit for a czar or a private dermatologist, he felt ashamed. He could not help remembering the hungry people of his own world. He could not forget the indigent nightmare to which both he and Cheryl longed to return.

After more than an hour and a half, they came to the end of the feast. They sipped the spiced, brandied coffee and tried to ignore the unusual feeling of satiation. Once or twice Mihalik thought that he was going to be ill, but his iron will saved him. He knew that it would be a while, however, before he'd be able to stand up. He burped.

"In some parts of the world," said Smith, frowning a little, "that's an indication that you're satisfied and that you enjoyed the meal. Not here, however." So much for his tolerance.

Mihalik ignored the remark. "Now that you've spirited us out of the Agency's clutches and demonstrated your stunning wealth, I'm wondering what your reasons are for all of this."

Smith gestured toward the remains of the meal, which Kalila was busily clearing away. "I'm not a rich man, Mr. Mihalik, by any means. I'm a minor Agency clerk. I have no private fortune. *Everyone* in London lives this well."

"What about Kalila?" said Cheryl.

"Oho!" Smith beamed happily. "I knew you'd ask me that. Well, when she finishes here, she goes home to a lavish suite as lovely as this one. And she has a domestic who will prepare for her something similar in grandness to what she prepared for us. And *her* cook has a cook. The Agency has provided for everyone."

"There's a catch in this somewhere," said Mihalik, "and we just haven't found it yet. Now all of this has been extremely pleasant; but a few hours ago you were scared out of your wits by something. Let's talk about that."

"The Second Squad," said Cheryl.

"Right," said Mihalik. "What *is* the Second Squad?"

"The executive branch of the Agency," said Smith. He smiled.

"You mean the police," said Cheryl.

Smith looked more uncomfortable. "Well," he said, "in a manner of speaking."

"What's the First Squad, then?" asked Mihalik.

Smith looked blankly at him. "What?"

"The First Squad."

"There is no First Squad," said Smith. He turned to Cheryl. "He's got a strong jaw, dear, but he's slow."

Cheryl smiled sweetly. "I love him just the way he is," she said.

Smith explained. "The Second Squad is the Agency's means of keeping crime under control. It's impossible to commit any sort of misdemeanor or felony anywhere in the world without the Second Squad knowing about it. They're probably even aware of this conversation we're having."

Mihalik and Cheryl glanced around the dining room, looking for peepholes or hidden cameras.

"The word 'Second' means 'one sixtieth of a minute,' you know," said Smith. "Not 'preceding Third.' They're the guardians of time."

Mihalik was completely lost. "How do they know when a crime has been committed?" he asked. "You mean they spy?"

"In a way, in a way." Smith seemed unwilling to say more.

"You're saying they watch everybody *all* the time," said Cheryl. "Like the *National Enquirer* in our world."

Smith's eyes got large. "Oh, no. There are no monitor screens in this apartment, no concealed microphones."

"Then how do they do it?" said Mihalik impatiently.

"They wait until after a crime is committed, and then they apprehend the culprit," said Smith. "Just the way a police force is supposed to work: democratically, with full respect for the rights of the citizen."

"Uh huh," said Mihalik. It wasn't always that way in his own 1996.

"I still don't see why you claim that it's impossible to commit a crime, then," Cheryl said. "If they wait for someone to go ahead and, say, rob somebody, it's already committed. And if they're not spying, how could they be aware of this conversation? You're contradicting yourself, Mr. Smith."

Their host began to perspire. He quite evidently didn't enjoy pursuing this further. "It's very simple," he said, spreading his hands helplessly. "They wait until you've gone ahead and done it; then they go back to before you did it, and arrest you." He shrugged.

Mihalik looked at Cheryl; she looked back expressionlessly. "Hey," he said, "I was the first man to go back in time. I did that 'yesterday,' according to your calendar. I found out that it doesn't work; you can't really move about in the past. You get stuck on a single day. Time travel doesn't exist."

"In *your* world, in *your* 1996," said Smith, "time travel doesn't exist.

Yet. In our world it's been perfected, and the Agency controls it. The Second Squad polices it."

"All since yesterday?" asked Mihalik.

"We've had time travel for about twelve years," said Smith. "We got it from the future. They came back in time and gave it to us. Like a gift."

"So there was no Frank Mihalik in your world," said Mihalik, trying to grasp the idea.

"Yes, there was," said Smith.

"Remember, Frank?" said Cheryl. "The people at the reception knew who we were. And Mr. Smith said he recognized 'me' last night, before 'I' went back to join 'you' in 1939."

"I don't get it at all," said Mihalik. "If you had time travel all perfected for the last twelve years, why did your Frank Mihalik go back to 1939 yesterday?"

"He had to," said Smith. "Otherwise the people from the future would never have developed the solution to the problem you discovered. It sounds complicated, but you—Mihalik, our Mihalik—had to play by the rules. And so did our Cheryl. Otherwise the whole fabric of our universe might have unraveled in some cataclysmic resolution."

"Then where are they now?" asked Cheryl. "Your Mihalik and your me, I mean?"

Smith just shrugged.

"I get it," said Mihalik suddenly. "This Second Squad of yours is like some time-traveling FBI." Smith closed his eyes and groaned a little; it had taken Mihalik at least six minutes to digest that information. "So they don't *need* to spy on you. They always know who's done what. People are probably being arrested all the time in utter confusion, because they haven't yet committed the crime they're being hauled away for. How do the cops prove it, then?"

"Potemkin," said Smith. He seemed nearly exhausted.

"Who's that?" asked Mihalik.

"It was an early motion picture by the Russian director, Sergei Eisenstein," said Cheryl.

"No, I don't mean that," said Smith.

"It was about a battleship called the *Potemkin,*" said Cheryl.

"Not that, either."

"Named after a famous Russian prince at the court of Catherine the Great."

"No!" cried Smith. "Potemkin: Post-temporal Kinespection. It's a great boon to democracy because no one is ever taken into custody on suspicion. Every arrest is based on absolute evidence of a crime committed, witnessed by the Second Squad. There hasn't been a case of an innocent person taken in to Minitern during the last twelve years. And Potemkin's a great time-saver, too; the Second Squad doesn't have to worry about searches and staking out locations and all that sort of thing."

" 'Time-saver,' " snorted Mihalik. "That's rich."

"All this began just about the same time your second Man from Mars took over," said Cheryl thoughtfully.

Smith hesitated. "Yes," he said, "some coincidence, isn't it?"

"And they're using this Potemkin to keep tabs on us this very second," said Mihalik.

"Well," said Smith, "only if our evening together leads to some overt criminal activity."

"And if it does, they'd be busting down the door right this minute."

"I guess so."

"So they knew exactly when Cheryl and I would appear at that Agency party."

"Of course," said Smith. "That's why I was hurrying you out of there."

It was Mihalik's turn to be disgusted. "Then how the hell did we manage to escape?" he demanded.

There was a long, empty silence in the room. "There does seem to be some sort of paradox there," admitted Smith. Mihalik wished that he had more champagne, but he didn't want to ask Smith for it.

"You've never explained why you think we're in trouble," said Cheryl.

"Because you're unpersons, that's why," said Smith. "And here I am, feeding unpersons and chatting with them as if they ever existed."

Mihalik gently pushed his chair away from the table. "Well," he said quietly, "I think I've had my limit of this. I think it's time to find Dr. Waters. He must be in that Agency Building somewhere."

Smith barked a loud raucous laugh. "Dr. Waters!" he said in amazement. "Why do you think Dr. Waters would spare time to see you?"

Mihalik glared across the table. "Dr. Waters is the head of my project," he said in a low, tightly controlled voice. "He assumed the responsibility for my safety. We became pretty good friends during my training. He owes something to me, and I owe something to him and to the project."

"Dr. Waters probably isn't interested in your project any longer," said Smith with some amusement. "He has much more important things to worry about. Dr. Waters is the Man from Mars."

"Dr. Bertram A. Waters?" said Mihalik, stunned.

"Of course," said Smith. "But you saw his picture and didn't recognize him."

"See, Frank?" said Cheryl. "Didn't I say it looked like him?"

Mihalik shook his head. "I don't believe it. First, Dr. Waters is a dedicated scientist; he couldn't care less about ruling the world. Second, that picture shows a guy a whole lot older than the man I know."

Smith nodded. "Dr. Waters left our present twelve years ago, to go into the future for some kind of vital work. He stayed in the future for about sixteen years, and then returned to 1984. So he's older than if he had just lived in the present all the time."

Mihalik was trying to sort out this new information. "And you say that now he's the boss of the world?"

"That's right."

"And he's the head of the Agency, and that means he's given the order to hunt Cheryl and me down?"

"Right again."

"I'll never believe that," said Mihalik with finality.

Smith shrugged. "Suit yourself. I've tried to help you; but if you insist on sticking your own head into a noose, there's nothing more I can do." Kalila appeared with liqueur glasses and a crystal decanter. "We'll take that in the other room," said Smith. He indicated to his guests that they should precede him into the parlor. Mihalik and Cheryl took seats on a sofa, and Smith dropped into an overstuffed armchair. They sipped the sweet liqueur for a few moments and studied each other.

"All right," said Cheryl, "I'm willing to accept all this for the sake of argument. Now please explain those three slogans we see all over the place."

This was a safer topic for discussion, and Smith seemed more relaxed. "They belong to Minipeep, the Ministry of People. There is a massive program under way at the moment to resettle great numbers of people; the poor souls come from lands more crowded and poverty-stricken than here. Not everyone in the world is as rich and comfortable as we have it in London, I'm afraid; but the Agency is taking care of the situation. The goal is to have every individual in the world fitted into just such a rewarding life before the turn of the century. I think we'll succeed."

"That's truly amazing," said Cheryl. "Then that's why we've seen so few people about. Most of your population's been resettled."

"That's precisely it," said Smith, with a touch of pride. "I have a small part in the process, myself."

"And then the first slogan means—"

Smith interrupted. "It means simply that the less people there are, the more there is for the remaining folk."

Cheryl shook her head. "Your slogan's wrong. It should be 'fewer.' "

"I don't follow you," said Smith.

"LESS IS MORE is a phrase from a poem by Robert Browning," said Cheryl. "It was used as a general statement about art by the architect Mies van der Rohe. If Minipeep is using it the way *you* mean, it should be FEWER IS MORE. Or have you resettled grammer, as well?"

Smith looked at Mihalik and Cheryl and mused, "A fool and a pedant; what awful company to be arrested in."

The sentiment passed over Mihalik's head. "The second slogan, MARS IS EARTH, obviously refers to the Man from Mars."

"That's your first point of the evening, Mr. Mihalik," said Smith sourly.

"But I don't understand TOMORROW IS YESTERDAY."

Smith finished the last of his liqueur. "It becomes simple enough when you realize that the resettlement I mentioned takes place not in space, but in time. We find new homes for the huddled masses and the wretched refuse on some bright, prosperous day in some long-ago year. They are given a new start in the colonial Empire of the Past, and we are relieved of the burden of their welfare."

The implications of this casual statement horrified both Mihalik and Cheryl. They had spent only a year imprisoned in the past, on one "bright, prosperous day," and only their mutual love and will to survive saved them from madness. They considered what it must be like for the "colonials," who were doomed to spend the remainder of their lives repeating the same day endlessly, without hope of alteration or rescue.

"That's the catch," said Mihalik finally. "I knew we'd hear it sooner or later."

Smith pretended he didn't know what Mihalik meant. "We simply don't see it that way," he said. "In any event, you have no right to make judgments about the way we handle our affairs; you don't even belong to this world. I suppose *your* world is governed better."

"No," said Cheryl, "we come from a place that's pretty terrible in a lot of ways. We are hungry and cold and frightened. But at least we don't solve our problems by casting millions of other people into a bottomless pit and forgetting about them. And we don't have an Agency looking over our shoulders every moment of the day."

Smith made a disdainful gesture. "No, you don't have resettlement, and you don't have the Agency; but I'll bet neither of you ever tasted a Château Latour before, either."

"Your Château Latour is too expensive," said Cheryl.

"That," said Smith, "is a matter of opinion, my righteous young lady."

"Yes," Mihalik said, "but we know *your* opinion. I wonder what the people you've dumped into history would say about it. They've had the

chance to spend a few years watching the same dead leaves blow by at the
same time every afternoon. It gets very boring, let me tell you."

That didn't concern Smith. "Only if you have no other occupation," he
said. "Boredom goes hand in hand with idleness. I can't bring myself to
fret over such beggars."

Cheryl held up a hand. "Forget it, Frank," she said disgustedly. "You
can't reason with him."

"Well," said Mihalik in bewilderment, "what are we going to do?"

"You might stay here," said Smith, affable once more. "Learn to love
our world. It isn't difficult. It sounds to me as if your own has very little
to offer."

Mihalik stood up and took Cheryl's hand. "Come on, honey," he said,
"let's go see the chief. Somehow in this place they've forgotten the meaning of 'home.' "

As they left Smith's apartment, they heard him laughing. Mihalik
slammed the door behind him. It was still very cold outside.

Checking into the Hyatt Infinity

When Mihalik and Cheryl arrived at the Agency Plaza, they learned
that things were generally as Smith had described them. This Agency,
whatever it was, had entirely replaced the previous world order. "Man
from Mars" was now merely an ornamental title, and the word "Mars"
did not appear anywhere on the building's directory. They found Dr.
Waters' name, and learned that his offices were on the 111th floor.

"Bet he has a nice view," said Mihalik, as they rode up in an express
elevator, listening to gentle instrumental versions of songs they couldn't
identify. Such piped-in music had disappeared from their own world as a
result of an international movement; a petition had been signed by over
one and a half billion people. Hearing the soft music now gave the time
travelers a melancholy nostalgia.

Immediately beyond the bank of elevators was a corridor leading to a
checkpoint; the way was guarded by several armed men and women, all
wearing the same style silver and blue uniform the general had worn at
the party. One of the men stepped forward as if to block Mihalik's way.
"Yes?" he said in a gruff voice.

"I want to see Dr. Waters," Mihalik said. "It's me, Frank Mihalik.
And Cheryl. He'll want to see us, just let him know we're out here."

The man in the Agency uniform gave them both a quick but thorough
scrutiny, then turned to a speaker mounted in a wall. There was a small
holoscreen there, too, but Mihalik couldn't see to whom the soldier was
reporting.

"You know," said Cheryl, "if Smith's story were completely accurate, the Second Squad would know we're here, and these guards would have been ready for us."

"I don't know what to believe," said Mihalik. "I'm just waiting until I can hear it all from Dr. Waters himself."

The soldier returned, his expression respectful. "Just walk right through here, please," he said. "Right down the corridor and past that officer at the desk. He'll buzz you through. Dr. Waters' office is just beyond that."

"Thank you," said Mihalik. He was on his best behavior, and minding his manners. He let Cheryl go through first. Whatever his relationship had been to Dr. Waters in the past, Mihalik was now going to meet the ruler of the world. Everything around him indicated that this was a no-nonsense kind of place. He suddenly got the unhappy notion that this interview might not be so easy as he had figured.

They went by all the security checks as swiftly as though a guardian angel hovered above them. In a way, that was true; Dr. Waters had personally ordered that Mihalik and Cheryl be shown every courtesy. As they approached nearer to Waters' suite, the carpeting was more luxurious. Mihalik had never walked on anything like it, not even during the three-day all-expenses-paid holiday he had been given just before his leap through time. He had gone to Russell Stoverworld in Orlando, Florida.

Dr. Waters walked through the door to meet them. "Frank!" he said, smiling. "And Cheryl! Marvelous to see you both! It's been a remarkable day, hasn't it?"

"Dr. Waters—" began Mihalik.

"Frank, come into my office. Sit down, be comfortable. I want to hear all about your adventure. Sorry I couldn't be at your reception. No rest for the weary, you know. Look out there, isn't that beautiful? Lonely at the top, though, just like they say. Cheryl, you look lovely. Did you like the past? 1939, wasn't it? World's Fair, I understand. Bit of a muddle about bringing you back, I believe. We've got that all worked out now, I hear. Best men and women working around the clock. Never happen again, I promise you. Well."

Mihalik was struck dumb with astonishment. Dr. Waters *never* spoke that way. He was a thoughtful, reticent man. When you were with him, you were always aware that his powerful brain was constantly observing, cataloguing, evaluating, and deciding; but he rarely shared whatever important conclusions he reached. He was a tall, slender man, strong, but not in a bulky way. He had—or he *had* had, in the proper 1996—black hair in a sharp widow's peak; a narrow, straight nose; deep dark eyes that people unfailingly described as "magnetic"; prominent cheekbones that gave his face a long, somewhat sinister appearance; and his one affectation—a carefully trimmed mustache of the sort film stars wore when the city of Hollywood still existed. He liked stylish clothing, and customarily wore a dinner jacket and black tie in the evening. Someone had once remarked, accurately, that Dr. Waters looked like Satan played by a young Erroll Flynn.

The Dr. Waters who stood smiling at Mihalik was older, grayer, and a little slump-shouldered from the weight of his duties; he had eliminated the mustache. Mihalik thought the man looked no more like his project's administrator than the giant photograph had. And on top of that, it seemed that Waters' whole manner had changed as well. Mihalik glanced at Cheryl; she gave him a little shrug to indicate that she was just as perplexed.

"Dr. Waters," said Mihalik, trying desperately to calm down a little, "we met this man Smith who said—"

"Smith!" cried Waters. "Yes, of course you'd run into him. Told him to go to that party and take care of you. The man can be a little hard to bear sometimes, thinks he knows absolutely everything. He used to give me a lot of trouble a few years ago, but I changed his tune. He'll argue with you all night if you let him, but the thing to do is tell him right off you won't stand for it. He won't dare use that on me anymore. Loves me like a brother. Of course, I'm the ruler of the world now, so maybe that has something to do with it. Just as hard to put up with as the arguing. Ha ha! What did he tell you? Some rot about putting you right back to work, no doubt. Well, never mind him. How would you and Cheryl like a vacation? You've earned one, no doubt about it. Where, though? Anywhere you like, you just name it. There's nobody in Venice this time of year, but I wouldn't recommend it."

Mihalik took a deep breath and tried again. "Sir, there's been some kind of terrible accident, and you're the only hope we have of setting everything right. Even if you aren't the Dr. Waters we knew, you must have the knowledge and imagination necessary to help us. This isn't our world. This isn't the 1996 we left; it's all different. We've got to know if we can get back to our own, or if it's been destroyed forever and replaced by this. Can you do something, or must we spend the rest of our lives here?"

Dr. Waters seated himself comfortably behind his desk and gazed thoughtfully for a while at the panoramic view of London. From the 111th floor, the city looked even less like the London of Mihalik's world. There was a scattering of buildings here and there; once in a while a road joined a few blocks of houses or apartment buildings; there were several large blocky edifices that must have been the various ministries; but all in all the city was comprised mostly of large parklike expanses, clad now in snowy white. The peaceful stillness was by far the most alien quality of this false universe.

The ruler of the world turned at last and faced Mihalik. "Put your minds at rest," he said. "You won't have to stay among us, if that's your choice. Glad to find a home for you. Get right to work on it. Sad to hear that you're rejecting our simple, rather comfortable society. It's been a little project of mine, you know, getting the world into decent shape. Don't know what your world is like, but it must be something special, if you're in such a rush to return. Do my best for you, of course, but it's not so easy. Not just a case of tapping your heels together and wishing. You're not Dorothy, and your separate reality's not Kansas."

"It's not a matter of rejection, Dr. Waters," said Cheryl. "It's just that everything we know, everyone we love, our own past and our own future, all of that is in another world different from this. We just want our own place, better or worse than yours as it may be."

Dr. Waters nodded sadly. "And I suppose there's another Dr. Waters there, too, eh? Not like I am, I guess. Different in some ways. If you don't have time travel, then your Dr. Waters hasn't gone into the future. He's younger, am I right? Still has the mustache, no doubt. Well, maybe you're quite correct; maybe my younger self was more likable." He sighed. "When you get older, you'll see that the road from youth to middle age is not so straight as it seems. I often wonder how I got here myself. Where were the turnings? A small choice, a decision that didn't seem important at the time—thousands of them add together, and what you're left with is what you see every morning in the mirror." His voice trailed off.

Mihalik wondered why it was so difficult to keep Dr. Waters' mind on the point of the conversation. "This Smith guy mentioned something about the Second Squad, and that Cheryl and I could expect trouble from them."

"Oh, yes, of course," said Waters. He looked uncomfortable. "That's quite true. You're supposed to be arrested. Ought to occur just as you leave this office. They'll take you away, toss you into Minitern, probably never see you again. You'll be resettled, if you survive. Best thing for everybody. We'll find a nice sunny day for you. Even let you pick the year. Any year you like. You just name it."

Cheryl got quickly to her feet. "But why?" she cried.

Dr. Waters looked even sadder. "Have to," he said. "You're unpersons."

"Smith called us that," said Mihalik. "What the hell does it mean?"

The Man from Mars toyed with a small round glass paperweight on his desk. The paperweight had a bit of pink coral embedded in it. He didn't look up at Mihalik as he explained. "You're not the real Frank Mihalik, or the real Cheryl—that is, the ones we sent through time yesterday, to keep the strands of temporal unity untangled. You're the Frank and Cheryl from some other universe, coexistent with ours. So you're not even human beings; you're figments of the cosmic imagination. A disruption of our conveniently regulated society. Well, we know how to deal with disruptions. Cause you no unnecessary pain, I assure you. Though there may be a good deal of necessary pain if you're particularly hard to persuade. The Frank and Cheryl of this world would have gone off happily to be resettled, proud of the chance. LESS IS MORE, you know. But you're not them; they're gone."

"That's right," said Mihalik, slamming a fist on Waters' desk. "We're here and they're not. Where did *they* go?"

Dr. Waters' smile brightened. "Have you ever heard of the Paradox of the Infinite Hotel?" he asked.

"No," said Mihalik impatiently.

"Time travel is a mother lode of paradoxes," said Waters. "Have a fondness for them, myself. Kind of a hobby of mine. Studied them all in the future. Don't pretend to understand them all the way they do centuries from now. They have them all sorted out there. But the Hotel, now, I do comprehend. Imagine that there's a hotel with an infinite number of rooms."

"What does this have to do with getting Cheryl and me home?" Mihalik said. There was a kind of animal snarl in his voice.

Dr. Waters ignored him. "And there's a guest in every room in the place, get it? Now a convention comes in late in the day. Big convention. Even an infinite convention, with no reservations in advance. They're all tired from traveling. People want to go up to nice clean rooms, wash up, take a nap, go out for dinner. Maybe find some girls."

"What's the point?" shouted Mihalik.

"So the desk clerk is a little upset because all his rooms are taken, and he has to deal with all these grumpy salesmen or whatever they are. Then he has a brilliant idea. He goes to Room 1 and knocks on the door and takes the guest from that room and puts him in Room 2. Then he puts the original Room 2 guest in Room 4. He puts the Room 3 guest in Room 6. See? What he's doing, he's putting all the old guests in all the even-numbered rooms. There's an infinite number of even numbers, so it's no problem. They'll fit. Then he takes the infinite number of new convention people, and puts them in the now vacant odd-numbered rooms. It all works out very well unless too many of them call down to the desk for early wake-up calls. And they better not all want ice at the same time, either."

Mihalik was furious. He wanted to grab Dr. Waters the way he had grabbed Smith's shirt, but he restrained himself. "You're saying that every Frank and Cheryl in all the infinite possible universes just moved over one, like playing musical chairs."

"Something like that," said Dr. Waters. "Gratified you can see my meaning. You're not real, not by the standards of this universe."

"I wonder if all the Franks and Cheryls are having this problem," said Mihalik. He shivered as he glimpsed the vast array of Mihaliks, all lost in this same terrible vision.

"Many of them are settling down comfortably in whatever situation they find themselves," said Dr. Waters. "As you should. Accept resettlement."

"No," said Mihalik. "We're going to find our way home."

Dr. Waters thought for a moment. "Why don't you and Cheryl come with me? I have something to show you. It might change your thinking about our world."

Mihalik only grunted; Cheryl came toward the desk. "If you can help us get home," she said, "we'll do anything you ask."

"You should be learning," said Dr. Waters, "that you can't choose among alternate realities as if you were looking at tomatoes in a grocery store."

"We know that," said Cheryl. "But why can't you just reverse whatever process brought us here in the first place?"

"Come with me," said Dr. Waters. He smiled at both of them.

A Small Token of Our Esteem

It was getting late. Mihalik's watch had stopped, but he had heard bells somewhere tolling twenty-one o'clock. He was sitting with Cheryl and Dr. Waters at a table in a large hall. There were other decorated tables around them; Mihalik turned to see how large the crowd was, and he realized that he couldn't see the far end of the room. There must have been thousands of people, all seated at small round tables made festive with vases of mixed blue and white carnations. There was a head table with a rostrum set up, and a small, elderly, pink-haired woman was speaking into a microphone. She was extremely nervous because of the presence of Dr. Waters.

"It's been absolutely marvelous working for the Agency all these years," she said. She glanced around at the people at the head table. "I want to thank my supervisor, and my foreman, Mr. Sokol, and I want to thank all the other men and women who worked with me in the Delitescence Section for making it so pleasant. I love you, and I'm going to miss you all." Tears began to stream down her face.

Another woman, younger and wearing the Agency uniform, stood up and joined her. "Thank you, Diota," she said. "I'm sure they'll all miss you, too. Go sit down, dear, that's it. Hurry up, now. Next I'd like to introduce Captain Telek Shalcross, who is retiring after nearly thirty-eight years in the Second Squad. Captain Shalcross was recruited in 1874, and spent most of his years with us policing the settlements of the sixth and seventh centuries. He has chosen for his retirement home a day he visited twice in the line of duty, September 23, 681 A.D. Let's have a nice hand for Captain Shalcross."

There *was* a nice hand, and Shalcross came to the microphone. He was tall and broad-shouldered, with a military bearing that made him seem even larger. "I have only one regret," he said. "I wish I could take this uniform with me. I've worn the silver and blue for most of my life, and it will be strange to dress as a civilian again. Especially in seventh-century clothes." For an instant a smile touched his lips, then disappeared. "It is an honor and a privilege to serve the Agency, and all the difficult times and hardships I've known have been repaid tonight, just to glimpse Dr. Waters here with us. That's all I have to say. God bless you all."

"See?" said Dr. Waters. "They all love the Agency. All happy about being resettled. All these wonderful people, loyal workers and friends, retiring tonight. They don't have to worry about what the future will hold. If their old age will be lonely and wretched. They know exactly what their declining years will be like, because they've picked their resettlement sites themselves. They've searched through extensive catalogues of pleasant, halcyon times and chosen the very perfect sort of day. Whatever their preferences. Most people go for June or September. Have a number of winter enthusiasts, however. Makes no difference. We've preselected the years for prosperity, peace, and health conditions. I think it's wonderful."

"If they had anything bad to say about the Agency," said Cheryl, "they wouldn't be here, because the Second Squad would have arrested them this afternoon."

"A valid point," admitted Waters. "Unlikely, though, that any such person would have stayed on with us until retirement age."

One senior employee after another spoke his thanks into the microphone, and then was hustled out of the spotlight. Everyone seemed animated with anticipation; no one seemed particularly anxious. It all tended to bear out Waters' words.

"Do these people know what happens after they're abandoned on their chosen day?" asked Mihalik. "Do they know they can't go anywhere because at midnight they'll be whisked back to their precise point of arrival? Every day starts at that same place, wherever they may have traveled during the previous hours. And they can't acquire anything because at midnight, when the next repetition of the day starts, all they've gathered disappears. Their only permanent possessions will be just what they take with them from the present. That means they have to go out each morning and find food or medicine or whatever they might need. They can't put up a supply for a few days. They can't afford to get sick or injured. And none of the things they do will have any effect on the past; when the day starts over, none of the true local inhabitants will remember the previous version of the day. Broken things will be magically mended. New friends will be strangers again. There isn't the slightest sense of continuity. It can drive a person insane."

"I know, I know," said Dr. Waters. "And these people understand that. A difficulty, I agree. Preferable, even with all that, to the over-crowded, starving world we had before. Flaws in the system. We're not perfect, never claimed to be. But we take precautions. All these retiring men and women are settled near a good food source. As you say, each midnight everything returns to the condition it was in when the resettlee arrived. Means the food supply is inexhaustible. They cannot go hungry. Same is true for most of their needs. We do our best."

Suddenly Cheryl sat up very straight. "That captain," she said. "He visited his resettlement day twice in the line of duty. And the Second Squad—I never made the connection before. They have no problem at all traveling through time, backward or forward. Time travel has been *perfected.* You don't *need* to strand these folks on isolated days in the past. It doesn't have to be that way at all. You're doing it for other reasons, something you're not telling us."

"Of course," said Dr. Waters reasonably. He smiled.

"What are you hiding, then?" asked Mihalik.

"Not going to tell you. Tried persuasion, showed you how nice we can be. Showed you all these marvelous people. Just didn't dent your thick skulls. Now we'll have to try threats and ugliness. Hate to do it. You're so much like Frank and Cheryl, my friends whose places you've taken. But you've forced me. We have other catalogues, you know. Catalogues of particularly gruesome days, in years so bad they've become legendary. We could throw you down anywhere we choose. There are some days in America in 1968 that would make the French Reign of Terror seem like a field trip to the zoo. My favorite is 1361 A.D. A Black Death year. Some perfectly horrendous weeks to choose from right here in England. All we have to do is show a holofilm of one of those days, and criminals confess

anything. But we won't bother entertaining you with films. Just pluck
one of the worst dates in recorded history out of the hat, and kick your
contumacious asses into the middle of it."

Mihalik cleared his throat. It was very obviously time to regain control
of the situation. He gave Dr. Waters his cool, devastatingly calm smile.
"Thank you for everything," he said, "but I believe that once again it's
time for Cheryl and me to be going." He got slowly to his feet. Cheryl
looked at him, wondering what he was planning. She pushed her chair
back and stood up, also.

"You're going nowhere," said Dr. Waters, still seated. "The Second
Squad—"

"The Second Squad can't touch us," said Mihalik, "or they would
have by now. We're invisible to them because we're not of your world and
we just don't exist in your future."

Dr. Waters gave a satisfied grin. "Because in a few hours you'll find
yourself filed away in some perilous and dreadful year, with other villains
just like yourselves locked into days on either side. But unlike prison, you
won't be able to communicate with the people in the other cells. All that
will exist for you is your own grim, narrow hole in the calendar."

Mihalik let out a deep breath. "Dr. Waters," he said, and then he
swung a powerful blow that smashed the Man from Mars in the face.
Mihalik grabbed Cheryl's hand and half dragged her away; they ran
toward the nearest exit. They didn't stop to see what reaction they had
caused. Mihalik could hear the beginning of a loud uproar. He was moving as fast as he could, and Cheryl was not far behind. A woman in an
Agency uniform was guarding the exit; Mihalik slashed at her throat
with the side of his hand, and the woman collapsed. Then he was through
the door and running for the elevators.

"We've got it made," Mihalik called over his shoulder.

"Hope so," gasped Cheryl.

"Second Squad," said Mihalik, punching the elevator button furiously,
"would have prevented that. No other security people around."

"Then we *don't* exist in this future."

"Right. Either Dr. Waters will catch us and do what he threatened, or
else we're going to escape."

"How?" asked Cheryl.

"Don't know yet." The elevator arrived, and Mihalik pushed Cheryl in
ahead of him. The doors closed; the elevator dropped toward the ground
floor. For a moment there was peace except for the lilting melodies from
the hidden speaker. Mihalik looked at Cheryl; she was a brave little
woman, he thought. She's been through so much, and she's still holding

up. He gazed into her beautiful green eyes and wanted to hold her, to kiss her moist, sensuous lips. But this was not the time or the place for that.

Twice into the Same River

They ran out of the Agency Plaza and down the marble steps. "Damn this snow!" Mihalik cried. He hated cold weather. It was night, and the pale beams from the streetlamps made the drifts glitter like crushed diamonds.

"Where are we going?" asked Cheryl.

"Don't know yet."

"There must be somebody—"

Then Mihalik knew. There was one person in this world who could help them, who would be glad to help them. "Ray," he said.

"But Ray's in New York," said Cheryl.

"Dr. Waters was supposed to be in New York," said Mihalik. "We were supposed to be returned to New York. The project was in New York. But in this world, the project means the Agency, and all of that is here, in London. Ray will be here, too."

"Unless he's been resettled," said Cheryl. "How do we find him?"

Mihalik thought for a few seconds. "Phone book," he said. There were so few buildings nearby, however, where there might be pay phones. "We have to go back into the Agency Building." He grimaced; he didn't like that idea at all. They ran back up the marble steps and into the building. There were several phones against a wall opposite the elevators. There were no phone books, not of the kind Mihalik was familiar with in his own world. The holophones were different, too. For an instant Mihalik was afraid. He wondered how long they had before the pursuit arrived.

"Look," said Cheryl breathlessly, "there's a button on the phone marked *Info.*" She punched it and the screen lit up. A synthesized computer voice asked what information they wanted, and Mihalik gave it Ray's name. He murmured a prayer and waited. A few seconds later, a section of a page appeared on the screen. There was Ray's address and phone number. "I'll remember the address," he said, "and you remember the phone number."

"All right," said Cheryl.

The voice asked if there was other information they required. "Can I make a collect call to that number? I don't have any coins."

"Yes, sir," said the voice. "Your name, please?"

"Tell him it's Frank Mihalik."

"Just a moment, please."

And then the screen was filled with Ray's familiar, grinning mug. Ray was more than just Mihalik's backup, the temponaut who would have plunged into the past if Mihalik had turned up lame or with his liver suddenly lilied. Ray was crony and compotator, tennis partner and paraclete. He was the loyal Patroclus to Mihalik's Achilles. Ray was almost as good as Mihalik at everything a time traveler needed to know; Ray was even *better* at certain things, like being funny at press conferences. Mihalik was often stuck for a good evasive quip on such occasions, though by means of electronic stimulation of the brain Dr. Waters had inserted more than a thousand into Mihalik's memory. Indeed, the primary reason Mihalik had been chosen over Ray—and this was a fact wholly unsuspected by either man—was Cheryl. Ray didn't have a girl friend or even a wife. Some of the project's psych people felt that in an unexpected crisis that might be a disadvantage. They had been correct about that; thoughts of Cheryl had kept Mihalik going when there was little else motivating him to survive.

"Back so soon?" said Ray jovially. "The good old days not what you expected?"

"Ray," cried Mihalik, "it's great to see you. You have to listen carefully." He sketched the situation briefly, emphasizing that "time was of the essence," that they were being threatened with "a fate worse than death," and that only Ray's presence indicated that Providence had, after all, "fitted the cloud with a silver lining." The project's chief had loaded Mihalik up with clichés, too, because Dr. Waters hated to see so much blank space in Mihalik's mind just going to waste.

"So it's *not* you," said Ray thoughtfully. "It just looks like you. And just talking with you could get me thrown away into the trash, on some Godforsaken prehistoric day before the invention of beer. The SS might be coming up the stairs right now."

"The SS?" Mihalik asked.

"The Second Squad," said Cheryl helpfully.

"Is that Cheryl's voice I heard?" asked Ray. "Is that the real Cheryl with you?"

"She seems real enough to me," said Mihalik.

"But then, who *wouldn't?*" Ray shook his head. "Never mind. You say you're in trouble. Tell me where you are, and I'll come get you. Any friend of mine is a friend of Frank's. Even though you've never met him, I'm sure you'd like him. And I'm sure he'd want me to give you a break."

Mihalik didn't try to follow that logic. "We're in the lobby of the Agency Plaza."

"Hiding out under their noses, huh? Very clever," said Ray. He laughed. "Across the street and to the right, about seven blocks, there's a service station. You lock yourself in the men's room, and Cheryl locks herself in the ladies' room. Wait for me; I'll be there in about half an hour."

"All right," said Mihalik. "Ray, you're our only hope."

"I know. You're lucky I'm not jealous or resentful or anything like that, because this would be the perfect opportunity to clean your clock. You're lucky that we're such great pals. Of course, you don't have any idea what our relationship is like in *this* 1996; you're banking on our friendship in *your* 1996. But you always were an intuitive lad."

"Love to chat with you, Ray," said Mihalik, "but we're kind of pressed for time."

"I'm on my way. I'll knock eleven times." Then the holoscreen went blank.

"Eleven?" Mihalik asked Cheryl. She just shrugged.

They found the gas station easily enough, and did as Ray had directed. It was cold in the rest rooms, and the minutes passed slowly. At last, as Mihalik was studying his hairline in the mirror, there came twelve knocks on the door. "Ray?" he called.

"That's me."

Mihalik unlocked the door, and felt a great wave of relief when he saw his faithful sidekick. "You knocked twelve times instead of eleven," he said.

Ray hugged Mihalik fiercely, even though, for Ray, it had been only a day since he had seen his friend. "Then why did you open the door?" he asked.

"Because you said you were you," said Mihalik. "Let's go get Cheryl."

Soon the three climbed into Ray's flashy red car, and headed up the avenue away from the Agency Plaza, toward Minitern. Ray began making frequent turns, as if eluding hypothetical shadowers. In a few minutes Mihalik, at least, had no idea where he was. "Where are we going?"

"Let me know one thing," said Ray. "Where do you *want* to go?"

"Home," said Cheryl. "Our home. Our own 1996."

"Well," said Ray confidently, "there's only one person who can help you do that. Dr. Waters. You say that he's not very receptive to the idea at the moment. So we'll outthink him."

Mihalik snorted skeptically. "The three of us combined couldn't think in an hour what Dr. Waters can think while he's shaving."

"Frank," said Cheryl, "let's listen to Ray's idea."

"Thanks," said Ray. "Now here's my plan. We're going to bundle you off to the future, centuries from now. The people there perfected time travel, then came back to give it to us. That's where Dr. Waters went in 1984 to get a complete education in chronics. When you meet him there, remember that he won't know what's happened here during the last twelve years. He won't know about yesterday or today. He'll be even younger than when you first met him in your world. He'll be glad to help you, and the people of the future will probably have a simple solution to your predicament."

"That sounds perfect, Ray," said Cheryl. "It's brilliant."

"There's only one hitch," said Ray. "If, in the future, your arrival there or the results of your journey cause some kind of unpleasantness, they'll know about that, too. They'll be in a position to prevent it, unlike our SS. And then, too, you may not go into the future, after all. You may end up stuck back on that day in 1939."

In the silence that followed, the windshield wipers made dull, lonely noises. "I like to hear about the risks in advance," said Mihalik.

"Well, that's them," said Ray. "The brighter side of the coin is that there's a very good chance you'll end up just where you want to be, back in your very own 1996. The people in the future may be maneuvering things toward a happy ending, if they like your looks. In that case, you won't need to go to their time. That may be why you haven't been caught by the SS. The people of the future may be clearing a path for you."

"If that's true," said Cheryl, "we won't have any trouble from now on, either."

"Right," said Ray. "We'll see."

Paradoxes and nonlinear time-flow made Mihalik feel the same way he did when he tried to read poetry that didn't rhyme. "So where are we going?" he asked.

Ray's sleek car squealed around a corner, and Agency Plaza stood before them about a mile away. "Oh," said Cheryl.

"Don't worry," said Ray. "We're all well-known faces in there. I'll be able to get us into the transmission room. I can set the coordinates and all the rest. If you haven't been stopped by now, you can assume that you'll get away clean."

They left the car in Ray's assigned place in the parking garage, and once more hurried up the icy marble steps. Ray led them to the elevator, and they rode up to the project's facilities on the fifty-seventh floor. No one challenged them. Mihalik began to feel more confident; it was beginning to look as if Ray was right. They said hello to a bored Agency man —guard or janitor they couldn't tell—and hurried to the transmission room. It didn't resemble the equipment Mihalik had used, but this world had the benefit of a helping hand from the future. The two nervous time travelers took their places on the transmission stage while Ray went about the business of setting the controls; evidently, once perfected, the procedures involved with time travel were not especially complicated.

"I wish you could stay here longer," said Ray, when he'd finished getting everything ready. "After you leave, there won't be a Frank or Cheryl in this world."

"Maybe your own will come back," said Mihalik.

"Maybe," said Ray dubiously. "Anyway, give my regards to the Ray in your time. Are you all set?"

"All set," said Mihalik. He took Cheryl's slim hand and pulled her close. "Once more into the Unknown!"

At that moment they were interrupted by danger in the form of Dr. Waters and six armed Agency soldiers. "Stop them!" cried the ruler of the world.

Mihalik silently damned all theories and the people who inflicted them on normal folk. "Push the button!" he yelled.

"Wait!" shouted Waters. "Listen! I've got something important to tell you! When you hear this, you'll think twice about taking your chances with another jump through time." He looked from Mihalik to Cheryl. He eyed them magnetically.

Before Mihalik had a chance to make a courageous sardonic reply, there was a flicker of amber light, a sizzle, a snap, and a moderate clap of thunder. It was obvious that a few things had changed slightly during those seconds. The room looked just a little different, larger and brighter; the electronic equipment was bulkier and less sophisticated; the armed guards were gone; Dr. Waters was younger, smiling, and once more sported a devilish mustache; Ray was pretty much the same, except now he and Dr. Waters were dressed in olive green jumpsuits, the same as Mihalik and Cheryl wore. Most happily of all, a buffet table was set up, but this one did not bear fantastically abundant and sumptuous food; instead, there were platters of frozen Milky Way bars and caramel apples without the apples and sheets of little candy buttons stuck on paper. To drink there were bottles of Vernor's ginger ale, the Official Beverage of the Conquest of Time. Civilization had gone back on the candy standard.

"Ray was right," said Cheryl with wonder. "We're *home.*"

"Good old Ray," said Mihalik, helping her down from the transmission stage. They turned to receive their welcome. It wasn't so elaborate as their reception in the false 1996, but it was infinitely more pleasant. That thought led Mihalik to another: he felt grateful that they had managed to find the right suite, somehow, in the Infinite Hotel. They had come a long way, and they could use some rest.

"I'll bet you're glad to see me," said Dr. Waters.

"Wait until we tell you about it," said Mihalik.

"That can wait," said Dr. Waters. "First, I'm sure you'll want to rest and get cleaned up. Then we can talk."

"Have you ever thought about shaving off your mustache?" asked Cheryl.

Dr. Waters looked at her, bewildered. "No," he said slowly.

"Don't," said Mihalik. "Don't ask me why, just don't."

"Anybody want a jawbreaker?" asked Ray.

Mihalik turned and looked at his faithful backup man. It was nice to be back.

Book Three

Just Because
Everything Is Different
Doesn't Mean
Anything Has Changed

Dr. Waters was holding a large box of gold foil-wrapped chocolate-covered cherry-flavored processed food product. Real cherries had disappeared years before during a worldwide frenzy of hatred directed against anything that grew on trees. Trees needed to grow on land, and most people believed that housing was more important than fruit. For a time, many nations operated their own orchards; then it was learned that high officials in certain countries had made themselves wealthy by tearing down low-income housing projects and leasing the property to the government as prime nectarine acreage or guava plantations. The public rose up in its wrath and its anger could not be appeased. In those days, the expression "I do not care a fig" took on a whole new meaning. It seemed that chaos would overthrow democracy and totalitarianism alike. Then, miraculously, in 1992 a scientist named Rod Marquand, nephew of the physicist Zach Marquand, learned to grow quinces, whortleberries, and grapefruits on vines that climbed up buildings like claw ivy. Soon fruits of almost every variety were making a comeback, no longer dangling from space-wasting trees, but sagging ponderously from elegant, rapidly spreading creepers. Many buildings were entirely clad in green leaves, and people could reach right outside their windows to harvest guavas, plums, walnuts, satsumas, cranberries, or almost any other fruit. Except cherries. It was too late for cherries; they had sadly been the victim of the indignant fury of the masses. Marquand tried his best to recreate the cherry by sophisticated botanical methods, but all he could come up with was a kind of maraschino grape that fooled nobody.

"Here," said Dr. Waters, "have another one." His magnetic eyes sparkled with good humor.

"I couldn't eat another thing," said Mihalik.

"What I'd really like," said Cheryl, "is a hot bath and a clean jumpsuit. We weren't in the alternate 1996 long enough to have either, and there was a terrible lack of washaterias in 1939. We had to take our clothes down to the East River and pound them on rocks."

Dr. Waters and Ray laughed. "That's the past for you," said Ray in his gentle, cheerful manner, "always primogenial. You can't get away from it."

"I guess not," said Cheryl. She took a sip of club soda.

"But you're here now," said Dr. Waters, "and all those experiences are behind you. I know you'd like a little time to rest up and relax, and let me assure you that you'll have it. You don't know how critical things are here. I've worked out a rather delicate assignment that needs someone with experience in handling emergencies. None of our field operatives has suffered the kind of bad luck that you ran into. As soon as you're able, I'd be grateful if you'd come into my office to discuss the matter with me. Maybe in ten days or two weeks. Enjoy yourself in the meantime."

"Fine, boss," said Mihalik. He glanced at Cheryl, whose face had gone pale. "What's the matter, honey?" he asked.

"Dr. Waters just said something about 'field operatives.' What kind of field operatives?"

"Agency field operatives, of course," said Ray.

There was no need for Cheryl to explain it to Mihalik. They just looked at each other; they weren't home, after all. They had arrived in a 1996 very similar to their own, but it was still not the right one.

"Close, but no cigar," said Cheryl.

"You're just now realizing that you're not in the right universe," said Dr. Waters.

"Yeah," said Mihalik. "So how did you know we were coming? You seem to have expected us."

"My equations predicted it." Dr. Waters didn't bother to elaborate. "They tell me how to send you home, as well. To the correct reality."

"Don't tell me," said Mihalik, "we'll have to do you some kind of favor first. This delicate assignment you were talking about."

Dr. Waters shrugged. "I'd send you home immediately, if I could. Believe me. But we're engaged in a sort of time war, with a rebel group trying to destroy the Agency. We'll have to root them out of the past before we can regain control of the cross-temporal matrix."

"And you want us to do the rooting for you," said Cheryl.

"It seems only fair," said Ray. "You're going to create the rebel army yourselves. You're responsible for the whole mess in the first place."

"I wouldn't do something like that," objected Mihalik.

"You can't help it," said Dr. Waters sadly. "You're doomed to lay the groundwork for the Temporary Underground. It's your destiny, it's fate. You can call it kismet, Frank, or karma. It's in the cards."

"In the cards," said Mihalik. "Do your equations tell you all this, too?"

"More or less. I have other means of knowing the future, but that's not important now. Listen, Frank, I don't hold it against you. About founding the Underground, I mean. I can't expect you to love the Agency. It doesn't exist where you come from. You can't understand how vital the

Agency is in maintaining order in a cosmos that doesn't particularly enjoy order. I can tell you this much, though: you aren't going to attack the Agency directly. You aren't going to lead the revolution yourself. But things that you do and say are going to impress men and women of an insufficient morality, and they will exaggerate and distort your ideas. From that corruption will arise the Temporary Underground, and we will have to fight them on battlefields all up and down the thoroughfares of time. We are fighting them now. In a sense, we have always been fighting them. And we need you. Both of you."

Mihalik considered Dr. Waters' words for only a few seconds. "You can count on me, sir," he said. He had cast his lot with the forces of truth and justice. It seemed like the right thing to do at the time.

"And me, too," said Cheryl.

"I knew you'd have no problem making up your mind," said Dr. Waters. He looked at both of them in turn; his eyes were serious and stern, yet at the same time friendly and wistful, and a little magnetic, and courageous and weary and brown. "Ray will get in touch with you next week, and we'll give you a briefing. Our ESB techniques of implanting essential knowledge are much advanced over those in your own world. Your mission will be to a time far in the past, but you'll have nothing to fear: you'll fit right into whatever era we send you to."

Frank and Cheryl in Duel Roles

The ESB training made the assumption that virtually everyone would hold a sword in the right hand, so quite naturally it was just Mihalik's luck that the Cardinal's Guard who attacked him was a left-hander.

"Monsieur," said Mihalik, "has no one troubled to inform you that you fence perversely? Surely the cardinal would not countenance such an abominable disregard for convention."

"I pray to advise you, monsieur," said the guardsman, "that the cardinal does not concern himself overmuch with convention. His Eminence cares only for victories, and I am compelled to admit that in that regard I have always provided him with great satisfaction."

Their rapiers touched briefly, and Mihalik retreated beyond the other's reach, observing the fighting style of his foe. "You mean, monsieur, that you have managed to survive. That may not—*will* not—always be the case. In any event, it is not the fierce lion alone that outlives the victims of his fangs and claws."

"I fear, monsieur, that I do not apprehend your meaning." The guardsman gave a little flourish by way of salute, then drove forward to the attack.

"Timid rabbits that flee the battle also survive their more conventional brothers." Mihalik fell back a few steps in mock retreat, drawing his angry opponent toward him. The guardsman started a lunging attack from low position; Mihalik tapped the man's blade on the outside, turning it in, and in the same motion scored a bloody touch on the guardsman's shoulder.

"Damn," muttered the cardinal's man. Mihalik's stinging taunt about fleeing bunnies had made the guardsman careless. He drew back now with more respect for Mihalik's clever swordplay.

Despite his inexperience in dueling left-handed swordsmen, Mihalik knew from the instant they crossed blades that this man of the cardinal's was as good as vanquished. A red mist seemed to float before Mihalik's eyes, and a grim fighting smile played upon his lips. He waited, inviting in octave, certain that his opponent would eventually display a fatal weakness. The guardsman guarded in sixte, as he would in a practice match with foils; it was an error in real combat that would cost him dearly. Mihalik noticed immediately that the other man's elbow was bent too much and the undersurface of the forearm was entirely exposed. He extended his rapier and began a feinting attack; the guardsman parried but did not riposte. Mihalik recovered forward and lunged, his sword's point thrusting under the other's guard, piercing the cardinalist's forearm. The guardsman fell back quickly, changing the sword from his left hand to his right.

"You waver, monsieur, as you retreat," Mihalik criticized. "Your difficulties arise from your lack of balance."

"You perceive correctly, though it pains me to admit it. However, I have defeated many a confident musketeer possessed of superior equilibrium, but insufficient stamina."

Mihalik smiled. "Oh la, monsieur! You force upon me the observation that our encounter must be brought to an early end." He lunged, and the guardsman fell back; he lunged again, and once more the other man retreated. Mihalik stood up straight and dropped his point, inviting attack. As the guardsman extended his rapier, Mihalik relaxed on guard, his blade in octave. The cardinalist lunged forward, attacking Mihalik's front leg above the knee, intending to pierce the thigh and restrict Mihalik's movement. Mihalik counterattacked, thrusting forward and drawing his front foot back at the same moment. The unbalanced left-hander ducked his head as he continued his downward stroke—and Mihalik drove his point through the man's throat. The guardsman gave a gurgling cry and fell to the courtyard's stone pavement.

Mihalik glanced around quickly, to see which of his comrades most needed his aid. Porthos was toying with a young guardsman who was hardly more than a boy; it seemed that the boastful Musketeer was reluctant to end the youth's life, and was giving him a lesson in the finer points of swordplay. Athos had already dispatched one foe and was pressing a second unmercifully. Aramis was reciting a psalm in a cheerful voice as he dueled; he did not seem to be in any immediate difficulty. Cheryl was still disguised as a man, and she also seemed quite in control of her opponent. Mihalik took the opportunity to catch his breath. He watched as Porthos disarmed the boy, sending the rapier clattering across the stones. "I beg of you, my son," said Porthos sadly, "don't retrieve the weapon."

"I must," said the young guardsman. He ran after it.

Mihalik was closer to it. He scooped up the sword and refused to relinquish it.

"Then I must surrender," said the boy. "The cardinal will not be pleased."

Porthos put his huge hand on the young man's shoulder. "When you tell him that it was Porthos of the King's Musketeers who defeated you," he said, "the cardinal will have nothing but admiration for your courage."

Athos joined them. The fleeting joy of victory faded rapidly from his face; then he was the grim inscrutable man who commanded the awe of everyone who knew him. He nodded to Mihalik and to Porthos, but he did not speak.

"Come along, Aramis," called Porthos. "Finish your sermon and have an end to it. You need not quote Holy Scripture to your man; he'll meet the Author himself soon enough."

"As you say, my friend," said Aramis. With an elegant combination of binding and thrusting, he drove his rapier through the luckless guardsman's heart.

"How unfortunate that His Eminence could not spare more of his loyal defenders this afternoon," said Porthos. "This was barely worth the inconvenience to five such stalwarts as us."

Only Cheryl still battled in the chilly March afternoon. The ringing of her blade against the guardsman's echoed in the stillness. Slowly she drove her man back; she lunged and he retreated out of reach, trying to avoid her flashing rapier. It seemed to Mihalik that she was weaving a deadly net of steel around the cardinal's man. At last he was brought up against a wall of the courtyard; he grunted, unable to retreat farther. She looked at him calmly, dropping her point into low position, allowing him a gracious final chance. The man snarled a few unintelligible words and launched a furious flailing attack. Cheryl did not flinch. She held her ground, taking his blade on hers, deflecting it, and riposting immediately.

She slipped inside his guard and impaled him. He fell forward, tearing the sword from her hand.

"Very pretty," said Mihalik, as Cheryl stooped to recover her weapon. She smiled at him.

"You two young lads fight as well as anyone in France," remarked Aramis.

"From the lips of one of France's greatest swordsmen," said Cheryl, "that is the supreme compliment."

Athos gave a short-lived smile. "It was well earned, without a doubt. And our dinner is also well earned. Let us retire to consider the proper care of our weary bodies, which have served us so well this afternoon."

"And let us not neglect our spiritual selves," said Aramis.

"No," said Porthos lightly, "we must remember to light a candle at our convenience, and attend mass sometime in the future, and perhaps even go to confession, though in my case all such activity is only for the sake of good form and custom. The cardinal's villains leave me no spare time to commit an honest sin for which to repent."

They all laughed heartily and walked arm in arm out of the courtyard, in search of honor, fame, and a fine roast fowl.

Reporting for Work in Someone Else's Novel

Paris: City of Light, Capital of the World, the city that is like a woman with flowers in her hair. Paris: the tree-lined boulevards, the bookstalls and intimate cafés, the artists and poets, the city of lovers. But she was not always so. In the days of Louis XIII, Paris was a city of poverty and misery, burdened by the policies and taxes imposed by the King's chief minister, Cardinal Richelieu. Revolts against the cardinal were plotted all over France, by peasants and by dissatisfied noblemen. In this time of intrigue and danger, Frank Mihalik and the lissome Cheryl hoped to stay alive long enough to complete the mission Dr. Waters had given them.

Cheryl's auburn hair was cut short and hidden beneath a dark wig in the style worn by gentlemen in the mid-1600s. Her features were regular but ambiguous in gender: dressed in masculine clothing in the uniform of the King's Musketeers, with a plumed hat riding her artificial ringlets, Cheryl appeared to be a young man, old enough to seek his fortune, young enough so that the lack of a beard and a man's sterner expression did not arouse suspicion.

Mihalik and Cheryl shared a single room above a butcher shop in the Rue de Charpie. Unlike other newly made musketeers, they had no man-servant to act as squire. Cheryl explained this to those who inquired by pleading poverty, though it was clear from her clothing that her concept of poverty included a certain allowance for style and fashion. The truth was that they did not trust the generally dull-witted yet inquisitive lackeys available for hire. In any event, they did not plan to remain long in the seventeenth century.

"It's kind of fun to be able to handle a rapier so well," said Cheryl one morning.

Mihalik grunted; he was wolfing down large chunks of stale bread dunked in a rather coarse red wine. "I still feel funny stabbing another man to death. I don't enjoy killing people."

Cheryl gave a sad smile. "Dr. Waters told us not to worry about that. This isn't real life, here. These people aren't real. We're not really killing anybody." Her expression was dubious, however.

Mihalik didn't share that view, either. When he'd skewered the guardsman earlier, the dying man shed dark red blood and fell to the ground in a very persuasive imitation of death.

The day was as gray and chilly as winter could be. Mihalik and Cheryl dressed in their musketeers' doublets, with rapiers belted securely in place, and soft floppy leather boots protecting their feet from the muck and mire of the Parisian streets. They walked to their headquarters, the Hôtel de Tréville.

They were greeted warmly by the other Royal Musketeers who lounged, gambled, bragged, fenced, joked, drank, and otherwise entertained themselves while filling up the house of their captain, Monsieur de Tréville. The story of the encounter with the Cardinal's Guards had passed from Musketeer to Musketeer, growing a little in each telling. By midmorning, Mihalik and Cheryl had attained quite a little reputation of their own, which did not suffer by its connection with the godlike trio of Athos, Porthos, and Aramis.

"Messieurs," said a Musketeer whose name Mihalik did not yet know, "Monsieur de Tréville has ordered that you wait upon his pleasure in his chamber immediately."

"Thank you, Guichard," said Cheryl. She shot a glance at Mihalik, who read nothing in the look. He wondered if Tréville would be angry or joyful about their defeat of the cardinal's men.

Cheryl rapped lightly on Tréville's door. "Come in," called the captain's strong voice. Cheryl grasped the knob and opened the door. Mihalik followed her in; Athos, Porthos, and Aramis were already assembled before Tréville's great desk.

"Ah, Juvin," said Tréville, addressing Cheryl by her nom de guerre. The captain stood and offered his hand; Cheryl removed her magnificent plumed hat and her gauntlet, bowed, and shook Tréville's hand.

"You will recall my comrade from Ste. Clothilde," said Cheryl, indicating Mihalik.

"Yes, of course. You have made a great beginning to your career, Monsieur Chauvet."

"Thank you, monsieur," said Mihalik. He too shook Tréville's hand. Cheryl nudged him, and Mihalik came smartly to attention beside the unsmiling Athos.

"Perhaps you wonder why I asked you to appear before me this morning," Tréville began.

"It must concern our unfortunate collision with the men of the Cardinal's Guard," said Porthos, trying to hide his satisfied smile.

"Ah, yes. That." Tréville's face clouded for an instant. "I must get to the King, to explain that little contretemps before Monsieur le Cardinal explains it from *his* point of view. But no, you will receive no congratulations from me; you were but performing your duty as Royal Musketeers. And you will receive no condemnation, for reasons I suppose you already understand well enough. I have asked you to attend me for quite another purpose."

"Then it must concern the King," said Athos. "Or more precisely, the Queen."

Tréville's expression did not change, but his glance lingered for a long silent moment on the face of Athos. "Yes, my friend," he said at last. "I wonder if it is necessary for me to speak to you of the matter at all. But perhaps your young apprentices do not share your perception. It is important that they, too, have all the facts that you have evidently already gleaned from some secret source.

"For some time, my Musketeers, I have known of a rumor that threatens to shake the very throne of France. Whether it is true or not I cannot say, but that is not of very great importance. The rumor itself is the danger: it is that our Queen, Anne of Austria, the beautiful and gracious wife of Louis XIII, has been replaced by a twin, a woman so precisely like the Queen in all respects that not even the King himself suspects that it is an imposter who accompanies him at court."

"If not in the boudoir," said Porthos.

Tréville's eyes closed, like a man enduring a kind of agony. "You do our King no credit with such an observation," he said coldly.

"Forgive me," said Porthos, "but, to be sure, it is common knowledge—"

"If I may continue," said Tréville. "According to the stories, the genuine Queen is a captive in the Bastille, a prisoner of the Red Duke, Cardinal Richelieu. No one knows his motives or his schemes, but they cannot bode well for the Queen, or for France."

"You wish us to search out the truth in this matter," said Aramis placidly. He held a slender volume, a book of prayers with his place marked by a lady's handkerchief.

"Yes, that is the case. You must perform this task with utmost delicacy, secrecy, and tact. The fate of France may depend upon your actions. The fate of our dear Queen—a queen, but also an innocent woman caught in the tangled plottings of the cardinal—that, too, is in your hands."

"But have no fear," said Athos, "for there is no one else in France so capable as we three. We five, now that we are of that number." He bowed politely to Mihalik and Cheryl, who returned his elegant salute.

"I am not fearful," said Tréville, "for I trust your skill and judgment. But I do not sleep well these nights, and I shall not until this affair is concluded. Now go, and make your plans well. I will do everything I can to aid you in your inquiry. I pray you to report to me daily, and do nothing to arouse the suspicions of the cardinal or his men."

Some time later, over a midday meal of roast saddle of hare, the five musketeers began to devise their scheme. "It is not an easy thing Monsieur de Tréville has set before us," complained Porthos.

Cheryl swallowed some ale and wiped the foam from her lips. "But it may not be impossible, either," she said. "We must place someone in the palace itself, someone who is not well known to the King, the cardinal, or the guards."

"Then it cannot be myself," said Aramis, "for I have a slight acquaintance with certain ladies of the court. And Athos and Porthos are also too familiar. Juvin, you or your young countryman, Monsieur Chauvet, may be perfect for this role."

Mihalik felt a chill wind whispering down his neck. He wanted to tell Aramis that there was no way in hell he'd march into the palace of King Louis XIII and begin poking around in all the corners. "I accept the assignment gladly," he said. He shivered.

"Well said," cried Porthos. "And remember that we will defend you with all our abilities, though we must remain outside the palace walls. You will have our encouragement and support and good wishes. And if you sound an alarm, we will hurry to your side as quickly as we can. All for one, and so forth."

"I will be in your debt," said Mihalik. This was just the kind of thing his beloved old mother had warned him against; Mihalik had always been too eager to go along with the crowd. He didn't want Athos, Porthos, and Aramis to think he was some sort of coward and a weakling. He didn't want to look like a chicken in front of Cheryl. The Musketeers' opinions were important to him even though, as Dr. Waters would insist, the three swordsmen didn't really exist.

The Kids from the Future Play the Palace

Aramis, through one of his connections at court, was able to secure for Mihalik a position that gave him a certain amount of liberty to investigate the royal apartments unobserved. His contact, Madame de Romiers, was lady-in-waiting to Queen Anne. The lady, swept away by Mihalik's rugged good looks and charmingly odd accent, fell in love with him almost instantly. Mihalik was glad Cheryl could not know about it. Sometimes Madame de Romiers permitted herself certain liberties of a physical nature that shocked Mihalik's sensibilities, which had been formed, after all, in the more inhibited and prim world of the late twentieth century. The French aristocracy of the 1600s seemed to be a lewd and licentious lot, and their behavior frequently embarrassed Mihalik.

Madame de Romiers always made such conduct entertaining, however, if not entirely acceptable by Mihalik's standards of decency. "You are in danger," she whispered one evening. They had met in a place arranged in advance by Aramis. Mihalik did not know what she had said; he was staring into her lovely gray eyes, suddenly forgetful of his mission. "Please, monsieur," she said, "you are in terrible danger. I am sure that something has happened to our beloved Queen. There are spies and agents everywhere."

"But is that not usually the case?" he asked.

"That is true," she admitted, "but these are not the usual spies whom I have come to recognize. There are new and strange people at work, and I wonder if even the cardinal himself is in control of them."

Rebels of the Temporary Underground, no doubt; Mihalik was sure of it. He wished that Cheryl were near enough to be consulted. He wondered if he'd have to protect the safety of the entire world, of the entire future, without help from Dr. Waters' Agency. It was a cruel and unfair baptism of fire.

Yet he felt comfortable and safe beside Madame de Romiers. It was evident that she, too, returned his feelings; although married to a wealthy wine merchant, she lived a lonely and unfulfilling life at court. Her days were spent attending to the trivial needs of Anne of Austria, avoiding the traps and schemes of Monsieur le Cardinal, and staying out of the clutches of every lecherous nobleman she chanced to meet. She recognized in Mihalik a forthright spirit who honestly liked her, unlike the many men who, though clad in silk and brocade, concealed malignant souls beneath their rich costumes.

Each day brought new information, but Mihalik was unable to make sense of most of it. There were countless plots and counterplots: some of them were formed by courtiers to overthrow the King; some of them were directed at the cardinal; some of them seemed to be more all-inconclusive, possibly devised by the Temporary Underground to wrest control of this era from the Agency. But was that perhaps only Mihalik's imagination at work? He had no tangible evidence that the rebels were present. He did his work in the palace and hoped that Cheryl was able to interpret things correctly. Their lives depended on that.

Sometime later, Mihalik was preparing for bed in his tiny apartment in the palace, exhausted after a long day of arduous labor. Just as he had slipped into his woolen nightshirt, there came a frantic knocking on his door. "Who is it?" he called. There was no reply, but the knocking came again. Mihalik grabbed his rapier and went to the door.

He was surprised to see Madame de Romiers, who could not afford to be seen in this part of the palace. "Monsieur Chauvet," she said breathlessly, "your life is in imminent peril. Please, let me come in."

"Of course, madame," he said. He silently prayed that this was no trick of hers, a pretense to allow her the opportunity for yet more shameless body contact. He stood aside and she swept by him, her exquisite gown of satin and lace rustling so loudly, Mihalik was sure even His Eminence must hear it.

Madame de Romiers turned to him, her expression anxious and afraid. "Do you love our Queen?" she asked.

Mihalik merely nodded.

"Then you must learn of the dark secret that the Red Duke wields as a weapon, directed against the very heart of France."

"You are speaking of the Queen's twin," said Mihalik.

Madame de Romiers was astonished. Her face flushed. "How do you know of this?" she whispered.

Mihalik gave her a modest smile. "I am not what I seem," he said. He rather liked cloaking himself in a little mystery.

"I have known that from the moment we met." Her long lashes slowly covered her gray eyes, and she looked down at the floor in some emotional distress.

As much as Mihalik felt inclined to pursue their personal relationship, there were more vital matters to attend to. "You claimed that I am threatened, even now," he said. "By whom? And for what reason?"

"You are certainly more than you seem, Monsieur Chauvet, even though it is only now that my belief has been proved true. But others have not only entertained their suspicions, but also acted upon them. A creature of the cardinal's is preparing, even as we speak, to end your life this very night. We must—"

A loud, urgent rapping interrupted her. Mihalik glanced at Madame de Romiers; she shrugged, not knowing if the visitor was the assassin or a more welcome guest.

"Who is it?" called Mihalik, trying to sound unconcerned.

"Cheryl," came the reply.

"Oops," said Mihalik. He was uncomfortable, discovered by his girl friend with the opulent Madame de Romiers in his suite; but he was relieved, as well. "I am not alone," he murmured to his sweetheart as he opened the door.

"Who do you have in there?" asked Cheryl. She was only a little jealous. She was still dressed as a young man, though not in the uniform of the King's Musketeers. Mihalik closed the door again behind her.

"Madame de Romiers," said Mihalik, "I have the privilege of presenting to you my countryman, Monsieur Juvin."

"I have observed Monsieur Juvin on several occasions," said Madame de Romiers, "but until now I have been denied the pleasure of his acquaintance."

Cheryl accepted her hand and bowed gallantly over it. "Madame," she said, "you have been denied but little while I have learned only now how empty my life has been." Madame de Romiers smiled at this extravagant flattery.

"What you have told me, madame," said Mihalik, "you may also trust with Monsieur Juvin. We are closer than brothers."

"Then you are both in danger. You must leave the palace tonight, this very hour."

"Already?" asked Cheryl. "The crisis has come?"

"Yes, apparently," said Mihalik.

Madame de Romiers looked frightened. "Richelieu's men are everywhere. There is no safe way to transport you from the palace. We must find a way to hide your identities from the guard." She thought for a moment. "If we were able to enter the suites belonging to the ladies attendant on the Queen—"

"Yes," said Cheryl, "that is just what I was thinking. But can we get there safely?"

Madame de Romiers shook her head. "I do not know. It is a risk that must be taken."

Cheryl nodded reluctantly. Mihalik still didn't know what stratagem had been decided. The three slipped from his quarters and began the journey to the apartments of the ladies of the court, which were two floors below and in the farthest wing of the palace. They moved quickly and quietly, but even so they were surprised by a guardsman, not more than fifty yards from their goal. "I was told to expect you," he said with a crooked leering grin.

Mihalik's rapier sang as he ripped it from its scabbard. The guardsman's smile grew wider. Mihalik waited for the guard to attack; the man was hesitant to begin the battle, but it was not for lack of courage. He was waiting for the arrival of others who would make the risking of his own blood unnecessary. Mihalik had to dispatch the man before the reinforcements arrived. The red mist floated again before his eyes; he lunged and compelled the guard to defend himself. The cardinal's man parried and riposted, and Mihalik fell back a few inches, guarding now in sixte. The guardsman drew back as well, stalling. Mihalik began a flashing attack, his blade ringing in the narrow passageway as he sought to discover his opponent's weakness. There was no time for a slow and methodical duel. Pressed desperately by the fury of Mihalik's onslaught, the guard began to show how inadequate was his skill. Mihalik scored once on the forearm, once through the shoulder, and yet another hit on the wrist.

The guard opened his mouth; he was going to shout for help. "Quickly!" cried Madame de Romiers. Mihalik did not hear her plea. He captured the man's blade on his and slid by it with a falling lunge. His point slipped between the guard's ribs, and the cardinal's man fell to the carpeted floor, his call for aid stillborn on his lips.

Gasping a little from the exertion, Mihalik led the two women down the corridor. Madame de Romiers touched his arm when they reached the entrance to the ladies' apartments. "I must go first," she whispered. "Even among the Queen's ladies, there are doubtlessly traitors. If no one is about, I will lead you into my suite, where we may assemble a hasty costume to cloak your true selves."

Mihalik understood at last, and he wasn't pleased by the plan: he would have to escape from the palace dressed as a woman. Cheryl was in an even more implausible situation—she would be a woman dressed as a man dressed as a woman. Well, mused Mihalik, it worked for Shakespeare's characters all the time.

It did not take long for Madame de Romiers to choose garments for them. Over her masculine attire, Cheryl put on the costly apparel of the Queen's lady-in-waiting. She abandoned her high boots and slipped her feet into a pair of Madame de Romiers' pumps. The final touch was a wig in the current fashion, blond rings and curls piled high upon the head. "You would make a charming lady," said Madame de Romiers.

"Thank you," said Cheryl. She was ill at ease, but Mihalik thought that she was probably more than a little pleased with the compliment.

After a moment, Cheryl looked as if she were beginning to enjoy the masquerade.

Not so Mihalik himself. He had no idea what some of the items were, or how they operated. Madame de Romiers alternated between amused teasing and nervous bullying. "No, not that way!" she cried. "The other way around! How did you ever get to be a King's Musketeer, knowing so little about a lady's undergarments?"

At last, however, both time travelers were dressed according to the lady's specifications. After the last perfectionist touches of makeup, Madame de Romiers stepped back to survey her accomplishment. *"Parbleu!"* she cried.

"What is it?" said Mihalik anxiously. "Do you hear the guards?"

"No, no, it is not that," she said. "Look." She held up a mirror.

Mihalik saw nothing in the mirror but his painted face beneath a towering blond wig. He presented a rather attractive picture, all in all, but nothing spectacular. "What do you see?" he asked.

Madame de Romiers turned to Cheryl. "Do you not agree?" she said. "Is he not a marvelous likeness of the Queen herself?"

"I am?" said Mihalik, astonished.

"He is?" said Cheryl, likewise surprised.

"Certes," said Madame de Romiers, "and I am one who should know. But there is no time for wonderment. We must make haste."

"My rapier—" said Mihalik.

"You must leave it," said the lady. "To carry it would invite disaster."

Reluctantly Mihalik agreed. They left the apartment and hurried back the way they had come. Leaving the palace, fortunately, was a simpler matter than finding a way in.

Many minutes later, at a gate used primarily by servants and tradesmen, Madame de Romiers bid them both farewell. "I may never see you again, my darling," said the Queen's lady. Cheryl moved away to give the other two a bit of privacy.

"You must not tell yourself such a thing," said Mihalik gallantly. He kissed her lightly, trying to keep his tall blond wig from bumping her tall blond wig.

"Adieu, then, my hero," she whispered. Her cheek was wet with tears.

"Adieu," said Mihalik. He drew away. The beauty spot she had placed beside his nose was starting to itch like crazy.

Mihalik and Cheryl had not gone more than a hundred yards before the catastrophe occurred. To Mihalik it seemed as if the moon turned as red as a crushed tomato, and the stars began to vibrate and hum with an evil energy, and then they exploded. It was a detonation of darkness, however, and it swallowed Mihalik up and silenced his thoughts. There was no way to measure time in that total absence of light, and Mihalik floated about, not living and not dead, until there was another explosion. This one was of pain.

There was a solid chunk of agony at the back of his skull, and it beat there like a second heart. Every movement exaggerated the pain, so Mihalik tried to stay as motionless as possible. Even breathing brought tears to his eyes, and the grinding soreness claimed all his attention. It was almost an hour before he thought to wonder where he was.

Queen for a Day

"Hello?" he called.

There was no answer. The only sound was the steady drip of water somewhere close by. Mihalik's senses began to awaken and report information, little of it cheering to his fearful mind. He lay on a damp, cold stone floor. There was a litter of straw beneath him, and he was aware of the sharp ends sticking into his bare shoulders and neck. Now that he was fully conscious he realized that his head was shut up in some kind of . . . mask. Some kind of heavy iron mask. "Oh, no," said Mihalik. "Oh, no. Oh, no."

He got to his feet, which were bare; he had kicked off Madame de Romiers' shoes at the first opportunity. He was still clothed in her layers of garments and devices, over which he wore her tightly bodiced gown of ruffled taffeta. "Guard!" he shouted. There was still no answer.

The cell was small and dark. The only light came from the smoky flickering torch that lit the corridor beyond his cell door's small grill. There was not enough room to exercise his cramped muscles. Each minute, marked by forty or fifty throbs of his aching head, passed with vicious slowness.

Finally, after a minor eternity, a man came with a wooden bowl of food. "Where am I?" croaked Mihalik.

"Be quiet," snarled the guard. "I'm not supposed to talk with you."

"But can't you see there's been some kind of mistake?"

"I see nothing." He dropped the bowl beside Mihalik's legs. There was a shackle around one ankle, and it was chained to the stone wall.

"Why have I been arrested?"

The guard gave him a wicked grin. "You'll learn the answer to that from the cardinal himself," he said. For some reason the man thought his words were particularly clever or funny, and left the cell laughing to himself. Mihalik called after him to no avail; there was an echoing bang as the guard slammed the door closed, a loud snap as he fastened the iron lock. Mihalik was once more alone. He picked up the wooden bowl and ate ravenously. Every bite caused him renewed pain.

He measured out the days by the meals: there was a bowl of gruel in the morning, and a thin stew of fish or mutton at night. The bowls were always brought by the same taciturn guard. Twice a day Mihalik pleaded for an audience with his captors, for a chance to prove that a terrible mistake had been made. All he earned for his troubles was sly, sadistic laughter from his jailer.

As the days passed, Mihalik's mind began to weaken. Entombment in the dank, fetid cell alone might have driven a man mad; the horror of the iron mask multiplied his sense of hopelessness. In the beginning, he counted on Cheryl's resourcefulness to rescue him; she was the only person who might know who and where he was. When no rescue came, he guessed that she too was a captive, or dead. He believed that he was a prisoner of Dr. Waters' enemies, the Temporary Underground; as his sanity wavered, he began to suspect that Madame de Romiers had led him into this trap, that Cheryl had abandoned him, and that both women were secretly in the employ of the rebels.

"You think I am Anne of Austria?" he shouted into the darkness. There was no reply but the startled squeaking of a rat. "How can I be the Queen? Look, I'm not even a woman!" It did no good.

Mihalik plotted his escape, but each idea died in frustration. He had no weapon with which to overpower the guard; he could not escape for long, dressed in the grimy, tattered dress of one of the Queen's own ladies; even if he did elude the rebels, he was trapped in this false past with no means of returning to his own time and reality.

At last, when the hysteria had given way to a quiet, calm acceptance that was beyond despair, Mihalik was told that he would be given an audience with the King's minister, Cardinal Richelieu himself. The guard's manner had changed dramatically; he now addressed Mihalik as "Your Majesty," even though it was clear from the bits of beard that stuck out beneath the hideous iron mask that the prisoner was not a woman. Mihalik was conducted by four armed guards from the damp dungeon in the Bastille to the cardinal's apartments in the palace.

"Ah," said Richelieu, when the soldiers had left the room, "it is good that we have this talk."

"Talk?" cried Mihalik. "I want to know what's going on. I demand that you remove this mask. I demand that you release me."

Richelieu studied Mihalik in silence for a long moment. He was dressed in his red robe and red skullcap; he looked like Charlton Heston with a pasted-on beard. One long bony forefinger stroked his carefully trimmed mustache. "Very few people make demands of me and live to witness the results," he said at last. His voice was very soft.

Mihalik felt no fear; he wondered why that was. "Your Eminence," he said, "either I am the Queen, in which case I may speak as I like; or else I am not the Queen, in which case you've made a monstrous error that will prove dangerous for you."

The cardinal smiled. "And in that event, I would be wise to hide my blunder. In an iron mask, in the deepest, darkest pit in the kingdom. Or in an unmarked grave almost anywhere. It seems that it would be well for you to be the Queen. What have you to say now?"

"I say that I am not the Queen. I am not even a woman. Have your guards no eyes? Look, I'm a man!" Tearing the material of the filthy dress, Mihalik presented his most persuasive argument.

Richelieu said nothing while he considered the matter. "Perhaps that seems to you like adequate proof," he remarked dryly. "But I must disagree, monsieur; it is no defense. I have known the King too long and too well. I am aware of his, ah, predilections, and the fact that the Queen may not be a woman does not startle me so much as you may have hoped."

That remark upset Mihalik. He didn't know what to say. The interview was rapidly degenerating into the irrational, but that was nothing new for time travel. "I take it, then, Your Eminence believes me to be the Queen. And that you have a double to take my place. Is your double also a man?"

The Cardinal seemed vexed. "No," he admitted.

"Don't you think that Louis XIII, however unusual his predilections, will discover the change in his royal wife?"

Richelieu uncovered his chilly smile again. "The Queen may be the King's consort, but that does not mean that Their Majesties really do, ah, *consort*. If you understand my meaning. Our secret may go unguessed for quite a long time."

Mihalik had the strangest feeling that he was dealing not with a fictionalized version of a historical personality, but with a shrewd and clever agent of the Temporary Underground. It was an unlikely notion, but it wouldn't go away. "I know for certain that I'm not the Queen. That means if Your Eminence has planted yet another duplicate on the throne, there is a third woman—the genuine Queen—running around. Did you capture her, too? Is she in another cell, with another iron mask hiding her face?"

"You have come at last to the flaw in my scheme; but so long as the two of you are kept out of sight, all will be well. I cannot bring myself to end the life of the Queen, and I am not sure at this moment which of you that is. So you will have to grow content with my hospitality. I trust things have not been too terrible in the Bastille. I intended that this talk should have cleared away my doubts, but I see now that my hopes were in vain." He clapped his hands twice, and a guard entered the chamber. "Convey this lady back to her cell, and pay no heed to her ravings. She is quite mad, the poor creature."

The guard put a rough hand on the prisoner's arm. "Stop!" cried Mihalik in a panic. "I'm not the Queen! You've got to listen to me!"

"To the Bastille," said the cardinal. He had already lost interest in the matter, and was examining some papers on his desk.

We Meet the Enemy, and He Is Them

The guard released Mihalik's arm. "I am not what I seem," murmured the guard.

"Oh, really?" said Mihalik. "Neither am I."

"I've come to rescue you. I've come to take you back to the twenty-first century."

Mihalik's heart beat wildly. "Thank God!" he said. "Can we get me out of this dress and this iron mask?"

"No, we don't have a minute to spare. They'll take care of the mask back in our time. Right now we have to get away from the palace; that won't be difficult because I have the cardinal's safe conduct."

"What about Cheryl?" asked Mihalik. "I haven't heard anything about her since I was captured."

"Who?" asked the guard.

"Cheryl. I was beginning to imagine she'd left me here holding the bag."

"I don't know anything about any Cheryl. I was just sent to get you."

Mihalik walked alongside his rescuer, through the foul muddy streets of seventeenth-century Paris. "Victory is almost in our grasp," said the guard.

"Hooray for us. You know, no one has ever really told me what this war is all about. What is the Agency fighting for? What are the Underground terrorists fighting for? I don't know. Power? That doesn't make sense, not the way they're going about it. What *good* is the past to them, anyway?"

"Nobody answers my questions, either," said the guard. "Mostly it's like a great big game of hide-and-seek down all the alleyways of time. But I think we're working on some way to make the present more responsive to changes in the past."

That chilled Mihalik. He didn't want anybody—neither the Agency nor the Underground—to experiment with altering the present. It was an immensely disturbing notion. "I hate to admit this," he said, "but sometimes it seems to me that the Agency is doing the wrong thing. Sometimes I think that there isn't much to choose from between the two sides. The Agency may be just as sinister as the Temporary Underground."

The guard stopped suddenly in the street. "Say," he said calmly, "what did you say your name was?"

"Mihalik. Frank Mihalik."

"I don't know any Frank Mihalik," said the guard. He drew his rapier. "I was sent here to recover Brother Fortunati, but it looks like I've stumbled on an Agency spy."

"Oh, hell," said Mihalik. "Would you really kill me like this? Would you leave me here dressed like this, with this goddamn mask on my head?"

"We have no pity in the Temporary Underground. That is a weakness and a luxury. We've come to expect that from hors like you."

"Say what?"

"Hors. From *hora,* the Latin word for 'hour.' It's a contemptuous name we have for you people who believe in time."

"Oh. Well, why don't you just leave me here? I can't hurt anybody or interfere with your plans, stuck in this storybook."

"I can't do that. I have to—" The guard was silenced by a crashing volley of thunder. Mihalik looked up; the sky was bright and cloudless. The guard seemed to be frightened by the noise, and he was now cowering on the ground in terror.

"What's wrong, man?" asked Mihalik. "You're behaving like a superstitious savage." Then he saw that the guard was not writhing in fear, after all; he was writhing because three gaping holes had been blown through his body. The man's blood pumped out upon the mossy cobblestones and trickled away toward the Seine. The guard stopped writhing.

"Come, Chauvet," called Athos. Mihalik turned and saw his four companions—the Three Musketeers themselves and Cheryl. They carried primitive firearms. Of course, thought Mihalik; that's why they're called musketeers. They understood that in certain circumstances, rapiers made little sense. "We persuaded Juvin not to abandon you," Athos said.

Mihalik gave Cheryl a hurt and puzzled look from within the iron mask.

"Dr. Waters sent a courier to fetch me," she explained, a bit flustered. "We thought you were dead, that the cardinal had disposed of you days ago. Then we got a message from one of our spies in the Cardinal's Guard, one of the men who delivered you to the palace from the Bastille. We came to your rescue as soon as we heard the news."

"I'm so glad," said Mihalik coolly. He didn't want to have anything more to do with the time war or anything connected with it. He wanted to find his way back to his own crummy world, where at least the Agency and the Temporary Underground didn't exist.

"Your young friend lost hope several times," said Aramis with a serene smile. "As the King's Musketeers, we require proof before we give our friends up, but perhaps customs are different among your countrymen."

Mihalik frowned at Cheryl, but she still could not see it. "Were you really so quick to leave me behind?" he asked.

She looked as if she was ready to cry. She did not answer.

"May I ask you something?" said Porthos. "Why are you barefoot and wearing that hideous iron mask and that disgustingly filthy gown?"

Mihalik laughed bitterly. "It's just a custom where we come from," he said. "I'm the April Fool."

A Mind Unused to Activity Stirs Uneasily

Mihalik and Cheryl were fetched by a tall handsome young man in the blue and silver uniform of the Agency. He looked absurdly out of place among the foppishly costumed Musketeers at the Hôtel de Tréville. His name was Private Brannick, and he had black hair and steely eyes, and it didn't seem to bother him at all that he was out of place. "You get used to that, shuttling up and down the catwalks of time," he said.

"But doesn't your appearance cause problems?" asked Cheryl. "Don't the natural residents of the past notice you? Doesn't that change history sometimes?"

Private Brannick shrugged. "It might," he admitted. "It would, I mean, if this were the real past; but this isn't the real past. Didn't you realize that?"

Mihalik had realized no such thing. "How could this not be the past?" he asked. "How can you go back in time to anything *other* than the past? I mean, it has to be the past, by definition."

Private Brannick laughed indulgently. "The Three Musketeers never truly lived, you know. You've just had a little vacation. Ask Dr. Waters to explain it all to you. It's just like a holoshow, with better-than-usual special effects."

"Vacation!" cried Mihalik. Brannick had pried off the iron mask, to Mihalik's great relief, but Brannick had brought no spare uniform or change of clothes. Cheryl was in her musketeer outfit, and Mihalik was in his tattered and beslimed gown. No one seemed to be taking his recent torment seriously, and he felt like busting this Brannick guy in the face.

"Now, now," said the Agency man, "Dr. Waters warned me about your irrational spells. We'll just slip out of sight here, and fling ourselves back to the present."

"To *your* present, you mean," said Cheryl. "We'll still be stuck in this wrong universe."

"It doesn't seem wrong to me," said Brannick. "It doesn't even seem wrong to these French guys. It seems wrong only to you, so I think we can safely say that if anything is wrong around here, it isn't the universe's fault. I'd say even you two were beginning to fit in rather well. If you'd just start thinking of our world as 'right,' everybody would be happy."

"You know," said Mihalik thoughtfully, "this whole situation reminds me of something else. A book or a film or something."

They ducked behind an arras, and Private Brannick performed some operation with some bit of equipment. Almost instantly they were thrown forward more than three centuries to Dr. Waters' laboratory in the Agency Building. There was no one to greet them this time.

"It reminds me of something, and it's nagging me," insisted Mihalik. "I wish I could think of what. Something very obvious."

"Dr. Waters will want to meet with you after dinner. It's now about noon. You can refresh yourselves and rest until then. I think Dr. Waters will send someone for you when he's ready."

"Thanks," said Cheryl. Private Brannick nodded and left the quiet laboratory.

"It will come to me," said Mihalik.

"Whatever are you muttering about?" asked Cheryl.

"I want to get this goddamn dress off. Let's go down to our quarters. I need a bath, too."

"I'll say," she said.

An hour later, when both had showered and changed into the official Agency uniform, Cheryl went into her room and closed the door to take a nap, and Mihalik lay on his bunk and stared at the soundproof ceiling. He was desperately tired, but his body wanted to fade away into pleasant dreams, and his mind was too agitated. The circumstances were tantalizingly familiar. It irked Mihalik that he couldn't put his finger on it; it was like trying to wrestle a popcorn hull from between his teeth. The more he thought, the farther the answer seemed to be. His mind's tongue just wasn't strong enough. The popcorn hull stayed lodged.

At last, Mihalik's exhausted body won out and he fell asleep. He had a disturbing dream. "Good," he told himself, "maybe my unconscious mind is working on the problem even while I'm asleep." He saw himself in a small rickety boat buffeted by the strong current of some vast, dark river. It is the Orinoco. It is the Kasai, before it joins the Congo above Kinshasa. It is Tinker's Creek, behind my grandmother's house, and I am still a boy. There are shining fish in the depths, their hungry eyes bulging at me, their fat lips osculating like the kisses of faithless mermaids. The water is cool and inviting, and my brow is so hot. I would slip into the coffee brown river but I know that to do so is death; still I tease myself with the idea and it is exciting. I may yet leap in or some person may push me.

Yes, there are other people in the boat. There is a woman, a slim beautiful woman with auburn hair and eyes the color of the veldt grasses after the rainy months. She tempts me with unfinished smiles, but I am strong and brave and trust no one, because this is a dream and even my best friends have screwed me up in dreams. She is Cheryl, yet in some sinister way I know she is an ally of the water creatures who wait for my living flesh.

There are men. I can't count them. There are many men, and they pay no attention to me at all. They are not friends. Are they waiting for me to die? They must desire Cheryl, they must want me to fall overboard, yet none of them approaches me. It is Cheryl who glances at me with heavy-lidded eyes. She would tell me how cool the water is, how it would take away this fever, make me whole again.

There: I have learned that I am not now whole. What is wrong? A fever. I have a fever, a terrible fever, and I am not in my right mind. Of course I'm not, I'm dreaming. No, even for a dream I am not thinking clearly. Otherwise, how could I imagine that gentle, devoted Cheryl could ever suggest such things, that she could ever threaten horror and death? Cheryl is all that is good and clean in the world, the only un-spoiled, generous spirit I have known, the only person I can love without reservation. And that includes Dr. Waters *(the real* Dr. Waters), who, after all, even in our own universe, cares more for the results of his scientific inquiries than for the safety of his volunteers. Yes, I love Cheryl, and it is my duty to guard her and keep her safe from these men and from whatever dwells in the reeking and filthy water, so I go to her and she is glad. She comforts me. She puts her cool white hand on my brow.

What is this fever? What does it mean? I feel very weak suddenly; Cheryl whispers to me, but it does no good. I have no strength at all, and if the men came now I could not defend myself or Cheryl. I must not think about that; I have enough experience with dreams to know that if I think something must not happen, it will certainly hap—

Mihalik awoke, thrashing weakly on his bunk. His head ached and he felt feverish. There was an awful taste in his mouth. "Cheryl!" he cried.

She hurried from her room to his. She sat beside him and stroked his hair. "There, there," she murmured. "It was only a dream."

"I know that," said Mihalik impatiently, "but it was important. Fever has something to do with what I was trying to remember before. And traveling. A girl and a group of men."

"It's almost time to see Dr. Waters."

"Damn it, I won't be able to rest until I think of it."

"Just take it easy, honey," said Cheryl. "Forget about it for now. We'll talk about it later."

"Easy for you to say. You don't have the fate of our whole universe resting on your shoulders. Whatever's on the tip of my tongue is the key to this phony reality. I'm sure of it."

Pay No Attention to That Man Behind the Screen

Private Brannick arrived to escort them to Dr. Waters' suite, where the head of the Agency was just finishing his dinner. They joined him at the table and were each served a delectable tangerine ice and a glass of Dr. Pepper. A large platter strewn with barbecued rib bones stood in the middle of the table, and there were white cardboard containers of fried dumplings and moo shu pork with one leftover pancake. A cobalt blue cocktail shaker was half filled with liquor, and a martini glass stood neglected by Dr. Waters' hand, empty but for a pearl onion. Dr. Waters looked benignly from Cheryl to Mihalik. Private Brannick stood shifting his weight a few feet away, trying to be inconspicuous.

"Well, now," said Dr. Waters.

"There's a lot we have to talk about," said Mihalik. He had felt a certain quality growing in him lately, a kind of daring, forthright recklessness that was pleasurable but risky. He had always been a good follower, he had always prided himself on his tremendous skill at being second in line. If someone else would break the ground, if someone else would send back instructions, Mihalik was the very best there was at being runner-up. He had been the first to travel through time only because he thought that Dr. Waters had solved every problem, had, in effect, blazed the trail. Mihalik fully expected merely to obey orders and do nothing on his own initiative; the way things had turned out, though, it had taken him a little while to find this new inner strength. It made him feel clever and tough and powerful. It excited Cheryl, too, and he liked that.

"What do we have to talk about?" asked Dr. Waters, puzzled.

"We have to talk about getting back to our universe," said Mihalik.

"Tedious, Frank," said Dr. Waters. "Don't be tedious."

"It's the most important thing on our minds," said Cheryl.

"Anybody want the last of the moo shu pork?" asked Dr. Waters. Obviously he didn't want to talk about their dilemma.

"Look, sir," said Mihalik, banging his fist on the table, but not heavily, "you sent us back to Louis XIII's France for some reason of your own, just like—"

"Just like the Wizard of Oz," said Cheryl.

Mihalik stared at her. His mouth opened, then closed. "That's it!" he shouted. "That's just what I've been trying to remember all afternoon! The Wizard said he'd help Dorothy get back home, if first she did this one little thing for him. She had to steal the Wicked Witch's broom. Just like you had us go back to the seventeenth century and clear out the Temporary Underground for you. Well, we did, and now we're back. And you have to help us go home."

"What's this Wizard jazz?" asked Dr. Waters. He looked at Private Brannick, who only silently shook his head.

"It's a film in our universe," said Cheryl. "With Shirley Temple as the little girl."

"So what happens?" asked Dr. Waters. "Does the Wizard get her back home?"

"It wasn't Shirley Temple," said Mihalik.

"Yes, it *was* Shirley Temple, I remember her tap dancing with Bill 'Bojangles' Robinson, who played the Licorice Man who ferried them across the Root Beer River."

"I don't give a damn about any of that!" cried Dr. Waters. *"What happens?"*

"Oh, the Wizard can't help her," said Cheryl. "It turns out that it doesn't matter, anyway, because the girl is actually dying of blackwater fever, and all of this Oz business is just a delirious nightmare she's having in the hospital, and all the people in the dream are really the doctors and nurses taking care of her."

"So she never does get home?" asked Private Brannick sadly.

"Well, she dies, see," said Cheryl, "but at the end you see her going up to Heaven, which looks just like Oz but all her family is there, just like at home. They all died of the fever, too."

Dr. Waters drummed his fingers impatiently on the table. "You're telling me that none of this is real. You're wrong, folks. It *is* real. *You* may not be real, Frank, and *Cheryl* may not be real, but all the rest of this is real. If you died right here on the spot, I promise you that the rest of us wouldn't blink out of existence. You're not God, Frank."

"I never claimed that I was." Suddenly, Mihalik's eyes opened wider. "Do you remember, Cheryl, the other Dr. Waters said something about how it wouldn't be so easy to get back home? Not like just tapping our heels together and saying 'There's no place like home'?"

"Yes," she said breathlessly.

"Damn it," said Mihalik. "I'm getting confused, trying to keep straight which Dr. Waters said what. We've met three of you already. You seemed more substantial than the last one, because this universe looks more like ours. But this one and all the others are just blurry, distorted copies of the real universe."

Dr. Waters laughed softly. "You can make up theories like that all night if you want to. The important point—the only truly important point—is that you are here, whatever you want to think about this universe. It's your problem, not ours."

"But you have to help us!" said Cheryl.

"Show me where it says that," said Dr. Waters. He took out one of his expensive imported cigarettes and leaned a tall white taper over to light it.

"Then you never meant to help us," said Mihalik. He raised himself halfway out of his chair.

"Now, now, Frank, you've always been hotheaded. I'll do what I can, which isn't much. I'm a chronicist, not a wizard. But I owe you something. First, though, I want you to tell me exactly what you accomplished on your mission."

Mihalik looked blankly at Cheryl. "We don't know," she said.

"Well," said Dr. Waters impatiently, "did you run up against the Underground?"

"Of course we did," said Mihalik. "You could have given us a little more information before we left here. It took me a full day to figure out that the Musketeers were the good guys and the Cardinal's Guards were the rebels."

Dr. Waters squinted a little. "When you left here, we didn't know who the rebels were. But I'm pretty sure they weren't the Cardinal's Guards. They weren't, at least, the last time I checked."

"But the Musketeers couldn't have been, either," said Cheryl.

"That's right," said Dr. Waters.

"Then who the hell *was* the Temporary Underground?"

Private Brannick cleared his throat loudly. "We, uh, we've since learned that they've taken over the Flemish textile industry. You should have infiltrated the society of Flemish merchants."

Mihalik looked at Cheryl. "I didn't see a goddamn sign of any Flemish merchants, did you, Cheryl?"

"Nope."

"No Flemish merchants," growled Mihalik. "No Dutch uncles, no German shepherds, no English muffins, no Spanish moss, no Portuguese men-of-war, no Swiss cheese, and no Maltese falcons."

Private Brannick frowned and took a warning step toward him. "Remember where you are, Mr. Mihalik," he said softly.

"Can't take a joke," said the chrononaut. "That's the trouble with all you time fascists, no sense of humor. So if the Musketeers weren't the Underground and neither were the Guards, who the hell was that guy who was looking for Brother Fortunati?"

Dr. Waters raised his eyebrows. "Fortunati? He's one of the Commander's right-hand men."

"Who is the Commander?" asked Cheryl.

"The top dog of the Temporary Underground," said Private Brannick with a murderous expression. "The head honcho. The big noise in the mutiny department. A number 1. The bee's knees and the clam's garters, as far as sedition goes. He thinks he's hot stuff and a real pipperoo, but he's not so tough. He's nothing to write home about."

"Sounds like Brannick's spent too much time on the sidewalks of New York sixty years before he was born," said Mihalik.

"Oh," said Dr. Waters with some amusement, "Brannick's all right. That will be all, private." When the uniformed man left the suite, Dr. Waters smiled again. "He'd love to get his hands on the Commander, but that guy's slippery as an eel. The Commander likes to hide in the most Godforsaken places and eras. We found him once on Samoa in 220 A.D. Who would have thought to look for him there?"

"Who *did* think to look?" asked Cheryl.

"Your buddy there," said Dr. Waters.

"Me?" said Mihalik.

"Well, the *real* Frank Mihalik did."

Cheryl raised a hand. "Let's not start that business again. We thought the Cardinal's Guard were the enemy. We decimated them, and then we came back. If we were wrong, it wasn't our fault. We didn't have the right information."

Dr. Waters sighed. "I guess it's ultimately my fault. Anyway, no harm done; we can accomplish our objectives by sending another mission back to the same time. There won't be a single Flemish textile trader alive in that century when we're through. But I do owe you something for letting me know where that Fortunati bastard is holed up."

Mihalik relaxed a little. "Then you will help us, after all?"

"Certainly, Frank, certainly! What do I look like, some sort of tyrant, some awful despot of time? Ha ha, we're old friends, even if we've only just met. Now what do you think would be the best thing to try?"

"I don't know," said Mihalik thoughtfully. "The other Dr. Waters—I mean, the second Dr. Waters, in the universe we visited just before this—

well, he said that we ought to go into the future, where they've got all this sort of thing figured out."

"That makes sense."

"Wait a minute, though," objected Cheryl. "It made sense before, too, and all it got us was a quick trip to another wrong universe."

"It might work this time," said Mihalik. "We're starting out a lot closer to home than before."

"But there are an infinite number of universes, Frank," explained Cheryl patiently. "You keep forgetting that. We can get closer and closer from now until doomsday, and still never find our way back."

"Now, now, my dear girl," said Dr. Waters, fixing his magnetic gaze on the distraught young woman. "You are correct, after a fashion. However, the differences between any two universes may be so small that for all practical purposes you may call them identical. Suppose you land in another wrong reality, but the only reason it's 'wrong' is that two tiny grains of sand in the Sahara Desert are transposed in position. Would you ever know about it? Of course not. That 'wrong' universe would seem completely 'right' to you. And I don't need to remind you that a universe exists for every possible combination of details: for every transposition of every grain of sand, or drop of water, or atom of hydrogen, or anything else you care to mention. There are a staggeringly vast number of universes that will seem 'right' to you."

Cheryl jumped up. "The problem with your line of reasoning is so big, I don't even need to discuss it," she cried.

"Well, *I* don't see it," said Mihalik glumly.

Cheryl didn't pay any attention. "Have you noticed, Frank," she said, "that when we try to reason our way out of some situation, nothing happens? And that when we just *act,* things change?"

Dr. Waters patted the air soothingly with one hand. "Have you noticed, Cheryl, that when things change, they change for the worse?"

Cheryl had no answer to that; she sat down again and waited for Mihalik to make some contribution.

"I like what Dr. Waters just pointed out," he said. "Our trouble is that we've been going off half-cocked. Our own Dr. Waters wasn't entirely sure about what he was doing—that's the way it seems to me now. He just punted the both of us through some trapdoor in the air, and we landed entirely by accident in 1939. Then that crazy Marquand guy zapped us with his lightning bolt just because it seemed like a good idea to him. No calculations, no preparation, no safeguards. And look where we ended up then."

"Some awful place where everybody always has enough to eat and somebody else to cook it for them," said Dr. Waters. "Frightening."

"You had to be there to see how terrible it was," said Cheryl.

"And then," Mihalik went on, "the second Dr. Waters shunted us here. He was aiming for the far future, so his technology couldn't have been much better than the Dr. Waters in our own world."

Cheryl shook her head. "Yet he claimed that time travel had been perfected, too."

"Time travel, maybe," said Dr. Waters, "but not inter-reality travel. That's something altogether different. As it happens, I don't have that kind of universe-leaping perfected, either, but at least I have a lot of promising equations and a plausible model to base my experiments on. If you'd be willing to volunteer, I'd be glad to provide whatever limited assistance I can."

"You want to send us off, willy-nilly, into the infinite congregation of universes?" asked Cheryl. She looked dubious.

"You've already done it twice," said Dr. Waters, smiling in a kindly way. "You're no worse for the experiences, are you?"

"We've been incredibly lucky," said Cheryl. "There are more ways for a universe to be wrong than to be right. The next time, we might end up in a universe with no Dr. Waters at all, no time travel, maybe not even human life."

Dr. Waters shrugged. "There is that chance, I must admit. But come on, aren't you game? Aren't you up for the adventure?"

"I know that I am," said Mihalik. "Adventure is my profession."

"Good lad," said Dr. Waters.

"If only you had some kind of emergency recall mechanism," said Cheryl wistfully. "Some kind of insurance."

"I'll give you insurance: I'll make the trip with you. I'd love to visit another plane of existence. You know that I wouldn't take the risk unless I was pretty certain of success."

"All right, then," said Cheryl, "let's do it."

"Fine," said Dr. Waters, standing and beaming at both of them. He went to his desk and pushed a button. "I signaled Ray. He'll meet us at the transmission stage."

"Good old Ray," said Mihalik.

"He'll have to operate the screen. He'll push us through to my selected universe, and then draw us back after sixty minutes. If it seems acceptable to you, we can send you there permanently. How does that sound?"

"Great," said Mihalik, "unless something horrible happens during that hour."

Dr. Waters frowned. "I'm disappointed in you, Frank. Where's your explorer's zest for discovery?"

"Oh, I'm not worried for myself, sir. I was just concerned about you and Cheryl. You don't have all the temponeering training I've had. Besides, the universe and I seem to be reaching an understanding."

Dr. Waters laughed. Together the courageous trio left the suite and took the elevator to the laboratory. Ray was there to meet them, just as Dr. Waters had promised; both Mihalik and Cheryl shook his hand and promised to be careful. "We've been doing a lot of this lately," said Cheryl. "Saying goodbye to you two, I mean."

Dr. Waters and Ray were amused. They took their positions: Ray at the controls of the apparatus, the three adventurers on the transmission stage. "Ready?" called Ray. "Counting down now: five, four, three, two, one, *switch on!*"

There was a flicker of blue light, and Dr. Waters disappeared.

"My God!" cried Cheryl. "Come back! Don't go without us!"

"It's that damn movie again," muttered Mihalik. "The Wizard going off in the balloon, leaving Dorothy behind in Oz."

"My fault," called Ray, "I forgot to split the beam. I'm sorry. I'll split it in two, now. Counting down again: five, four, three, two, one, *switch on!*"

After another shimmer of blue and a rolling crackle of thunder, the world went dark. There were coiling mists on the ground and a faint yellow glow everywhere. Mihalik and Cheryl looked around in terror. There was nothing to see. They were nowhere at all.

Book Four

Time Is What Keeps History from Happening All at Once

Mihalik and Cheryl said the same thing at the same time:

"*Now* you've done it," said Mihalik.

"*Now* you've done it," said Cheryl.

Usually when they said the same thing at the same time, they thought it was cute. It was a sign of how close they were and how similar their thinking was. Now they just glared at each other.

"Frank—"

Mihalik turned and stalked off through the swirling mist.

"Frank—"

He whirled and glowered at her. "I don't even want to *talk* about it."

"Well, what are we going to do?"

"I said I didn't want to talk about it." He turned around again and marched through the dimness.

Cheryl watched him anxiously for a few seconds. This wasn't like him, she knew. He seemed really afraid.

The palely loitering fog didn't cause Mihalik much terror, and neither did the absolute lack of other things to look at, the absence of the sky, the ground, the horizon, *everything*. Yet he had never experienced such mad, paralyzing horror before. There was no terror, but the horror was tremendous. Still, he had been trained—well trained, expensively trained— to shrug off fear.

Mihalik took a deep breath and shrugged off the fear. The *horror* was still there, though.

He shrugged off the alarm, the dread, and the panic, too; but the horror hung right in there. "Here's where I start to earn my money," he thought, but deep inside he had no real relish for it. The horror grew out of the beginning of the hint of the idea that he wasn't a real hero, after all. One cruel part of his mind nagged him: "A real hero wouldn't have felt that horror. He wouldn't even have recognized it. He would have stepped right into this nothingness the way you step into a warm bath. But no! *You're* horrified! You're so horrified you can't think straight! And you *aren't* thinking straight, are you? You don't even trust yourself to talk to Cheryl. What, do you think *she's* not afraid? She didn't have your training. A *real* hero would be concerned for her first, but *you*—" The cruel voice in Mihalik's head was prepared to go on like that throughout

eternity. In fact, it *did* go on just like that for as long as Mihalik continued to draw breath. What made him truly a hero was that he stopped
paying attention to it. After a while.

There was something about this place—this nonplace—that was hard
on your nerves, besides the obvious loneliness and unreality of it all.
There was a tension in the air, a hovering, penetrating potential for yet
more horror. Mihalik had felt that sort of thing before, but never to this
numbing degree. It was like walking into a dentist's waiting room after
hours, or when you know you don't have to have any work done on your
own teeth. Still, just the whine of the drill or the sight of it clipped up
into its resting position is enough to give you a quick jolt of alarm. The
drill sits there like the most patient metal viper in the world, and you feel
an inverted thrill stab through you, starting somewhere near your groin
and clawing up toward your heart. The difference was that you could
turn and walk away from the dentist's office; here, you could turn and
walk, but there didn't seem to be any direction at all labeled "Away."

"Frank—"

Mihalik jumped, startled. "Don't sneak up on me like that," he said.

"I'm sorry," said Cheryl. She put her hand on his arm. She wondered
if he was quivering with worry or chill. "What are you doing?"

Mihalik laughed sardonically. "Oh, nothing much," he said. "Just killing time. That's a joke, Cheryl. What we ought to be doing is saving time,
I guess. I mean, we have no time to lose, right?"

For a moment, Cheryl couldn't tell if Mihalik's time puns were a good
sign or a bad sign. Because she was a hopeful, cheerful sort of young
woman, she concluded at last that things were getting better by the minute, because at least her beloved Frank was no longer stumbling witlessly
around in the clinging fog. He was bantering with her. That *was* a good
sign; soon they'd put their heads together and analyze the situation and
list the positive points and the negative points and figure their options
and come to a mutually agreeable decision. Then it would be simply a
matter of putting their plan into effect—that was Frank's part, of course;
he was the truly dynamic one of the team. Cheryl believed (though she
would never have spoken it aloud to him) that she had a deeper understanding of the ways of the world in general, and that she was quicker to
adapt to changing conditions; but she did not hesitate to award her boyfriend all honors in the action department.

But not just yet. While she watched, Mihalik's smile, which had never
really progressed further than causticness, slipped back into what was
very clearly a grimace of distress. Mihalik himself slipped down into the
wafting coils of yellowish mist. He was sitting up to his neck in the stuff,

with just his handsome head visible. "Well," he said, letting out a sigh, "here we are."

Now Cheryl was beginning to get impatient. "That's great, Frank," she said, standing over him with her hands on her hips, one foot tapping invisibly, enunciating her irritation in case it hadn't come through in her tone of voice. "Here we are: *that's* your contribution."

He shrugged. "Let's hear yours," he said.

Cheryl opened her mouth, realized she didn't have anything further to add to "Here we are," and closed her mouth again. Her foot continued to tap, but it slowed down bit by bit.

"Might as well rest here for a while," said Mihalik. "Gather our strength while we can. We never know what dangers we may have to face soon. Let's just take five here. Smoke 'em if you got 'em."

"Dangers, Frank? What dangers? There isn't anything here at all, dangerous or otherwise."

He looked up at her through half-closed eyes. "Cheryl," he said, "I agree with you that there isn't anything here at all. That doesn't mean, however, that something dangerous might not show up here at any moment."

The notion dismayed her; she hadn't thought of that. Once again, she'd underestimated Mihalik's grasp of the situation.

My! People Come and Go So Quickly Here

Before they could carry the discussion any further, a patch of the fog a hundred yards away began to swirl about in an unusual and unnatural way. It twisted slowly upward, spiraling and climbing, and more fog rushed in along the ground to replace the fog that was rising toward the —sky. There wasn't any sky, of course, but you can't get away from thinking of overhead as "sky." The fog was forming a small cyclonic cloud, growing denser and rotating faster every second. The whirling cloud was soon a broad wall of dirty yellow, no longer a mist or haze but something resembling a miniature tornado. Yet the tornado was upside-down, thicker near the ground and tapering up into a conical spinning spindle of vapor. The base of the tornado spread outward toward Mihalik and Cheryl. When the diameter of the bottom was about twenty or thirty yards, the tall, tenuous point began to fall back into the center. What had been a rapidly turning cone became a disk, then a rotating sphere.

"It's slowing down, Frank," said Cheryl. The sphere was indeed coming to a gradual stop; now it looked like a solid ball of churning gases ten feet high.

Mihalik got up and began to walk toward it. "I've got to investigate it, Cheryl, honey," he said. "It's the only phenomenon we've got here."

She nodded, understanding that he was duty-bound. "Be careful, Frank," she murmured.

Before he crossed half the distance between them and the ball, it disappeared. It popped just like a soap bubble, with a vaguely metallic, ringing, echoing sound. The ball vanished, blowing away the curling yellow mists that hung nearby; in its place were four people. There was one tall beautiful woman speaking to three uniformed men. The woman wore brown trousers and black leather riding boots, a beige turtleneck sweater with the sleeves pushed up over her elbows, and she carried a riding crop tucked under one arm. She had a great mass of black hair that had been carefully coiffed at some time in the past, but now it was disheveled and awry and every few seconds she ran a hand through it to no great effect. She was tall and slim with a marvelous figure, and her face was beautiful in a theatrical kind of way. She reminded Mihalik of Elizabeth Taylor about the time she made *Cleopatra*. She was evidently very disturbed about something, because every few seconds she'd underscore her angry words with a slash of the riding crop, and the three uniformed men looked from her face to the ground with unhappy expressions. The woman pointed in the direction of Mihalik and Cheryl, and then she led her three aides through the once again innocent mist.

"Excuse me," said Mihalik, when the woman and her three underlings passed without noticing them.

The woman and the uniformed men went on by. It was as if the time traveler had not even spoken.

Cheryl stepped in front of the woman. "I'm sorry to bother you," she said, "but we're new here and we were wondering—"

One of the men grabbed Cheryl and literally tossed her out of the way. She stumbled and fell, then bounced right back to her feet. She ran after the small party and put her hand on the shoulder of the man who'd thrown her. She spun him around and slapped him sharply across the face. "Who the hell do you think you are?" cried Cheryl.

"Who is this?" asked the woman with the riding crop.

By this time, Mihalik had caught up. He turned on the man who'd treated Cheryl so roughly. "I'm going to give you three seconds, pal," he said angrily, "and then if I haven't heard one hell of an apology, I'm going to deck you. One. Two. Thr—"

"Who are they?" shouted the woman. Her tone reminded Cheryl of nothing so much as the Queen of Hearts yelling "Off with their heads!"

"—ee." And then Mihalik decked the uniformed man with one terrific straight right to the chin.

"Nice," said one of the other uniformed men.

The one on the ground got slowly to his feet, rubbing his chin and glaring at Mihalik. "That was a mistake," he said in a low, ominous voice. Mihalik laughed.

"Silence!" cried the woman. There was silence. "Arthur, you and Miguel restrain this man. Reilly, if your face isn't hurting too much, do you think you can handle the woman?" Reilly's expression was by turns humiliated, furious, and hateful. He nodded. "Good. Now, who the hell are you and what are you doing here?"

"I'll tell you, if you'll get your goddamn hands off me," said Mihalik. The woman nodded at Arthur and Miguel; they let Mihalik go. Reilly, however, still held on to Cheryl. "We're scientific explorers. We're time travelers who've been sent *across* time from one universe to another. Through some cosmic accident, we ended up here. We don't know where we are, and we don't know how we got here, and we don't have any idea how to get back where we came from."

The woman with the riding crop nodded. "That sums it up rather precisely, thank you. You're nobody." She looked at her aides. "Bring them along. We can't let them just wander around here." She turned and strode off through the mist. The uniformed men put their hands on Mihalik again and shoved him along after her.

"Well," said Cheryl, turning to Mihalik, "what do you think? Is she a good witch, or a bad witch?"

Mihalik gave her a sour expression. "Very funny, Cheryl," he said. He looked to the side, at Arthur or Miguel. "Do you want to tell me what's going on?" he asked.

"No," said one military man.

Mihalik turned to the other, who had one hand around Mihalik's upper arm, and the other hand firmly around Mihalik's elbow. "What about you?"

"My name is General Arthur Scott Leidecker. I've been in Her Majesty's service since the age of nine, when my parents were killed in a mysterious accident. I've risen through the ranks from private, the only one of Her Majesty's generals to do so. I know the names of all the men in my command, just as Caesar did. I think it was Caesar. Maybe it was Alexander or Belisarius. I know all the names, but I get the faces confused sometimes. It doesn't really make any difference, though; I have plenty of colonels and majors and other officers, and they all have clipboards with rosters. The men have a genuine affection for me, they'd follow me anywhere. They call me 'The Old Fogeater.' In the coming battle, Her Majesty has graciously granted me the honor of guarding her right flank, and everyone agrees that's her best side. I'm counting on my men, on my military brilliance, and the blessings of Almighty God to lead us to a great victory that will end this stalemate once and for all. I foresee an irresistible breakthrough that will crush the enemy and push our lines forward far beyond the present position, adding greatly to the domain and glory of Her Majesty, Queen Hesternia, who commands my loyalty and my love."

Mihalik didn't speak for a moment. He had been taken aback by Leidecker's little life story. "I don't care about any of that," he said at last with some bitterness. "I want to know where we are, and how we're going to get out of here."

"You aren't anywhere, señor," said Miguel, the other general. "That's the whole point. You're where there is neither time nor space. You're between universes. You're on the battleground where the fate of those universes is decided. As for getting out of here, *no one* gets out of here. You *can't* get out of here because you can't get into the universes from here."

"We got into *here* from *there,*" said Cheryl.

"You couldn't have," said Miguel simply.

"Well, now we know one important thing," said Mihalik. "We can forget about learning anything from these two idiots." He felt both Arthur and Miguel tighten their grips on him. He wanted more than anything to clip them on the jaw as he had Reilly. He suspected that he'd get his chance eventually.

"I can see that she's a busy woman and everything," said Cheryl to Reilly, "but do you think we could have a word with Her Majesty? I'm sure she could straighten this out quickly."

"It'll get straightened out quickly, all right," said Reilly viciously. "We'll just execute you. We don't have to consult Her Majesty about that, either. We're generals."

"They're going to execute us, Frank," said Cheryl.

"I heard him; don't pay any attention. He's just the kind of impotent son of a bitch who likes to frighten girls. I'll think of something."

"I know you will, Frank," said Cheryl. They smiled to each other while the generals forced them on at Hesternia's quick pace.

For a battlefield, this zone of twilight had its pluses and minuses. It was big and flat and dry. You didn't have to worry about the enemy riding down on you from some hillside, or picking off your men from some Devil's Den of a stronghold. That's because there was no topography at all. None. On the negative side, there seemed to be two obvious things missing that were necessary for the great battle: Hesternia's troops and the enemy's troops. No doubt they had some way to get around this detail, but the answer wasn't obvious to Mihalik.

When the Music Stops, Find the Nearest Army and Join It

Mihalik ticked off their choices on his fingers: one, they could join; or two, they could die. It was about as simple a problem as he'd ever faced: it could be solved with only one decision. "Well, Cheryl," he said as he sat in the mist with her, "what do you think?"

"You mean 'join or die'?"

"Uh huh."

"Really, Frank, what do you expect? We join."

"Good," said Mihalik. He just wanted to be certain that she agreed with him. He thought too much of her to make important decisions involving her fate without consulting her. She deserved at least *that* much consideration.

"I wish I knew what we were going to join, though," she said.

"Queen Hesternia's army, I guess," said Mihalik.

"I never thought I'd end up as a foot soldier," said Cheryl. "Things were so pretty back at the 1939 World's Fair. Things were so simple, so innocent. We should have stayed there."

"You know why we couldn't stay there," said Mihalik.

"I *used* to know, Frank; I'm forgetting fast. If you think we couldn't stay in that happy, carefree world because our duty was to come here and carry spears for this Hesternia person, well, maybe I should have just minded my own business when they wanted someone to volunteer to come looking for you. I should have just mourned you in my shabby little room in 1996. I didn't *have* to come looking for you, Frank. I did it because I love you."

Mihalik chewed his lip for a moment. "You did it because nobody else would volunteer, didn't you?"

"Well. . . ."

"Nobody else *did* volunteer to try and save me, *did* they? Not even good old Ray?"

"I'm sure Ray would have, sooner or later. I didn't give him a chance."

"Wait until we get home, wait until I get my hands on those guys. . . ."

They were sitting back to back in the gloom, with Miguel keeping a close eye on Cheryl and Reilly keeping watch over Mihalik. Reilly's jaw was bruised and swollen, and he looked like he was just slavering for an excuse to carve Mihalik up. Leidecker must have been elsewhere with Hesternia. "Forget about your false friends back home, Frank," said Cheryl. "We have to take our problems one at a time. We have to get out of *this* mess first."

"You're right again, honey," said Mihalik proudly. "Having you with me is almost as good as having Dr. Waters himself. So we'll tell Her Majesty that we'll be glad to join and follow her orders and help however we can in the battle. I hope that doesn't mean actually lasering other people. I'd never forgive myself if I've gotten you into real danger."

"I'll be all right, Frank, as long as you're with me."

"You've never been in combat, Cheryl. It can be a frightening and ugly experience."

"We'll face it together. If we please her, maybe Queen Hesternia will help us get home."

Mihalik frowned. "None of her generals sounded very hopeful on that score; but like you say, we'll see."

General Leidecker approached them, but Her Majesty was still off somewhere else attending to something. "Good news, fellows," said Leidecker heartily. Reilly and Miguel looked up at him disdainfully, as if he were the last person they wanted to see; neither said anything, though. "The Queen expects the battle to begin very shortly. That means we have to go rally our troops and make our dispositions. We can go anytime we like."

"What about these two?" Miguel jerked his thumb at Mihalik and Cheryl.

"I'm still in favor of pushing in the boron rods and shutting them down for good," said Reilly with a small tight smile.

Leidecker waggled a finger. "None of that now, Reilly. Her Majesty said that they were to be given a fair chance. She said that I was to make sure you didn't kill them unless they chose to be uncooperative. She said I was supposed to tell her *immediately* if you killed them against her wishes."

"You would, too, wouldn't you?" said Reilly with a sneer. "You'd rat. You'd rat on anybody. Everybody knows it, Leidecker. We all know what you're like; you're not fooling anybody, not even Her Majesty. Don't think she doesn't know about you. She knows, Leidecker. She knows just what you're really like, too."

"Because you told her, I'll bet," said Leidecker.

"Aw, hell," muttered Miguel. He had been squatting back on his heels, listening to Leidecker and Reilly bicker. Now he stood and walked up close to Mihalik and Cheryl. "What'll it be? Join or die?"

"We'll join," said Mihalik.

"Fine," said Leidecker, "you can be in my army. I don't think you'd be safe in Reilly's, and I don't think Miguel wants you in his, either." Miguel's expression didn't change.

"We'd be proud to be in your army," said Cheryl. "Where is it?"

Leidecker waved an arm vaguely. "Over there," he said. He whipped the arm over his head in a series of loops, faster and faster, and the fog began to rush in around them. Leidecker was making his own little up-side-down tornado, and it was spinning so fast that it made both Cheryl and Mihalik dizzy; they had to close their eyes. "Close your eyes," cried Leidecker over the roar of the wind. "It helps sometimes until you get used to this."

"Do you always travel like—"

There was a loud, ringing pop, and the three of them were in another part of the nowhere. Here there were trenches in the "ground." They weren't dugouts because the ground wasn't made of earth. The trenches looked like permanent regular features molded into the contour of what-ever the ground was made of, put there when the ground had been put there. There was less fog, but there was still some thin yellowish mist creeping down into the trenches and hanging around about knee level. In the trenches were hundreds and thousands of soldiers, all with black stuff smeared on their faces, all with rifles and soup-plate helmets, all with large frightened eyes and cleverly engineered bayonets, all with nervous tics and World War One British Army uniforms. They were waiting for something. They'd probably been waiting for it for a long time. They looked like if they had to wait much longer, they'd go whanging off like a busted guitar string snapping and whipping around at the end of the fret board.

"Well," said Cheryl. The rather historical-looking scene, almost banal in its implications, was at least more comprehensible than the vast empty place they had come from. To be sure, this place was still part of that skyless, sunless, earthless universe, but here there were more people and things. It made this nonplace seem more lived-in; it gave this nightmare a homey touch.

General Arthur Leidecker jumped down into one of the trenches. Ev-eryone immediately came to attention. Leidecker asked who was in charge of the unit. A captain saluted and identified himself; Leidecker nodded in a preoccupied way, indicated Mihalik and Cheryl, and then strode off down the trench, stopping now and then to cheer up a terrified young man or straighten someone's tunic.

The captain looked up at the brave temponauts. "Don't just loll around waiting for a bloody invite," he cried. "Get down here before you get your arses shot off." They turned and tried to gaze through the mist behind them; but if there were enemy trenches nearby, they were out of sight. Mihalik put his arms around Cheryl and handed her down gently to the captain, then jumped down nimbly beside them. "Rifles in that bunker," said the officer briskly. "I've got a lot to see to before the balloon goes up. You two take care of yourselves?"

"Yes, sir," said Mihalik.

"Good show. We'll be counting on you to do your part."

"For God and Admiral Nelson," said Cheryl under her breath.

"For the *Queen,*" said the captain over his shoulder. Then he was gone.

"God save the Queen," said Mihalik. He looked at Cheryl. "Well, here we are in the thick of it again. At least they're not using thasers or static guns. I hope we do as well with rifles as we did with the rapiers against the cardinal's men."

"We had the benefit of Dr. Waters's ESB training then," Cheryl reminded him. "Without that, I wouldn't have known which end of the rapier to hold. I know even less about rifles."

"They can't be that complicated," said Mihalik. "I'll get us a couple, and maybe one of these guys will give us a few pointers." He went down to the bunker and returned in a few minutes with two rifles, ammunition, and two helmets. "They wanted me leave a deposit on the rifles and the helmets," he said. "I couldn't believe it. I told them I didn't have any money at all with me. I had to sign for them, and they said they'd collect it after the battle, if we were still alive."

Cheryl laughed without humor. "I assume that if we're killed, we won't have to pay."

"Who knows, in this place?" said Mihalik. "They may have some way of—"

"Watch where you're pointing that thing, baby," said a sleepy-eyed young soldier. He was wearing a ripped, mud-stained uniform; Mihalik wondered where the mud had come from.

"Sorry," said Cheryl. She swung the old Enfield around by its sling, trying not to get in anyone's way. The soldiers were packed shoulder to shoulder in the trench, and it was easy to step on someone's foot or accidentally put an elbow in someone's eye.

" 's all right," said the soldier. He didn't sound British at all. He looked at them for a little while. "Helmets," he said at last. "All you got are helmets. You're dressed kind of informally for going over the top, aren't you?" Mihalik and Cheryl looked at their helmets, which they were holding in the hands that weren't holding Enfields. They clapped their helmets on their heads.

"We got our orders at the last minute," said Mihalik. "You know how it is."

The young man nodded. He closed his eyes and his head drooped; it looked like he'd fallen suddenly asleep. A moment later his eyes opened again halfway. "My name is Sopko," he said. He stuck out a grimy hand.

"Frank Mihalik." He took Private Sopko's hand and shook it. "This is Cheryl. She's a game little lady."

"She better be," said the young man. "You just call me Petie. I guess we're buddies now."

"Guess so," said Mihalik.

"Trench life demands that you have buddies," said Petie. "They die on you, though. You watch them get blown to bits in shell holes or machine-gunned down in front of you, you watch them gutted on barbed wire or bayoneted in no-man's-land. Then you make new buddies. Without buddies, what have you got?"

Neither Mihalik nor Cheryl had the faintest idea. "We're from New York," said Cheryl. "Where are you from?"

Petie looked at her curiously. "Nowhere," he said. "Where *is* there to be from?"

"New York, for one," said Mihalik.

"No such place," said Petie. "There *aren't* any real places. There's only this, and this isn't a real place. If you saw a place and it was real, it wouldn't be here; so then, if you saw a place and it was real, it wouldn't be here, so it wouldn't exist. It *can't* exist, QED. Take your New York, for instance."

"You may be right about New York," said Cheryl, "but I've been in some other places that were mighty persuasive about being real."

Petie laughed and shrugged. "Oh, sure," he said, "haven't we all? That doesn't prove anything, though. They're not real because they're not *here*. It's a simple test you can apply to anywhere you happen to find yourself."

There was a long silence while Petie seemed to go to sleep again, and Mihalik and Cheryl thought over what he'd had to say about reality. "You know," said Mihalik after a while, "I think the whole question of the nature of reality is pointless: you can never define reality. You can't say, 'This universe is real and that universe isn't.' I think I'm going to stop thinking about it and just deal with our problems. The hell with whether or not they're real problems."

"Psychosomatic pain hurts just as much as real pain," said Cheryl. She looked at her rifle. "Psychosomatic death may be virtually indistinguishable from the real thing, too."

"Think of all the universes as self-enclosed units bound in some kind of matrix, like motes of dust in a beam of sunlight. One mote has no knowledge of any other mote, and can't have any knowledge of the sunbeam, either. Then we, in our dust-mote universe—"

"Frank," said Cheryl wearily, "philosophers were going through all that before the time of Socrates. That's the oldest question on the books. You're defining reality again, and you just said you weren't going to do that anymore."

"I had trouble with enuresis when I was a kid, too," said Frank. "Eventually I triumphed, as I will this time also."

Cheryl kissed him lightly on the cheek. "I have the utmost confidence in you, Frank," she said.

Petie woke up again. "Miss anything?"

"Nope," said Mihalik.

"Damn it," said Petie. "Hoped the signal'd come and gone, and everything was over."

"A soldier's life is a tiresome one," said Cheryl.

"Who are we fighting, anyway?" asked Mihalik.

Petie laughed; it must have been a ludicrous question. "Those guys," he said, pointing in the direction of the enemy trenches, still invisible to Mihalik and Cheryl.

"What's it all about?" asked Mihalik.

Petie squinted his eyes. "You really don't know?"

Cheryl shook her head. "We're new here."

"Ah," said Petie, "some sort of miracle. Created out of nothing as adults, like Adam and Eve."

"No," said Mihalik, "we've been trying to tell you. We came from someplace else."

Petie shook his head slowly. "It's easier for me to believe the spontaneous creation theory."

"Whatever," said Cheryl.

"Why are we fighting them?" asked Mihalik.

" 'Cause they want to kill us," said Petie.

Mihalik looked at Cheryl. "Sounds like a good enough reason to me," he said.

"Uh huh," she said.

"See," said Petie, "the Queen—"

"Queen Hesternia?" asked Cheryl.

"Yeah. The Queen—"

"The strong-willed kind," said Mihalik. "She reminds me of a teacher I had in eleventh grade. Hesternia's got a nicer build on her, though. I'd like to get *her* all mussed up and muddy."

Petie's eyes opened very wide. The whites of his eyes completely encircled the irises. "You've *seen* the Queen?" he asked reverently.

"Talked with her. Gave her a piece of my mind, I hope to tell you," said Cheryl.

"I saw you arrive with the general, Old Foghead. But the Queen herself. . . . I've never known anyone who'd actually been that close to her." He looked at Mihalik and Cheryl with a kind of awe.

Mihalik just shrugged modestly. "She seemed all right, once you got to know her." He saw a faint greenish glow of jealousy in Cheryl's eyes and added, "I suppose she's just not my type, though." He put his arm around Cheryl's waist, and they kissed.

"It seems an odd time and place for a public display of affection," said Petie.

"So who knows?" asked Cheryl. "We may never have another opportunity. That might well have been our last kiss."

Mihalik gave Petie a wry smile at one side of his mouth. "No, it won't be our last kiss," he said, and he kissed Cheryl once more.

The Battle of Passchendaele, Back by Popular Demand

Petie was about to say something when a lieutenant clambered out of the trench and began to shout. "That's my platoon leader," said Petie with a sigh. "I guess it's show time, folks." The lieutenant drew his pistol and ordered his men to follow him. All along the trench, men carrying heavy packs and gripping 1917-vintage rifles started to holler and push and fight their way up the rickety wooden ladders. They were going over the top.

"Here we go," said Mihalik to Cheryl. "Stay back, and I'll cover for you. When everything quiets down a little, you can come up and join me. Either we're going to chase the enemy out of its trenches, or they'll punch us back here. You and I will be together again when it's safe."

"I'm going with you *now*, Frank," she said. "If we die, we die together."

"Cheryl—"

"You picked a fine time for a domestic squabble," said Petie. They watched the other soldiers scrambling out of the trench. Then Petie added his shout to the cacophony of the battlefield: "Let's go get 'em!" An instant later, Private Sopko was out of the trench, reaching down to help steady Cheryl while she climbed the crude ladder. Mihalik followed her and then all three were standing on the mist-shrouded ground, watching Leidecker's forces charging across the wire-strung, booby-trapped no-man's-land. Shells were exploding all around them, some from Queen Hesternia's artillery behind them, some from the enemy's artillery far ahead. The explosions made no mark on the ground, but there were plenty of built-in shell holes to jump into; these shell holes must have been provided at the same time the trenches had been laid out.

The artillery rounds didn't even scratch the ground, but the flying shrapnel was taking its toll. Mihalik watched tensely as dozens of men nearby fell screaming. No one seemed interested in rescuing and treating the wounded. Mihalik never saw anyone who looked like a medic.

"Frank!" shouted Cheryl over the noise of the bombardment. He had been lost in thought, his rifle hanging loosely from the sling in his hand. Now he realized how vulnerable he was and he began to move. He made his way forward toward the first shell hole where Petie and Cheryl were waiting.

"Sorry," he said, after he'd dropped into the shallow crater. "I was just thinking."

"You ought to practice thinking more often," said Petie. "That way when you get an idea, it won't freeze you up. Some people haven't thought for so long that when they have a real insight of their own, they get totally incapacitated."

"Say, pal," said Mihalik, "make all the jokes and snike comments you want. Even tough old veterans like you must get a little quaky when the big guns start to talk."

"Naw," said Petie, "I'm not nervous. I've been through this a hundred times before."

"Then let's keep up with the rest of the company," said Mihalik. "They're all ahead of us now. We got to keep moving."

"No, we don't," said the private. "How do you think I've lasted so long in this army? What we're doing, see, is we're guarding the rear. We'll just stay here until we don't hear any more shells going off. Then we'll run like hell, bellowing like heroes, and grab a place in the next trench. Or else, in the case of disaster, we'll just mix ourselves into what's left of our own company as it fights it way back to our original trench. There's been so many battles, and they always end with one side capturing a trench or two from the other side. From Tommy's point of view, it doesn't seem like anything changes one way or the other, but who am I to make judgments? We do what we're ordered to do, and we'll end up in some trench not far from here, waiting until the generals decide to order a new assault. The waiting is harder to take than the fighting."

"You make it sound so futile," said Cheryl.

"That's just what it is," said Petie.

A shell detonated a few feet from their hole. Instinctively all three people ducked down as far as they could and clutched their helmets tightly to their heads. If this place had had real ground, fragments of stone blasted out of the new crater would have injured as many men as the explosion itself. The only danger here, though, was from the shell itself; the explosion or the shrapnel could kill you. Other than that,

Mihalik, Cheryl, and Petie were perfectly safe, at least as safe as they'd
been in the trench. "It's a matter of statistics," said Petie, sitting with his
arms crossed on his knees, his rifle tossed casually to one side. "What are
the odds that one of those whiz-bangs will land right here in this hole?
Pretty slim, I'd say. If we got out of the hole, the enemy's sharpshooters
would have three fine plump targets to aim at. Let them aim at somebody
else."

"What do you mean, 'plump'?" asked Cheryl. She sounded annoyed.

"Never mind," said Petie. "Just be quiet and watch the war."

"So who *is* the enemy?" asked Mihalik. "The army of somebody just
across the border from Queen Hesternia's territory?"

"Uh huh," said Petie, "in a way."

"Nobody's ever told us what Queen Hesternia is the Queen *of,*" said
Cheryl.

The soldier raised an eyebrow. "She's the Queen of the Past. She rules
over all time that has already been and gone. Out there is the army of
King Proximo, who rules the future."

Mihalik and Cheryl exchanged dubious glances. "How can anyone
rule the past or the future?" asked Cheryl. "How did Hesternia get to be
Queen of the Past?"

Petie shrugged. "It's a crummy job, I admit," he said, "but someone's
got to do it."

"This must be an old war, then," said Cheryl.

Petie laughed. "It goes back a long way."

"I don't understand why there should be a war at all," said Mihalik.
"There's no way for the future to rule the past. What's past is past."

"What's past is Queen Hesternia's domain," said Petie. "It's a huge
empire, but it's not infinite. King Proximo, however, has an open-ended
empire that might go on through eternity. The Queen is jealous. She tries
to grab as much of Proximo's territory as she can, a little at a time. The
King never attacks; he's fighting to keep things at a standstill, but Her
Majesty won't let him relax. She never lets up. I said this war was futile,
and that nothing changes. That's not precisely true; Hesternia keeps
pushing, and the front lines move bit by bit. A year ago, we were back
there." He pointed behind them, beyond the trench they'd come from.
"A year from now, we'll be up there someplace. This war has been going
on since the beginning of the universe, and it will probably go on until the
whole universe itself dies."

"I see," said Cheryl, a look of dawning comprehension lighting her
eyes. "And so the present—"

"There really *isn't* any present," said Petie. "It's just a convention, an idea without concrete meaning. The present is always moving, just as the Queen's army is always moving."

"So the present is really just the point between the two armies," said Cheryl. "Wherever the front happens to be."

"That's oversimplified, but, yes, that's the way it works out. There would be no time-flow in the unreal universes if this struggle ended. Fortunately we've been able to push King Proximo back rather consistently; if his army rallies and drives us back, time-flow in the other universes reverses."

"Nobody's ever noticed time running backward, at least not where we come from," said Mihalik.

"You're not equipped to notice it," said Petie. "It probably occurs often, but your brain and your sensory organs make it seem as if your life were continuing along in one direction only, gliding on through the days as smoothly as a lubricated cat. It's like your eyesight; you actually see things upside down, but your brain takes the images and flips them for you. Likewise, your brain edits out the backward-running episodes, so you're never aware of them."

"That's the reason the Queen and her generals can't send us home, Frank," said Cheryl. "They rule over the past, and the past isn't any good to us. We've already been there."

Mihalik nodded thoughtfully. "What do you know about this King Proximo?"

"Nothing," said Petie. "I've never been close even to my own queen. I know even less about the enemy's king."

"Except that he rules the future, and the Queen is always nibbling away at his empire and adding it onto her own," said Cheryl.

"Sounds like opportunism to you, I guess," said the private. "Well, if Proximo can't hold on to his territory, why shouldn't Her Majesty take it if she can?"

Neither Mihalik nor Cheryl had a good reply to that. "I didn't think the philosophy of time would lead to this," she said. "A battle *through* eternity, *for* eternity."

"It's a living," said Petie. He leaned back against the wall of their shell hole and tried to go to sleep.

Mihalik and Cheryl waited until the soldier's breathing became slow and regular; finally he started to snore. Then the two people from 1996 conferred in whispers. "We have to get out of here," said Mihalik.

"I know," said Cheryl. "If we don't, we'll have no hope at all of getting home. What do you think we should do?"

"I think we should slip across this damn no-man's-land and see if King Proximo can be of more use to us."

Cheryl agreed in principle. "The only question I have," she said, "is how do we accomplish it?"

"Fleetness of foot," said Mihalik. "We leave the shelter of this little crater, and we haul ass after Hesternia's army. When we catch up with it we keep on running through it, and we join up with Proximo's army. Then we find Proximo. We'll have to wing it from then on."

"*I* wouldn't do it," said Petie. Mihalik jerked around, surprised that Petie had overheard them.

"Why not?" asked Cheryl.

"Because Hesternia's very jealous. She deals very hard with traitors."

"We never asked for this in the first place," said Mihalik. "We were coerced and pressed into service. Where we come from—" But Petie was asleep again. "Grab your rifle, Cheryl. Follow me, up and over. Then we race straight through the fog toward the enemy. Stay low and zigzag."

"You're going to be between two vast armies, and both sides will be shooting at you," said Petie.

"I put my trust in Providence," said Mihalik simply. "It's better than spending the rest of my life in a phony shell hole."

"I don't know about that," said Petie. "This is the most comfortable crater I've ever been in."

Kiss Yesterday Goodbye

"Goodbye, Petie," Cheryl said. "I hope you get through this battle safely."

"We all got to go sometime," said the soldier stoically.

"We got to go *now,*" she said.

"Come on, Cheryl," murmured Mihalik. Then he climbed out of the shell hole and started to sprint bent over, clutching his rifle to his chest, and making a zig or a zag every few yards. Cheryl followed him without a complaint. She was in good physical condition, so Mihalik didn't have to worry about her collapsing from fatigue in the danger zone.

The two chronatic explorers raced across the open ground, through the barbed wire into no-man's-land, and toward the rear of Hesternia's advancing army. Shells continued to burst all around them, and the explosions were constant and deafening. Soon Mihalik could hear nothing but a loud ringing in his ears. He looked over his shoulder and saw Cheryl, hunched over just as he was, closing the gap between them with every stride. Bullets from the enemy's rifles made a high-pitched zanging noise as they struck the ground nearby. Mihalik prayed that they wouldn't be cut down between the trenches. Soon Cheryl was running beside him, breathing heavily through her mouth. They were both nearing exhaustion; they didn't have enough wind to talk, so together they just charged silently ahead. There really wasn't anything to discuss, anyway.

They passed through the back ranks of Hesternia's forces and went on toward the vanguard. Mihalik felt Cheryl's hand on his arm, and he glanced at her. She pointed up toward the "sky." A World War One biplane—maybe a Sopwith Camel, but Mihalik had no detailed knowledge of early aircraft, not enough to make a positive identification—was circling overhead. If it belonged to King Proximo, it might be getting ready to strafe the advancing troops; if it belonged to Hesternia, it might be providing air support or spotting enemy gun emplacements. There weren't any other planes, so it was likely that this single aircraft was just a spy plane gathering intelligence.

In a few minutes, as they were forging their way through the front line of Hesternia's army, they saw the biplane leaving a message overhead. It was skywriting without a sky—in script, rather than block letters. The message was:

SURRENDER MIHALIK OR DIE

"Remember the Wicked Witch on her broom, spelling out 'Surrender Dorothy or Die' over the Emerald City?" asked Cheryl, panting between words.

Mihalik nodded. "How did Hesternia know about our plans? How does she know my name?"

"It's her job, Frank. She must know absolutely everything that happened in the past, whether she was physically present or not. Otherwise she wouldn't be the Queen of the Past."

"Well, I'm not going to surrender," said Mihalik. "Maybe to Proximo, but definitely not to Hesternia."

"Oh, Frank," said Cheryl breathlessly, "you're always so brave!"

That made him laugh right in the middle of one of his zags. "You're here with me," he reminded her. "I'm not being brave, I'm just being a hero. *You're* the brave one. You don't have to be here."

"You're sweet," she said. Then they put all their energy into running. Soon they'd outstripped the Queen's front rank and they were all alone, getting closer and closer to the trenches of tomorrow. When at last they reached the first of the enemy trenches, it was deserted. They jumped down into it and searched quickly for someone wearing an Army of the Future uniform. They found connecting trenches and tunnels and hurried through them, farther into Proximo's territory. They were beginning to get discouraged—there was no one to capture them, to take them to King

Proximo, to give them a chance to beg for freedom and help. They turned a corner and suddenly there was a dense crowd of futuristic defenders. Mihalik and Cheryl smiled to show they intended to do no harm.

"Drop those pieces," said a burly man with a thick black beard. He was wearing a blue and silver uniform that reminded Mihalik of the Agency's uniform he'd seen in one or another of the false universes they'd visited.

"Right," said Cheryl. She threw her rifle to the ground and so did Mihalik. They expected to be taken away to be questioned, but they were mistaken. The bearded man gave them each another rifle, the kind used by Proximo's infantry.

Mihalik looked at his new rifle, then at Cheryl. "Honey," he said softly, "I think we've been drafted again."

It's a Long, Long Way to Tipperary

"See them?" asked the sergeant, pointing back across no-man's-land, where the front ranks of Queen Hesternia's army were just emerging from the fog and smoke and mustard gas.

"Those guys?" said Mihalik, thinking fast.

The sergeant in the blue and white uniform glanced at him briefly, a pitying look on his face. "What happened?" he asked Cheryl. "Did your buddy here throw himself on a grenade to save his squad and miss?"

"No," she said pleasantly, "he's always been like this."

"Ah, well." The black-bearded sergeant coughed. "Then I'll take it slower. 'Those guys,' as he so aptly put it, are coming to do you harm."

"Naw, they wouldn't," said Mihalik. "I've met those guys. They're all decent sorts."

"I know that," said the big man, "I know they are. Believe me, though, when they get here, they'll be shooting and stabbing to make your hair stand on end. Why else are they carrying rifles? Ask yourself that one, my boy. Why else do the rifles have such devilish-looking bayonets? Not just for parade and impressing the girls on Lady Day. Now listen: me and my boys, we've been in this trench for a long time. A *long* time. And we've taken a vote and we've decided that it's about time we moved along. Headed back a bit, gave up a bit of ground if we have to. A strategic withdrawal, as it were, advancing to the rear. You're going to have to cover our backs. It's going to be up to you to see that we get away alive. It's heroic action I'm asking of you. I'm asking you now, do you think you're up to it?"

"Of course," said Mihalik, his chest beginning to swell up at the mention of the word "heroic."

"Wait a minute, wait a minute!" said Cheryl. "This isn't quite right. Those were our comrades, just a little while ago. Now you're telling us to shoot them down while you and your friends hit the dusty trail. You want us to hold off all of Queen Hesternia's army, just the two of us, while you turn tail. Why in hell *should* we?"

The sergeant thought about that for a second, maybe two. "I could bring up the matter of how you'd be executed as spies in a minute if I decided that you should be; but leaving that aside, think of it as Vietnamization."

"As what?" asked Mihalik.

"We're turning the war over to you who ought to be fighting it in the first place. We've been dying for *you,* you know, not that we haven't been glad to do it; but it's time you folks from the unreal universes began shouldering some of the responsibility. Now start shooting, because I'm beginning to see the whites of some eyes out there. Good luck, and watch out: these Mausers tend to shoot a little shorter than you'd think." With that, the sergeant ducked down and hurried around a turn in the trench, gone before Cheryl could get out another objection.

"What would happen if we ran after him?" asked Mihalik.

"They'd probably shoot us down as we turned the corner," said Cheryl.

"That's what I was thinking. So instead we'll stay here and fire into our buddies' advancing lines." He shrugged; it was all the same to him.

"Well, Frank, they never were our buddies, none but Petie, really; and he sure won't be up here in the front. We'll never live long enough to risk taking a shot at Petie. Let your conscience be clear. They'll overwhelm us here in the trench and we'll be dead meat long before Petie shows up. Don't worry about it."

" 'Dead meat,' " said Mihalik. There was a brief pause. "Cheryl," he said finally, "my conscience is clear. Why didn't that sergeant speak German and wear a German uniform?"

"Just start shooting, Frank. We'll learn the answers together in heaven."

Mihalik raised his Mauser and drew a bead on a faceless Tommy, some hundred yards away. Before he could squeeze the trigger, a calm, somewhat amused voice said, "Wait."

"What?" asked Mihalik. It hadn't been Cheryl's voice.

"I said, 'Wait.' " There was a young man standing beside them in the trench, wearing yet another sort of uniform. He didn't seem to have reached his twenties, yet his face showed that he'd experienced many of the cruelties of warfare himself, that life had not been easy for him, either. He put a hand on Mihalik's shoulder, and his touch was gentle but manly.

"Who are you, sir?" asked Cheryl. "And where did you come from?"

"My name?" The young man gazed off across no-man's-land, a brief smile upon his lips. "It doesn't matter, I guess, but I am Captain Hartstein of the Time Patrol. There's no one in the Time Patrol but me. It's a lonely job, or it would be if I didn't have—" Hartstein stopped himself abruptly. "None of that is important now. All you need to know is that I've come from the far, far distant future to rescue you from this untenable position."

"Good," said Mihalik, "that's just what I hoped would happen. You read the note we left in the time capsule at the Fair. It sure took you long enough. You put us through a lot of unnecessary inconvenience."

"Frank," said Cheryl in a loud whisper, "he's here to help. Mind your manners."

Mihalik was genuinely abashed. "I'm sorry," he said.

"Think nothing of it," said Captain Hartstein. "No, I didn't read your message in the time capsule. It's a long story. You see, in the near future —that is, *your* future—I mean, the future of your own lives, not of this nontime and nonplace—you will visit me, and give me valuable encouragement when I'm in a situation even worse than this."*

"We will?" asked Cheryl. "How can that be?"

"The twists and turns time can make," said Hartstein, smiling and shaking his head. "When you travel in time, you snag yourself around the lines of many other people. If some of them are traveling in time, too, your meeting may happen in your present but their past or future. Or their present, or any combination—look, we don't have time for a discussion of all this, just take my word for it. When I needed it, you tried to restore my morale. Now, later for me but earlier for you, I want to return the favor. I've come back to this point in your travels when you need assistance, and I'm going to take you out of here. In years to come, people will honor you as the Odysseus and the Penelope of Time."

"Gee," said Mihalik, obviously pleased. He liked the sound of that: the Odysseus of Time.

"So we won't have to kill our friends?" asked Cheryl.

"As you said, they weren't really your friends," said Hartstein patiently. "But no, you won't have to kill them."

"Good," she said. She dropped her rifle to the ground. Mihalik did the same.

"Now listen some more," said Hartstein. "The reason that you haven't

* See *The Bird of Time*, Chapter Eleven. "Oh, what a tangled web we weave. . . ."

been able to get home is very simple. You're in the future, and the future doesn't really exist. You've been in the future ever since you left the World's Fair—"

"But when we left there, we went back to 1996," said Mihalik. "It was just the wrong 1996."

Hartstein shook his head. "It was the right year, the right month, but the wrong day," he said. "Remember? You arrived exactly twenty-four hours later than you departed. So you were technically and effectively in the future, which is all fantasy, unreality, and not to be trusted. You've been in the future ever since. There's no such thing as the 'real' past or the 'real' future. Never mind about that now; it's something Dr. Waters will have discovered with his calculations before you even get home. Your only hope is to get back to your present, which will be the seventeenth of February, 1996. All the many months you've been gone will not have passed in your present. Remember, though, that as long as you're as much as one minute in the past or one minute in the future, you'll be trapped in one unreal universe or another. You *have* to find the present. . . ." And with those words, Hartstein's image began to fade away like a dream, like the snows of yesteryear, like a projected image in a darkened room when the lights are turned up brightly.

"But how?" called Cheryl.

Hartstein's disembodied voice came to them weakly. "You better close your eyes so you'll be in tune with the Infinite," he said.

"A line from *The Wizard of Oz*," muttered Mihalik. "Even from him."

"Close your eyes, Frank!" cried Cheryl.

They both closed their eyes, but they heard and felt nothing. They stood like that for a long time, until they began to feel foolish and a little afraid. The army of Queen Hesternia should be rushing upon them very soon. First Cheryl opened her eyes, then Mihalik. They looked around. The trenches were gone; the dim and foggy battlefield had vanished; the frightening world of between-time was now somewhere else, as it was supposed to be. The two explorers stood in a broad bright meadow of flowers, beneath a clear blue sky and a warm heartening sun. Mihalik looked at Cheryl, down at the flowers, and up at Cheryl again. His expression twisted sourly. "Poppies," he said disgustedly.

Book Five

The Future Is
Just Like the Present,
Only Longer

A Place Where There Isn't Any Trouble

Mihalik and Cheryl trudged southward through the meadow. They had picked that direction because it was generally downhill; there was nothing to see in the other directions except the gently waving red flowers. "If we come to a yellow brick road," threatened Mihalik, "I'm going to give up. I'm going to wait for Glinda to come take me by the hand. I'm not going to budge an inch. I've had it."

Cheryl was surprised by his vehemence. "I don't understand, honey," she said. "I thought you liked *The Wizard of Oz.*"

"If I never see that movie again, it will be just fine with me." He felt grumpy, and it actually cheered him a little to crush the innocent poppies underfoot. They didn't make him sleepy, and no snowstorm came to rescue them from an evil witch's spell. It was just a field of red poppies; there was no magic here at all. Mihalik was silently thankful for small favors.

"We used to watch it every time it came on, even though it was made back in the old 2-D days," said Cheryl. "Remember how excited we were when they put the 'Jitterbug' sequence back in?"

"Yeah," said Mihalik.

"So what's wrong?"

"It doesn't bother you that for the last few universes everybody we run into seems to have *The Wizard of Oz* on the brain? Doesn't it seem kind of coincidental, or strange, or even ominous to you?"

"How could Shirley Temple be ominous, Frank?"

Mihalik stopped walking; Cheryl went on a few steps before she realized that he wasn't keeping up. She turned around and looked at him questioningly. "There you go again," he said. "Shirley Temple. I told you before: it wasn't Shirley Temple, it was Judy Garland. And what was that phony stuff you told Dr. Waters about Bill 'Bojangles' Robinson being in the movie? He never had anything to do with it."

"Judy Garland?" said Cheryl, laughing. "Frank, try to make sense. That isn't even logical. Dorothy is a little girl in the book, maybe five or six years old. When the movie was made, Judy Garland would have been in her late teens, her young budding breasts thrusting against her childish gingham dress, her ripening hips swaying suggestively as she passed fearfully through the haunted forest, her full, sensuous lips—"

"That's enough, Cheryl. My God, Shirley Temple would have been just awful. She would have made the picture so sweet you wouldn't be able to stand it. At least Judy Garland had a real voice. I can't imagine Shirley Temple trying to sing 'Over the Rainbow.' "

"Sing what, Frank?"

" 'Over the Rainbow.' "

Cheryl looked at him blankly. "You remember *that,* which wasn't in the movie, but you don't remember Shirley Temple tap-dancing with Bill Robinson and Buddy Ebsen by the river, singing 'No Way to Stay the Day and Play?' "

Mihalik smacked his forehead with one hand. "Buddy Ebsen? You mean Davy Crockett's pal? What would he be doing in *The Wizard of Oz?*"

"Playing the Tin Woodman. He was one of the best all-around *hoofeurs* in Hollywood, Frank, and he made a great team with Bill Robinson. And Shirley Temple was a pretty fair little *hoofeuse,* for being only eleven. That's a lot closer to Dorothy's age according to the book, you know."

Mihalik began walking beside her again. They continued the argument as they went down the blossom-covered hillside; they came to a stream at the bottom, and followed it until they saw what were unmistakably the towers of a futuristic city on the horizon. They stared at it for a moment, then looked at each other. "Don't say—" said Mihalik.

"There's Emerald City! Oh, we're almost there, at last, at last!"

"—say it," finished Mihalik glumly.

Cheryl laughed at him. "Don't take it so seriously, Frank. I was just joking."

"Buddy Ebsen, huh? You don't remember Jack Haley at all?"

"Who's Jack Haley, Frank?" asked Cheryl innocently.

"The Tin Woodman!" cried Mihalik in frustration. "Look, MGM never could have gotten Shirley Temple for that picture. She was under contract to somebody else, Paramount or somebody."

"Studios traded stars all the time. I think MGM was going to let Paramount use Carole Lombard for a couple of pictures in return. Lombard didn't get around to making those movies for almost ten years, as it turned out, but they were great. First she did—"

"Carole Lombard died only three or four years after *The Wizard of Oz* was made," said Mihalik coldly. "In a plane crash."

Now Cheryl looked shocked. "You're thinking of somebody else, Frank. You're thinking of Will Rogers or somebody."

"You're telling me that I have Will Rogers confused with Carole Lombard?"

"Carole Lombard didn't die in a plane crash. She and Clark Gable became one of the best-loved teams in movie history. They made a whole series of wonderful comedies together. They had the best writers in the business working for them, back when movies were still made in Hollywood. They appeared on Broadway in a George S. Kaufman play written just for them, called *The Merry Whitlow,* and it made an even better film. S. J. Perelman adapted *The Taming of the Shrew* for them and called it *Wedded Blitz;* that was in 1940, and the war was going on in Europe, see? Then about 1947 Lombard got an Academy Award for her dramatic acting, as Daisy in *The Great Gatsby* with Tyrone Power."

"Carole Lombard died in 1942. Tyrone Power never played Gatsby, and I've never heard of those other pictures."

Cheryl only shrugged. "I can't help *that,* Frank. We all have our little areas of ignorance."

"Goddamn it, Cheryl," said Mihalik angrily, "I may be ignorant, but I know about movies. I know a *lot* about movies, Cheryl, because thick-skulled brutes like me are too stupid to read books, but we like to watch movies. The flickering light soothes us."

"Now, don't get sarcastic, Frank," she said.

"Why the hell are you telling me all this nonsense for, then?"

Cheryl folded her arms across her chest and turned away from him. "It isn't nonsense, it's the truth. Why would I make all this up? Just because you can't remember who played Dorothy. . . . You *are* a thick-skulled idiot sometimes. You move your lips when you read. You move your lips when you watch movies, too. I've seen you do it."

Mihalik stomped on toward the distant city, muttering under his breath.

"Frank?" called Cheryl, suddenly lonely and afraid of their quarrel.

He stopped and turned to face her. "Carole Lombard died in 1942," he said.

"She did *not.* She was married to Clark Gable until *he* died, and then a few years later she married Sizzlin' Sid McCoy. She introduced the stories on *Carole Lombard Presents* on television for years. Then she divorced McCoy and wrote two volumes of autobiography. She retired and died when she was in her mid-sixties, I think. Don't you remember?"

"Who the hell was Sizzlin' Sid McCoy?" asked Mihalik in a dangerously quiet voice.

Cheryl squinted at him. "Only the greatest pitcher in the history of baseball, that's all. Don't pretend you've—"

"Never heard of him." He shook his head. "Come on, we want to get to the city before dark."

They walked in silence, each thinking over what the other had said. It seemed absurd that either one was inventing all these names and dates, but the only possible explanation was too unpleasant to consider. It took a long time before Mihalik found the courage to express it. "Cheryl," he said at last in a profoundly sad voice, "you're not the real Cheryl."

"I'm real, all right," she said hotly, "but it's obvious that *you* aren't my Frank."

"You're from the wrong universe. You sure as hell didn't come from mine."

She looked at him in wonder. "I may not have come from your universe, all right; but that doesn't give you the right to call it 'wrong.' It was always 'right' to me."

He snorted. "And this from a woman who thinks Shirley Temple played Dorothy in—"

Cheryl began to cry. She just stopped in her tracks, lost the impetus of her outrage, and fell apart emotionally. The long adventure had all been too much for her. She was finally exhausted, finally pushed just a little too far. She sank slowly to the ground, put her face in her hands, and sobbed.

Mihalik didn't know what to do. This was always a difficult situation for him. A crying woman was more intimidating to him than a dozen murderous Finnish pirates. It's the way heroes are supposed to be, and Mihalik was made from the genuine material; he was helpless around hysterical women. "There, there," he said. It didn't seem to help.

"What are we going to do?" asked Cheryl, gasping the words between sobs. She looked up at him with reddened, puffy eyes.

"Do? We'll do what we always do—we'll keep on until we get where we're going. Come on, old girl, the sun's getting low in the sky."

"Oh, Frank," she said, drying her tears and sniffing, "you're so dependable." He just smiled down at her and offered her a hand.

All's Fair. . . .

As they drew nearer to the city, it became increasingly obvious to Mihalik and Cheryl that it was not, in fact, a city. The buildings were, however, disturbingly familiar, disgustingly familiar. The most unusual aspects of the skyline were the tall, skinny pyramid and the big ball; that is to say, the Trylon and the Perisphere. It was the 1939 New York World's Fair, the World of Tomorrow, for Peace and Freedom and All That Jazz. It was missing only one important thing:

New York City, which ought to have surrounded the Fair like a fist around a penny.

Encircling the Fair there were only endless meadows of flowers—the poppy fields Mihalik and Cheryl had crossed, tulips, daffodils, geraniums and poinsettias, marigolds, morning glories, all without regard to season or climate, all blossoming together in a bewildering display of color and scent. From the edge of the Fair, Mihalik and Cheryl looked back over these fields of flowers, wondering how the Fair had been torn loose from its secure moorings in 1939 and brought here. Wherever here was.

"Remind me to pick up another pickle pin for Ray," said Mihalik, as they went through a turnstile and found their way to the reflecting pool on Constitution Mall. They sat down on a bench and watched people going by. Neither felt like talking for a long while.

At last, Cheryl noticed something. "These people," she said slowly, "they're not dressed in the same kind of clothing the people in 1939 wore."

Mihalik looked closely at a man nearby, who had on gold pantaloons and a green vest. That's all, no shirt, stockings, or shoes. "They sure look odd," said Mihalik.

"Well, we're not in 1939, that's for sure," said Cheryl.

"They had a city around this thing back then. All right, we're here. That Captain Hartstein brought us here for some reason. Now it's up to us to figure out why. There must be some clue here that will get us home —I mean, get each of us home to his or her right home. That is—"

"I know what you meant, Frank," said Cheryl. She stood up. "I see something over there that you're not going to like. You're not going to like it even more than you didn't like finding this Fair here."

"Maybe I don't want to know about it, Cheryl," said Mihalik. "Sometimes I'm better off just not knowing about certain things."

"Yes, but this is an important detail. Our whole future may ride on this one unsettling little incongruity."

Mihalik thought for a few seconds, chewing his lip. "I'll tell you what," he said at last, "why don't we get something to eat first? Maybe ride a few rides, go see something like The Story of Diphtheria in the Medicine and Public Health Building, take our minds off things for a little while, and then, when we're in a good mood and relaxed and rested, *then* you can tell me all about this thing I don't want to know about. Maybe a week from next Tuesday. For sure."

Cheryl laughed as if he were making a joke. "Ha ha, Frank. If I didn't know you better, I'd think you'd left your hero-training back in the trenches."

"There's always the danger of getting too much of a good thing," he said. "I've really enjoyed pitting my talents and abilities against the meanest obstacles the universe can think up. I really have. I think I've grown as a person on account of all our adventures; but I could use a vacation, you know? Too much of this and you start to lose your fine edge. All work and no play, right? Why don't we get something to eat and ride a few rides—"

"You already said that, Frank," said Cheryl impatiently. Around them in the deepening dusk, the lights of the Fair began to blink on. Colored spotlights lit the fountains. Cheryl took one of Mihalik's hands gently and pointed it toward a large, white marble-faced building, immensely tall and square and clearly out of place in the Art Deco environs. "What's that?" she asked. "It wasn't there before."

"That's where the Heinz Dome is supposed to be, damn it. Ray's going to be sore about this. We better not tell him that we lost the pin and then couldn't get another one. Actually, both Rays will be upset, mine and yours. We both have to keep our lips—"

"*Frank!*" cried Cheryl. "Forget the goddamn pickle pin! What the hell is that *building?*"

"It looks familiar, too," he said thoughtfully.

"It looks—"

"Oh, hell," he murmured. "It's the Agency Building. From London, remember? When we thought we were back home the first time."

They looked at each other. They didn't like the fact that the Agency Building had sprouted in the midst of the 1939 New York World's Fair, which didn't seem to be in 1939 anymore; but it was definitely something to be investigated, and they were getting tired and hungry, and they figured they might as well find out what they were up against *this* time. There was no point in delaying matters. They walked up the marble stairs to the row of glass doors.

A man dressed in the silver and blue of the Agency came out of the middle door and held out his hands to them. He was smiling broadly and his crinkly blue eyes were twinkling merrily. "Frank and Cheryl, here at last!" he said happily. "Welcome, welcome to your fate!"

"Thanks," said Mihalik grumpily, "but we've been welcomed before— several times—and our fates haven't been all that terrific up to now."

"All that's going to change, you'll see," said the man, never losing a millimeter of his enthusiastic smile. Mihalik could tell that smiling was what this man was paid for; he was a real professional, and he was good at it, too.

"Is Dr. Waters here or what?" asked Cheryl.

The man waggled an index finger back and forth. "All in good time, my dear, all in good time," he said. "You'll have your chance to ask questions later. I'm sure you'd like to freshen up a little, relax in a hot bath, put on some clean clothing."

It was a wonderful suggestion. Both Mihalik and Cheryl realized that it had been a long time since they'd had a chance to wash, and as for their clothes, well, it was time to bail out of them altogether and into whatever their host would provide. "Thanks a lot, Mr.—"

"You can call me Bwana," said their new friend, smiling. "No connection with the ancient Swahili word."

Mihalik looked at Cheryl. " 'Call Me Bwana.' Wasn't that a picture—"

"Bob Hope and Hope Lange," she said. "1963. Anita Ekberg was in it, too."

"Bob Hope and *Edie Adams,*" said Mihalik coldly. "Anita Ekberg was in it, too."

"Hope Lange."

"Edie Adams."

"Stop, stop, you're both wrong!" said Bwana, chuckling. "It was Bob Hope and Suzy Christenson."

"Who?" asked Mihalik.

"Who?" asked Cheryl.

"Never mind. And it wasn't Anita Ekberg, it was Diana Dors. Come along, we have a lot to do."

Mihalik jerked his thumb at the plump Agency man. "How'd he know we were coming?"

Bwana looked back over his shoulder and smiled. "This is the future, folks. We know everything here."

"You should have guessed that, Frank," said Cheryl.

He didn't bother to reply. "Hope Lange," he muttered under his breath. "Suzy Christenson." Then he repeated a phrase Bwana had used —"All in good time, my dear, all in good time"—but Mihalik spoke it in the high threatening voice of the Wicked Witch of the West. He shook his head in resignation and followed Cheryl into the building.

The Unexpected Reintroduction of Social Stratification

They were led to separate suites where cheerful servants, all clad in blue and silver, helped them undress, run baths, dry themselves with big fluffy towels, and slip into fresh new blue and silver outfits. Cheryl found this luxurious and wonderful; Mihalik found it fussy and annoying. Their suites adjoined, and when Cheryl had made the transition from weary, travel-stained adventurer to squeaky-clean guest of the Agency, she rapped on the communicating door.

"Yo," called Mihalik.

"Are you decent?"

"Let it be a surprise," he said. "Come on in."

Cheryl opened the door and came into Mihalik's sitting room. He was sitting. "What do we do now?" she asked. She sat down on a silver and blue divan with cabriole legs.

Mihalik just shrugged. "I can't get over the feeling that we're prisoners. I *always* get the feeling that we're prisoners because we always *are* prisoners. So all we can do is wait around for Bwana and his friends to decide what they're going to do with us. Then we'll get shoved through into some equally rotten universe with just as many references to *The Wizard of Oz*, and this will keep on happening over and over until we finally drop dead from old age." He folded his arms on his chest and stared across the room, where large picture windows gave a lovely view of the Fair and the unending miles of flowers beyond.

"Frank, that sounds dangerously close to despair. Heroes aren't allowed to despair, you know."

He glared at her now. "You show me where it says that, you just go ahead and show me. Heroes can despair, baby. Heroes can even be afraid and heartsick and entertain thoughts of treachery. What separates heroes from the run of ordinary people is that heroes don't act on those emotions. They just keep plugging away. I'll keep plugging away, don't worry. Haven't I done an adequate job so far? I think I've done pretty well, all things considered, and I don't expect that to change. That doesn't mean I have to be enthusiastic about it."

"I need you to be strong, Frank."

He opened his mouth, thought better of it, and looked at her as if for the first time. His heart was flooded with a tender feeling for this alien Cheryl, so like his own Cheryl except this one came from a universe that was populated with insane motion picture producers and casting directors. "I'll be strong," he murmured. "For you." He almost rose from his chair to go to her, when the front door opened and their happy, obnoxious host came into the room.

"Well, well, well!" cried Bwana. "All cleaned up, I see! You both look handsome. How are you feeling?"

"Swell," said Cheryl.

"Hungry," said Mihalik.

"Ah," said Bwana. "Well, you'll have to wait just a little longer before dinner. You have an important appointment to keep." He looked from one to the other with glittering eyes, as if his surprise was so wonderful he could barely keep his excitement from brimming over and sloshing onto the thick silver-and-blue carpet. "The King wants to speak with you. The King himself!"

"Wow," said Cheryl. She'd already met a queen and she hadn't been very impressed. She wasn't impressed now, knowing that she was about to meet a king. Royalty was a luxury of inferior universes, she had de-

cided, one that her own could scarcely afford. She had grown contemptuous of places that still played at class distinctions.

Bwana was startled by her tone. For the briefest instant his implacable
cheerfulness wavered, but then he caught himself and was immediately
chuckling as if something amusing had been said. "You've been treated
roughly in some of the realities you've visited," he said. "I ought to have
anticipated your feelings. Your attitude is quite out of place here, my
dear. This is a wonderful happy world, and the King is everyone's idea of
a charming, personable, generous, and thoroughly old-fashioned fairy
tale king."

"I suppose he was a prince once," said Mihalik.

"Of course," said Bwana, guessing what was about to be said, "and he
was charming then, too."

"Let's get this over with, then," said Mihalik. "I'm starving."

"Of course," said Bwana, bowing slightly and indicating the door.

Mihalik and Cheryl preceded him into the hall. As she passed by him,
Cheryl asked Bwana, "What exactly *is* your job?"

"Job?" he said, puzzled. "No one has jobs here. All work is done in the
past, by other people. We just dance and sing and play. It's very pleasant."

"Dance and sing and play?" said Mihalik.

Bwana shrugged, closing the door to the suite behind him, leading
them down the hall to the right. "Maybe it sounds shallow to you, but
that's how we laugh the day away—"

"—in the merry old Land of Oz," said Cheryl. She was starting to get
tired of it, too, just like Mihalik.

"Well, no," said Bwana, "this isn't Oz."

"Then where the hell *are* we?" said Mihalik. "You've never told us
that."

"The future," said Bwana, smiling. "I *did* tell you that. The realm of
Good King Proximo."

"King Proximo?" said Cheryl with a hollow voice. "The one who's
fighting the war with Queen Hesternia? I thought we left all that behind—"

Bwana shook his head. They had come to an elevator and were waiting
for it to come up a hundred and twenty-six floors to meet them. "You can
leave the past behind, but you can't leave the future behind. It's very
difficult, probably impossible."

"I mean, I thought we left that universe with Hesternia and Proximo
in it behind," said Cheryl.

"In the future, there's only one universe," said Bwana.

"What's that mean?"

"It's very simple. Whatever universe you come from, you end up here. This universe is the future for every other possible universe. They all lead here. Whatever happened in whatever version of the past, it has to evolve into this. This is the only future there is."

"Captain Hartstein suggested otherwise," said Mihalik.

"Hartstein," said Bwana disparagingly, "what does he know? He meant that all futures are equally probable, and that every time you go forward into the future, you find a different, random one. That has nothing to do with where you are now. This isn't 'the future' as you're accustomed to thinking of it. This is more like the *control room* of the future; we're actually outside of time, just as the World War One battlefield was outside of time, marking the position of the present. This is King Proximo's headquarters, from which he can look into time, into all the possibilities and realities."

Cheryl considered that as the elevator doors opened. They got in. "Then—"

"Up, please," Bwana instructed the elevator girl.

"Then he can differentiate among the universes? He can send us back to the correct one for each of us?"

Bwana laughed indulgently. "How the hell should I know?" he said fondly.

Mihalik almost clipped him on the jaw, but Cheryl restrained him. They rode the rest of the way up to King Proximo's throne room in strained silence.

In Which We Meet a Merry Old Soul

"Approach him slowly," whispered Bwana, "and when you get to the foot of the throne, kneel and wait for him to tell you to rise."

"The hell I will!" said Mihalik indignantly. "Who in blue blazes does he think he is?"

"He's the guy who's got your whole future in the palm of his hand," said Bwana.

"Do you want us to kneel on one knee or both?" asked Cheryl.

"Wait a minute," said Mihalik. "I don't kneel to anybody. I'm an American and we stopped kneeling to people a few years ago when we got our independence back."

"I'll kneel, Frank," said Cheryl. "You go ahead and stand if you want to. This is a different place and they have different rules, and you have to respect their customs."

"What if he wants to take your virginity?" said Mihalik. "Kings can do that."

"Take it where, Frank?" asked Cheryl.

"Please," urged Bwana, "cease this argument and follow me. The King is courteous and magnificent and all the rest, but sometimes he gets irked if people just hang around wasting his time. He's running out of it, you know. And no one's more aware of that than His Majesty."

Mihalik and Cheryl followed Bwana across the polished ebony floor. They looked at each other. "The King of the Future is running out of time?" said Mihalik.

"Curiouser and curiouser," said Cheryl.

"I thought Proximo's kingdom was infinite," said Mihalik, "and that's why Hesternia wants to bite off chunks of it all the time."

"Don't ask me," said Cheryl. "I'm new here myself."

They reached the foot of the throne. King Proximo beamed down at them. He was a chubby, jolly, red-faced, bearded and mustached old gentleman. He looked like a king from a deck of playing cards, complete with long gray hair done in a kind of Prince Valiant style. He wore a crown and held a scepter and looked every inch a king. He chuckled as Bwana abased himself at his feet. "Sire," said Bwana, "Your Majesty, these are our visitors from the past." Then Bwana backed away slowly, staying as close to the glossy black floor as he could without flopping on his face.

Mihalik and Cheryl both knelt. It seemed the right thing to do. "Good boy," whispered Cheryl.

"I figured, who's it going to hurt if I kneel a little?" said Mihalik.

"It's so kind of you to visit me in my loneliness," said Proximo, smiling broadly.

"Are you so lonely then, Your Majesty?" asked Cheryl.

"No, no," he said, laughing, "not at all. I just thought you'd appreciate hearing another quote from your favorite movie."

"It isn't *my* favorite movie," said Cheryl. "My favorite movie is *Shane*, with Glenn Ford."

"Glenn Ford!" cried Mihalik.

King Proximo looked at him and exploded with merriment. He said pleasantly, "I have a reputation for being a pussycat, but that doesn't mean I tolerate bad manners. So you two have gotten yourselves into quite a pickle, haven't you?"

"It seems so, Your Majesty," said Cheryl. Mihalik had clamped his mouth shut and decided that he wasn't going to say anything more unless he absolutely had to. Let Cheryl carry the ball this time. He tried to imagine Glenn Ford in *Shane*, but it was impossible.

"And you've come to me to fix it for you."

"Well, yes, Your Majesty. That is, no, Your Majesty, we didn't know we were coming here. We've mostly been sent places at the whim of other people. We haven't had any choice in the matter. We ended up here, and you're the person with authority over us now."

"You could have stayed out in the flowers," said Proximo. "You could have begun entirely new lives for yourselves, Adam and Eve among the carnations and mums. Instead, you've come to my capital and you've come into my court."

"We were brought here, Your Majesty," insisted Cheryl. "And we haven't asked for anything."

King Proximo glanced over their heads and winked at someone behind them; both Mihalik and Cheryl were too afraid to turn around. The King laughed gently. "Not yet, you haven't; but you would, if I gave you a chance, eh?"

"Possibly," admitted Cheryl.

"Ha ha. Good girl. I admire honesty in a person. Well, I think I know what you want, and the great and powerful Proximo has every intention of granting your request. Indeed, I think I will put your fates into your own hands. You may choose your future yourself. It will provide us all with a few moments of entertainment in this otherwise dull and care-ridden reign of mine. We will attend to that tonight, after dinner."

"May I ask a question, Your Majesty?" said Cheryl.

"Certainly, my dear."

"What did our guide mean when he said that you were running out of time? I thought your kingdom extended onward throughout eternity."

King Proximo could barely suppress his glee; a few titters did manage to escape his lips. Then he quieted himself. "I live backwards, just as Merlin did," he explained. "How else could one manage the future? I know absolutely everything that will happen, because I've already been there. I was created at the end of time, and I am living backward until I run smack-dab into Hesternia's ample bosom. Is she still carrying that riding crop? I'm not sure about that, the riding crop business. I've always been attracted to softer, more feminine women. Like you, my dear." He laughed heartily again. "When the time comes when Hesternia and I meet in some unimaginable place, the future will come to an end, and so will I." He laughed, less heartily this time.

"The future will come to an end, as *you* know it," said Cheryl, "but the future will still exist for us, won't it?"

"Oh, of course. But who cares about you?"

Cheryl decided not to answer that question. Mihalik had an answer ready, and an impertinent question of his own, but he was wise enough to keep his silence, too. When King Proximo realized that neither of his guests had anything further to say, he chuckled some more, rolled off his

throne, and made his way toward the far doors. Trumpets blared, courtiers bowed low, and there was the general flash and swirl of a Shake-
spearean monarch's entourage going offstage to allow the principals a few
moments of dialogue.

Beat the Clock

The dinner wasn't quite as sumptuous as Mihalik and Cheryl imagined
it might be: corned beef sandwiches (on white with *mayonnaise),* potato
pancakes, and orange Jell-O for dessert. The King seemed to enjoy the
meal tremendously—he laughed and joked all through it; but it was beginning to look as though he laughed at anything. His laughter was not
necessarily a sign of his good humor. After the dishes were cleared away,
he remembered the promise he'd made in the throne room. He coughed a
couple of times to tune his voice, then announced to his entire court,
"Our two guests wish to leave us."

There was an immediate chorus of disbelieving voices crying, "No,
how can that be!" and similar sentiments. To Proximo's followers, it was
incredible that anyone would prefer another time and place to this wonderful magic kingdom.

Proximo held up a hand for silence, and he got it. "Do not think
harshly of them, my friends," he said, smiling. "They come from the dim
reaches of antiquity—from within the shadow of Hesternia, let us not
forget—and so their minds are not so developed as ours. If they believe
they will be happier in their own world, then we will give them a chance
at that illusory joy. Frank, Cheryl, come here." The timorous chro-
nonauts approached the royal presence. "Ha ha, don't be afraid," said
the King. Mihalik felt like a four-year-old boy going up to get his picture
taken on Santa's lap: he was terrified. "Cheryl, my dear, you will get your
choice first. It has become evident that you are from a slightly different
universe than our friend Frank. Your universe is concealed behind one of
these three doors. Which one do you want, Door Number One, Door
Number Two, or Door Number Three?"

Cheryl stared at King Proximo with wide eyes. "What's behind the
other two doors?" she asked.

"Ha ha, can't tell you!"

"And I have to choose one of them? What if I choose wrong?"

"You go through it anyway."

"Into what?"

"Ha ha."

Cheryl looked helplessly at Mihalik. He looked helplessly back. "Take
Three," he said. "They never put the good prizes in the middle."

Cheryl looked back at the King. "You can't make me choose my fate blind like this," she said. "It's outrageous! It's—"

Proximo laughed delightedly and said, "It's the way we do things around here. Choose."

Cheryl's shoulders slumped. "Door Number One," she said.

There was a loud buzzer and the crowd groaned. "Oh, oh," said King Proximo with some amusement. "You get to spend the rest of your life on a desert island on a world with no other land masses at all and no other living things, with a hundred cases of King Norway Sardines, a Speidel watchband, and a fifty-dollar gift certificate from the Spiegel catalogue."

"I told you to take Number Three," said Mihalik.

Cheryl turned on him furiously. "I'll give you Number Three," she said. She raised a fist to hit him, but she was restrained by a courtier.

"And now you, Mr. Mihalik. My subjects have put something new behind Door Number One. It may be your universe, and it may not."

"Three," said Mihalik, feeling his pulse beating faster.

The rude buzzer sounded again. Mihalik felt his stomach tighten. The crowd groaned. Proximo seemed to smile even more broadly than ever. "Sorry, son," he said, "but you get to be a blind beggar in a city in central Europe in the twenty-second century, a time of famine and pestilence. You also get a year's supply of Eskimo Pies and the home version of our game, 'Time Spy.' But you've both been good sports. Let's give these people a big hand." The entourage applauded politely.

Mihalik wasn't going to be railroaded into such a dismal fate so easily. He was about to step forward and put his hands around the plump neck of the happy old King, when Cheryl interrupted. "Is this for real?" she asked. "I want to know, because if it is, we're both going to be very upset. When we get upset, we sometimes lose control."

"Is that a threat?" asked Proximo, laughing.

"Uh huh," said Mihalik.

"No," said the King, "it isn't for real. You've found me out. It was just a little stunt, a little after-dinner prank. Surprise, surprise, the joke's on you! But you are good sports, after all, aren't you?"

Mihalik let out his breath in a sudden loud snort. "Maybe I'll throttle you anyway, just for practice," he said.

"Go ahead, Frank, I want to watch," said Cheryl.

"Ha ha, always kidding, you guys," said Proximo. "Well, I guess you want to know what I'm really going to do with you."

"We are developing a certain curiosity," said Mihalik. "I will admit that much."

The King laughed boisterously, obviously tickled. "I don't know," he said.

"Listen," said Cheryl patiently, "whatever you do with us, it will be in the future, because it hasn't happened yet from our point of view. You're supposed to know everything that happens in the future, because you've already been there. You have to know what's going to happen to us. Do we get to our homes all right? Does this ever end?"

Proximo smiled and shook his head. "I don't know. I lie about things sometimes."

Mihalik took another angry step forward. "I can stop that easily enough," he said in a surly voice.

There was a little flurry of activity behind them at the great ebony doors of the banquet hall. Mihalik and Cheryl turned to watch, and they saw Bwana wrestling with a tall, slender cadaverous man dressed all in white. The tall man clasped his hands together and brought them down heavily on the back of Bwana's neck; there was the faint crack of splintering bone, and Bwana fell limply to the polished floor. The gaunt man strode toward the table, not bothering to bow to King Proximo. "Who's that?" asked Cheryl.

"Pay no attention to that man behind the curtain," said the King sourly, smiling.

"Oh," said Mihalik, "I get it: the power behind the throne."

"The real power," said Cheryl.

"Pleased to meet you," said the starved-looking man. "I'm the Historian. Ignore this fat puddle of jovial blather. What can I do for you?"

Mihalik was pleased by the Historian's businesslike manner. "We want to go home," he said.

The Historian considered the request for a bare second. "Easy enough," he said. "Is first thing tomorrow morning all right with you?"

Mihalik glanced at Cheryl. "Sure," she said.

The Historian took out a small notebook and made an entry. "Right," he said. "Did anybody save me a sandwich?"

A Stitch in Time

"You know who he looks like?" asked Mihalik, as he sat in the front row and munched popcorn.

"Who?" asked Cheryl.

"The Historian. If he had the right facial hair and outfit, he'd look just like Cardinal Richelieu. I mean the Cardinal Richelieu who tossed me into the Bastille in the iron mask. Some coincidence, don't you think?"

"If you say so," said Cheryl. "What's it supposed to mean?"

"I can't think of anything. It's just a resemblance, I guess. Though, come to think of it, Cardinal Richelieu was a power behind the throne, too." He tossed some more popcorn into his mouth. They were watching the Historian setting up his equipment for a special performance in their honor. King Proximo sat nearby on his throne, glumly laughing at everything that was said or done, but no one was paying him any attention. All eyes were on the Historian. He turned and addressed Mihalik and Cheryl.

"In your era," said the spider-thin man, "your scientists have yet to discover that the universe consists of infinitesimal phantom units, one of which is the chronon. Chronons are not particles, not waves, not wavicles. They don't seem to be made of anything. By manipulating them we can control time: our passage through it from past to future or in the opposite direction, or across it, from reality to reality. Your travels from universe to universe have been entirely in accord with the laws of physics as I have come to understand them. You have not been able to control these adventures because you have no concept of time as a tangible entity."

The Historian checked the digital displays of a wide bank of meters; he compared the figures to a sheet of paper on his clipboard and seemed satisfied. "Everything is ready," he announced. "I will demonstrate how simple it is to alter reality." He twisted a knob, flicked a switch, and punched a button. Nothing happened; that is, nothing seemed to happen for a few seconds. Then, on the eastern horizon, where an unfamiliar constellation hovered, the night sky began to lighten. Dawn came swiftly —*too* swiftly. The sky turned pale blue, then gray, then white, then orange, then . . . then something wrong came up over the edge of the world: a double sun, a magnificent and awful spectacle in the sky. There was a small white star and a much greater red star, each pulling spiral jets of fiery matter from the other. They climbed higher and turned the world into a landscape of freakish colors. The grass looked black, all the flowers were the wrong shades, and people's faces looked feverish and fearful. There were cries of dismay, but the Historian smiled calmly and raised one hand. "No need for alarm," he said gently. "I haven't permanently changed our reality; I've merely transported us to another reality. Here the sun is a double-star system, and the earth is in a peculiar orbit far enough away to sustain life. It was easy for me to ignore certain factors—the concentration of radiation from the giant star, for example, could kill us instantly if I hadn't chosen a reality where such radiation doesn't exist. There are an infinite number of realities, remember; and included among them are plenty in which the physical laws of our universe do not apply. I may construct an alternate reality out of any set of conditions, no matter how nonsensical they seem by the standards of our own experience. It is merely a matter of applying strict and coherent principles. Of course, these principles are a secret, handed down from Historian to Historian. It would be disastrous if everyone could change reality as he saw fit, anytime he grew tired or displeased with the world as it is."

King Proximo clapped enthusiastically. "Well done, well done! I salute your double star. You are an artist, a genius! You are the greatest Historian of all time. Now take us back to our own universe."

The Historian studied his king for a moment; Mihalik sensed that the two men despised and feared each other. "At your command, Your Majesty," said the Historian. He turned the knob, flipped the switch, and punched a button. The stars, a little above the horizon, became one, turned yellow, shrunk to normal size, and disappeared. It was once again night; the same unfamiliar constellation hung in the space where the sun had undergone its transformations.

Proximo's courtiers and the rest of the Agency workers leaped up and cheered. The Historian raised his hands modestly, then graciously accepted the ovation. He walked to where Mihalik and Cheryl were sitting. "Well," he said, "what did you think?"

"I'm still stunned," said Mihalik. "I dropped my popcorn."

"Sorry," said the Historian, pleased by Mihalik's reaction. He turned to Cheryl. "And you, young lady?"

"It wasn't what I expected, that's for sure," said Cheryl. "I don't know *what* I expected, really. I'd give anything to have the ability to change reality—"

"Some people are prepared to kill for that knowledge," said the Historian. "Of course, they're very easy to deal with. I just switch to a reality where these particular people don't exist. As I said, this science is the ultimate synthesis of all man's knowledge; it can be used for the ultimate good or the ultimate evil."

"We thought the same thing in our own time," said Mihalik, "about thasers and the charm bomb."

The Historian smiled indulgently. "Men have always believed that times were as bad as they could ever get, that life was as hazardous as it was possible to imagine. Of course, they were often correct about that— life as any person knows it may well be as bad as he can imagine, because he cannot foresee the next turn of the screw, the next thing that will make his existence even less secure. Yet I feel confident that nothing will ever surpass the power of the chronon. I have King Proximo's testimony that I have in my frail human hands the consummate force. The only safe thing to do with such a force, we've decided, is to make of it neither tool nor weapon, but art. The position of Historian is nearer that of an entertainer than a scientist. I am considered a great artist, a sensitive creator of imagined possibilities, rather than a technician wearing a white lab coat who fools around with electronics and the philosophy of science."

"What you do beats holoshows all to hell," said Mihalik.

"Thank you," said the Historian. "It should be apparent to you now, my friends, that I, and not King Proximo, am the one who may aid you in your long and weary quest for your true homes."

"I hadn't even let myself dare hope," said Cheryl.

The Historian smiled. "Don't let your hopes get too high even now. I cannot promise anything with absolute certainty. As I said, what I do is an exact science. The manipulation of chronons is a complex operation, but governed by certain laws and procedures. However, the infinite number of potential realities means that singling out specific universes can be a time-consuming process. For instance, what I did tonight—changing our sun into a double star—was child's play. There is an infinite number of realities in which our sun is part of such a system. It is a lower-order infinity, to be sure, but an infinity nonetheless; I could choose any one of them. However, setting you into precisely the universe you came from will require more searching. That is, of course, unless you're willing to accept a reality that is indistinguishably close to your own. One in which, for example, the leaves of a single tree in some vast forest are arranged differently."

"That would be fine," said Mihalik. "As long as the difference would never become apparent to me—to us, I mean."

The Historian shrugged. "In that case, I can virtually guarantee success."

"Oh, Frank!" cried Cheryl happily. She threw her arms around Mihalik's neck and kissed him.

Mihalik was unhappy about such displays in public. "Must I remind you, Cheryl," he began. He got no further; she let her arms fall to her sides and turned away, hurt and near tears. "I'm sorry, Cheryl, really I am. I just can't help remembering that you're not *my* Cheryl, however much like her you are. If we allowed ourselves to take such liberties, it would be a kind of faithlessness to the other Frank and the other Cheryl."

"Moral tap dancing," said Cheryl, sniffling.

The Historian looked uncomfortable. "If you'll excuse me," he said, his eyes cast down, "maybe we could talk again tomorrow and begin to make some tentative plans. I'll need a certain amount of data from you both, in order to set up my calculations."

"Sure," said Mihalik. "We'll both be at your convenience."

"Wonderful," said the man in white. "It will be nice to perform some practical good for a change, though my artistic displays are fulfilling in their own way." He nodded to them both and went back to his equipment.

Strawberries and Champagne Return with a Vengeance

It was eight o'clock in the morning. Mihalik had gotten into the habit of staying in bed as late as he could, because he never knew how long he'd have to go without sleep. Emergencies and changes in circumstances had been coming thick and fast, so he stocked up on food, water, and energy whenever possible. When the knock came on his door, he didn't really want to wake up; he always rose to some situation he didn't want to be reminded of. The knock came again, louder this time. Mihalik couldn't help it; he awoke grumbling. "All right," he said. He swung his legs out of the wide brass bed, dragged on the Agency clothes, and went to the door.

"Good morning," said a young woman. "I'm Corporal Roxas. I'm here to answer any questions you may have about the Agency, about your responsibility to King Proximo, or anything else that may have occurred to you since last night."

"Right," said Mihalik. "Come in, make yourself comfortable. Can I get some breakfast?"

"Just call down and they'll bring it up in a few minutes. Anything you like. Let your imagination run away with you." He ordered orange juice and Spoon-Size Shredded Wheat, something his father had written once on a scrap of paper when Mihalik was very young, but which didn't exist any longer in his world. Mihalik had always been fascinated by the notion of shredding wheat: how had they done it? It was a lost technological secret. They must have had to use a teeny tiny shredder, he thought. Grains of wheat were small stuff.

While they waited for the breakfast to be delivered, Mihalik did ask a few questions. "What do you mean by my 'responsibilities to King Proximo'?"

Corporal Roxas smiled. "You don't think all this comes cheap, do you?" she said, with a gesture that included the room, the imminent breakfast, the terrific view, the entertainment of the night before, the clothes, the little bars of soap in the bathroom, everything.

"I thought I was a guest," he said. He wondered how he could possibly pay any kind of debt. All he had was the clothes on his back, and they already belonged to King Proximo.

"You're a guest in the most euphemistic sense," said Roxas.

"I don't carry cash," said Mihalik, "and my checkbook is behind in another universe."

She waved a hand in dismissal. "The King isn't looking for that sort of payment. He has all the material wealth imaginable. He needs your loyalty and your help, in his constant battle against those who seek to undermine his leadership."

"Agents of Queen Hesternia?" asked Mihalik. "Here?"

"Well, *her* spies, of course, but there are other enemies. A man as influential and powerful as the King attracts commensurate opponents."

"Who are we talking about, precisely?"

She waved a hand again. "Oh, the Historian, for example."

"I didn't think they were best buddies."

"You're very perceptive, Frank. You don't mind if I call you Frank?" She smiled prettily.

"Of course not," he said.

"You don't mind if I take off my tunic? It's so warm in here." She began to pull the silver and blue tunic over her head. She was wearing nothing under it.

"Uh, miss, I'd appreciate it if you wouldn't do that. I come from a rather puritanical society, and I'm just not comfortable in rooms with half-naked corporals. It's an embarrassing flaw, I know, but you have to take me, imperfections and all."

"Oh, Frank, I'll take you any way I can get you," she murmured, slipping the tunic back on. She stood up and came to him, sitting beside him on the sofa. "Can't you see? I'm crazy about you."

"Don't kiss me."

"Is it her? Is that what you're afraid of? That auburn-haired wench next door? I'll scratch her eyes out. I'll drop her off the three-hundredth floor observation platform. Oh, Frank, can't you tell? I've been waiting for you all my life."

He was saved by another knock at the door. "Breakfast," he guessed.

"Frank, how can you think of food at a time like this?"

"According to my estimate," he said as he went to the door, "that crummy supper we had last night was our first meal in more than two and a half million years. I can't live like that." He opened the door and an Agency private nodded to him, standing by a service cart with a covered tray. Just as the private wheeled the cart by Mihalik into the sitting room, the front door of the adjoining suite opened. A tall, dark-haired, good-looking Agency lieutenant came out, an angry look on his face below a red hand-shaped mark across one cheek. He gave Mihalik a quick sullen look and went stiffly but speedily down the carpeted hallway. Mihalik gazed after him. Obviously he had been pulling on Cheryl the same thing that Corporal Roxas had tried to pull on him. He thought of the hand print across the lieutenant's face: good for Cheryl! Mihalik grinned. He closed the door.

"Your breakfast, sir," said the private.

"Thanks, kid. Do I tip you or something?"

"No, sir, it's been my privilege."

"Great. Now beat it."

"Yes, sir."

"And take this soiled dove with you."

Roxas was furious. "What?" she cried.

"Get out," said Mihalik calmly. "I caught a glimpse of your pal next door quick-marching toward the rear. Ol' Cheryl was in no more mood for your phony passion than I was. Now leave me alone. Cheryl and I have some serious planning to do."

"The King will hear of this," threatened Roxas.

"So will the Historian," said Mihalik. He was gratified again by her apprehensive expression; evidently he'd hit a sore spot. Getting out the door before anything more could be said, she nearly upset an end table and a pink alabaster lamp. She didn't give him another glance, and the door slammed behind her. A moment later Mihalik knocked on the communicating door between the two suites.

"Who is it?" called Cheryl.

"It's just me, honey," said Mihalik. "I had this Agency vamp in here, but I got rid of her as soon as I figured out what she was up to."

"They sicced one on me, too, Frank. Wait a minute and I'll unlock this." She opened the door, and they smiled at each other, unsure who was going to visit whom. Finally Mihalik stepped across into her sitting room. It was identical to his. The remains of a large and elegant breakfast, complete with two half-full champagne glasses, lay on the table.

"Sharp guy, though," said Mihalik. "Saw him when I opened the door to get my breakfast."

"How did he look?" asked Cheryl.

"Pained," said Mihalik. "They'll have to put his self-respect in a cast and give him crutches." They both laughed.

"What time are we supposed to see the Historian?"

"Nine. We have time to finish breakfast and relax a little."

"It won't take me much time to finish my breakfast," said Mihalik. "I didn't go overboard. I just got a bowl of cereal."

Cheryl smiled. "That lieutenant brought me a spiced baked apple plopped in heavy cream and Eggs Sardou and cream cheese crêpes topped with strawberries flambéed in kirsch. And a pitcherful of mimosas —champagne and orange juice. It's wonderful, Frank, even better than an aspirin in Coke."

Mihalik nodded. "You have any of those crêpes left, honey? I'm getting spoiled, I really like strawberries. We'll never see another one after we go home."

Cheryl sighed. "I know. I haven't even touched the crêpes. Mr. Wonderful didn't give me time—he made his pass during the baked apple. Let's finish off the breakfast. I'd rather share it with you, anyway."

They kissed and Mihalik felt a familiar blossoming of affection until he recalled that this Cheryl belonged to someone else. His emotions were confused, and he dealt with them by hiding them away out of sight. They sat at the table in Cheryl's suite and began to eat the excellent breakfast the Agency had provided. Halfway through the eggs, while Mihalik was still spooning the strange yellowish sauce to one side, the telephone rang.

"Don't answer it," he said.

"I have to, Frank," said Cheryl regretfully. "It may be someone important. I mean, how many people could know we were here?"

"The King or Bwana or your lieutenant, wanting to make a date to apologize for his behavior. He'll make another pass then, too."

"I know that, Frank."

"If it's my mother, tell her I'm not here."

"Your mother's in a feminist Sufi convent, Frank."

He looked at her sadly. "My mother's home, Cheryl. You know that as well as I do."

"It might be the Historian on the phone ready to send us home."

"Okay, answer it; see if I care." He resumed discarding the hollandaise sauce. It seemed to go on forever.

Cheryl's part of the telephone conversation was restricted to several well-spaced "uh-huhs." She hung up the telephone and came back to the table. "He wants to see us right away," she said.

"Who? The King?"

"The Historian. He has most of the universes in the universe sorted out, but he needs quite a bit of information to narrow down the choices. We'll have to work with him."

"All right. We'll go right after breakfast."

Cheryl looked wistfully at the eggs, the crêpes, and the champagne and orange juice. "He said *now.* His time is valuable, you know. He said right now, immediately, within the next seven minutes, if we really want to go home."

"Damn it." Mihalik carried the champagne glass in one hand and stuffed the flambéed strawberry crêpe in the pocket of his Agency uniform trousers. "Well, I'm ready," he said. "I'll eat the crêpe when I get a chance."

"You're a slob, Frank," said Cheryl. When his expression turned offended, she added, "A lovable slob."

"Yeah, you're right." He didn't sound mollified. "Come on. Where *is* his place?"

"On top. The 316th floor."

"He must have some view."

Cheryl shrugged. "Of what, Frank? The flowers? They'd be awfully tiny from up that high."

"This is still New York, Cheryl, what ought to be the Queens end of Long Island. He can probably see for miles: the beautiful brown ocean; the Hudson Riverless Valley; The Parking Lot, what used to be Connecticut, and all those parallel yellow stripes—"

"Where I come from, they didn't turn Connecticut into a parking lot."

"They should have, back when they had all those automobiles and things. They had to put them someplace."

"They made Connecticut into a wild game refuge, for the weird, sick people who liked them. Wild games, I mean. You can get prosecuted for doing that sort of thing in the other states, even in the privacy of your own home."

"Just as it should be," said Mihalik. "I don't even like the idea of setting aside a place for those perverts. It just encourages them."

"It keeps them off the streets, Frank."

He shook his head. "Never mind, never mind; it isn't important. Your world has its rules, my world has slightly different ones. It's pointless to argue about them now."

"You're right again, Frank. Let's go." They left the remnants of their breakfasts; with a little luck, they might be sent to their dismal homes before lunchtime.

Portrait of the Artist as a Shrewd Cookie

They rode up to the Historian's penthouse. He greeted them warmly and invited them in. Mihalik and Cheryl exchanged surprised looks when they saw the windows—the Historian had had them boarded up. There was no view at all. "Had to do it, I'm afraid," he said. "I didn't want to, but little stones kept hitting them. This high, they're moving at a tremendous rate of speed, enough to shatter even the supposedly shatterproof plastic."

"Stones?" asked Cheryl. "Three hundred and sixteen stories up?"

The Historian nodded. "The Coriolis Effect," he said, assuming that explained everything. All it reminded Mihalik of was a young woman who emptied wastebaskets for Dr. Waters back in his own time, whose name was Coriolis Mae Jackson.

"What can we do to help?" asked Cheryl.

"Let's sit down, shall we? This may be a time-consuming job. We might as well get comfortable." He indicated some armchairs and a sofa. The Historian, for all his acclaim and influence, had a suite just like the ones that had been given to Mihalik and Cheryl. Mihalik approved of that; he was glad the Historian wasn't a typical power behind the throne, one who used his position to acquire personal wealth and status, and who mistreated and oppressed the less fortunate. The Historian was Mihalik's kind of man, apparently just a regular guy, a Joe Doakes with a great talent.

They seated themselves and the Historian opened a spiral-bound note-book. "Do you think you can send us home today?" asked Mihalik.

The Historian looked up from his notes and smiled. "Impatient to leave our little paradise?" he asked.

"The King and his sycophants couldn't believe it, either," said Cheryl.

"It's nothing to me," said the Historian. "I can understand your eager-ness. After all, if you want to go looking for your heart's desire, you don't have to look further than your own backyard."

Mihalik frowned. "We don't have backyards where I come from," he said.

"Shut up, Frank," said the Historian. "You see, one or more separate realities are generated by each event. For example, if you two were to marry"—all three people blushed furiously—"one universe would con-tinue in a straight line from that moment, yet a second universe would split off in which you didn't marry. That's a simple instance; the trouble comes in when we try to define the word 'event.' You see, there are separate realities for the brief lifetimes and quirky behaviors of each subatomic particle in existence. A single unicellular organism can gener-ate billions of worlds all by itself. A creature as complex as a human being, possessed of conscious decision-making powers in addition to the random activities occurring on the cellular and atomic levels, leaves be-hind itself such an immensity of equally 'real' realities that it would be unfeasible to search among them for any particular one. The marriage example I gave, when taken in its entirety, would generate more than five hundred quintillion worlds for each participant. It would take longer than the whole lifetime of our galaxy to catalogue them. I can reduce that time by asking some specific questions and eliminating the realities that don't reflect your answers. Only a relatively small fraction of universes exist in which neither Judy Garland nor Shirley Temple played Doro-thy."

"How did you know we'd been arguing about that very thing?" asked Cheryl.

"My dear," said the Historian, "King Proximo knows everything that will happen in the future. I, on the contrary, know everything that happened in the past. And not only *the* past, but also *every* past."

"What do you mean, *the* past?" asked Mihalik. "Who decides which one is *the* past?"

"Shut up, Frank," said the Historian. "There are universes where Deanna Durbin played Dorothy. There are universes where Dorothy was played by the daughter of Gertrude Stein and Maxwell Perkins. Some universes have a young boy playing Dorothy, some in girl's clothes, some as a young hero. There are Dorothys of every age, sex, and color. There are realities without Dorothys at all, with the Scarecrow and his buddies addressing lines to the spot where she ought to be. Everything you can imagine exists somewhere; much more than you can imagine exists, too. In fact, the unimaginable outnumbers the merely reasonable by a huge margin."

"It sounds kind of frightening when you put it like that," said Cheryl with a shudder.

The Historian gave her a thin smile. "It *is* kind of frightening," he said. "Actually it's chaos out there."

"And you have it all at your fingertips," said Cheryl wonderingly.

"It's a creepy job sometimes," said the Historian, "but *somebody's* got to do it."

"I'll bet they really had to twist your arm," said Mihalik. "To accept all this power, I mean."

"Shut up, Frank," said Cheryl. She turned back to the Historian, something like awe or dawning rapture in her eyes.

"So tell me," he said, "who discovered America?"

"John Cabot," said Mihalik. "In 1497."

"Maroun abu-Taifa, in 1108," said Cheryl, "but the Muslims thought that colonizing was more trouble than it was worth. They had more important things to worry about, so America wasn't really colonized until the Finns started settling in Newfinland."

"Uh huh," said the Historian. He jotted down their answers in his notebook.

"You mean Newphoneland," said Mihalik through clenched jaws. "The phone company dissidents who wanted to—"

"Telephone company dissidents?" said Cheryl skeptically.

The Historian struggled to regain control of the interview. "This is very helpful," he said dubiously. "Now who won the War Between the States?"

"The American Civil War?" asked Mihalik. "The North. The Union."

"France and the Canary Islands," said Cheryl.

There were a few seconds of unhappy silence. "Well," said the Historian at last, "it looks like I really have my work cut out for me. I was hoping that you came from universes that were a little closer together."

"Is it going to mean trouble?" asked Mihalik. "Will we be stuck here long?"

The Historian smiled. "It depends on what you mean by 'long.' I've been here a long time, and King Proximo's been here even longer. You wouldn't even want to start using the word 'long' until a couple of hundred thousand years go by."

"What Frank meant by 'long,' " suggested Cheryl, "was in the neighborhood of days, weeks, or months."

"Yeah," said Mihalik.

"Possibly," said the Historian, "but possibly not."

Mihalik looked at Cheryl. "We're getting the runaround again," he said.

"You're recognizing it more quickly," she said. "That's a good sign."

The Historian held up a hand. "Listen, this is no runaround. I meant what I said: I can send you home. You can't expect miracles, though."

"We can't even expect unadorned reality," said Mihalik. "So what do we do next? While we're waiting?"

"I want you to think over my proposition," said the Historian.

"Proposition?" asked Cheryl.

"I want you to fight on my side."

Mihalik felt the sinking feeling he had felt a few times before. "We weren't aware that you *had* a side, sir. We thought it was Good King Proximo against Bad Queen Hesternia. How can *you* have a side? How can you line up three armies? You'd need a triangular battlefield with an equilateral safety zone in the middle."

"That's not where you want us to stand, is it?" asked Cheryl. "In the middle? With three different armies coming at us?"

The Historian was vastly amused. "You primitives from the past are like a breath of fresh air to me. Really, I couldn't have come up with such a ridiculous image if I used teams of stenographers and worked weekends. No, you just don't understand; I see that I'll have to explain it all from the beginning. What you think is a time war between Proximo and Hesternia is actually a conspiracy to deprive me of my rightful position as Mastermind."

"Uh oh," thought Mihalik, "here it comes. . . ."

"I'd be a great Mastermind, too," said the Historian. "That's just what eternity needs—a Mastermind of Time. Proximo can't handle the job;

he's stuck in the future. Hesternia's stuck in the past. The work requires someone who's able to roam around time and do what needs to be done."

"Just exactly what does need to be done?" asked Cheryl.

The Historian's eyebrows raised a bit. "Oh, this, for example." He reached forward a few inches and punched a button on the arm of his chair. Both Mihalik and Cheryl underwent an astonishing and none too pleasant transformation: they were turned into humanoid lizards. They remained the same size and weight, they stayed in their Agency uniforms, they even kept their proper eye colors. They were just lizards, gray-green lizards with long pink tongues and scales instead of hair.

"Oh, my God," said Cheryl softly.

"Don't worry," said the Historian. "Everybody in the world is a lizard now except me. As if our antediluvian forebears had been reptilian, rather than hominoid. The people down in the city are used to changes like this now and then. It keeps them on their toes, reminds them who they ought to be nice to when they pass me on the street. I'll change you back into people when I feel like it."

"We'd be ever so grateful," said Cheryl. She was terrified. Her long pink tongue lolled from one side of her mouth. She found, to her vast disgust, that she was glancing around the room, looking for flies.

"I wonder if lizards like crêpes Fitzgerald," said Mihalik, remembering that he still had one in his pocket.

"Will you get your mind on the important issue here?" cried the Historian. It was the most overwrought either of the temponeers had ever seen him.

"Sorry," said Mihalik, "I'm not used to this lizard business. It was just my scientific nature taking over, thinking up an experiment. You're a scientist, too; you should appreciate the unique opportunity—"

"I've been a lizard, too, don't kid yourself," said the Historian. "And no, they don't like crêpes. Not strawberry ones, anyway."

"You were beginning to explain the time war thing and how you'd like to be Overlord," said Cheryl. Maybe if she got the conversation back on that track, they could stop being lizards sooner.

"Mastermind," said the Historian. "We had Overlords and we got rid of them positively *eons* ago. By the way, how would you like to stop being lizards?"

"If it's convenient for you," said Mihalik.

"No problem." The Historian punched another button, and Mihalik and Cheryl went back to being human again. "See? Wasn't that something? King Proximo or Queen Hesternia can't do anything like that. Who would you rather serve—them or me?"

"You, definitely," said Cheryl.

"Then you're going home as soon as I can arrange it," said the Historian.

"You, for sure," said Mihalik. "You've got my vote."

"I'm so pleased."

"Do you want us to sign a statement or anything?" asked Mihalik.

"No," said the Historian, "your word is your bond."

"You bet," said Mihalik. "Well, we ought to be getting back to our suites. I left my wallet on the dresser."

The Historian smiled and stood up, walking them to the door. Suddenly his smile faded just a little. "Say," he said suspiciously, "you wouldn't be cooperating with me just to humor me, would you? So I'll send you home and not make you into lizards again?"

Mihalik and Cheryl both shook their heads vigorously. "We wouldn't do anything like that," said Cheryl. "We'd never be able to live with ourselves. Besides, we took an oath before we started exploring. We promised to be morally upright and all that. We didn't know what kind of people we'd be running into. If we broke that oath, Dr. Waters would never forgive us."

"Good old Dr. Waters," said the Historian. "He taught me everything I know."

Mihalik was startled. "You've met Dr. Waters?" he asked.

"Sure," said the Historian. "After he perfected time travel."

"So he *will* perfect time travel."

"I just told you so."

"When?"

"After you get back home."

"Then we *will* get back home?"

"I just told you so."

"Let's go, Frank," said Cheryl nervously. She could imagine Mihalik antagonizing the Historian into turning them into something even worse than lizards. Sticks, maybe. Dead sticks.

"Well," said Mihalik, "it's been nice schmoozing with you. Call us whenever you need more information."

"I will," said the Historian. "Night or day."

"I can't wait," said Mihalik. They beat it the hell out of there and back down the elevator to their own suites.

"Wow," said Cheryl tiredly as they sat in Mihalik's parlor and looked out over the flowers."

"The guy's crazy as a loon," said Mihalik.

"Crazy as a *powerful* loon. *Everybody's* crazy here. Everybody's crazy *everywhere*. Except us, of course."

Mihalik gave her a narrow, appraising glance. She knew just what he was thinking.

Give Me Liberty, or Give Me Something Almost as Good

Mihalik hung up the telephone. "God knows how many millions of years we are in the future," he said, "and all the operators still sound the same."

"Be grateful," said Cheryl. "The Historian could make them sound like Daffy Duck if he wanted to."

He shrugged. "If what Bwana said is true, then it doesn't make any difference what we do from now on."

"What are you talking about, Frank? Hey, are you trying to think again?"

"Just a little; sometimes I just can't help it. I mean, if every past, every *possible* past, leads to this single eventual future, then it doesn't make any difference at all if you're a good person or a bad person; if you give money to the Reformation Regiment at Christmas or massacre innocent puppies and kittens; if the good guys or the bad guys win this war or that war; if the wagon train makes it through to California. *Nothing* means anything! Whether the dinosaurs disappeared or not, whether mankind learned to speak and read and build cities, whether we drove back the Martians into their scummy little holes—*none* of it means a damn thing. Whatever might have happened in the past would lead inexorably to today. To us here in this room, waiting for the Historian to figure out what he's going to try next."

"Frank," said Cheryl thoughtfully, "that can't be entirely true. What if human beings never developed from apelike ancestors? How could the Historian himself be here to do what he does?"

Mihalik shrugged. "If intelligent earthworms ruled the world, then the Historian would be an intelligent earthworm who changed reality into one with intelligent humans."

"What if life never evolved on earth at all?"

"Then it came from someplace else, and the Historian would—"

Cheryl was too impatient to wait for him to follow her reasoning. "What if life never developed *at all,* anywhere, not on any single planet in the whole, entire universe?"

Mihalik didn't like that idea a bit. "Nowhere? A completely dead universe?"

"Yes. *Then* where would the Historian have come from?"

"Another universe, one where there were two of them." It was the likely answer, and both Mihalik and Cheryl knew it immediately. There was an answer for everything—and the Historian had it. What it added up to was the bleakest, most inhuman, most demeaning explanation of the purpose of life anyone had ever considered: life, pain, joy, struggle—all were less than nothing, less than futile. The goddamn universe couldn't care less what you or your species did; it was hurrying on to its absurd, flower-strewn *Wizard of Oz*/1939 New York World's Fair future with or without you. You could choose to come along, or you could slash your wrists in despair. Neither decision—or any other, at any other moment—would alter the outcome.

"Boy, is that depressing," said Cheryl.

"I don't even want to think about it," said Mihalik. "I'd go to bed and never get up again if it would mean anything. It *wouldn't* mean anything, though, so what's the point?"

"That's just it, Frank," said Cheryl tearfully. "What's the point? Why bother going on, trying to find our homes? Why bother rebuilding our lives? Why bother trying to make the future better for ourselves and for future generations? If we succeed or we fail, it's all going to end up like this. We might as well spend the rest of our lives watching fireworks over the Lagoon of Nations and being changed into bizarre figments of the Historian's imagination. We might as well just give up."

Those were just the words Mihalik needed to hear. He was suddenly thrown into action, as if a key had been turned, as if a powerful restraint had been removed. "*Give up?*" he cried. "Not on your pretty little ass! Nobody pushes Frank Mihalik and his chick around like that, not even some pissant Mastermind with omniscience, omnipotence, and powers far beyond those of mortal men."

"You make him sound like God, Frank," said Cheryl shakily.

"God, ha! We'll see what he looks like when I get through with him!" He picked up the telephone again. "I want to talk to Bwana," he told the operator. He looked at Cheryl. "Bwana's still laid up. The Historian worked him over pretty hard last night."

"Maybe we can send him a basket of fruit," said Cheryl.

"Hello, Bwana? Frank Mihalik here. Yeah, the visitor from the past; you remember. I was wondering if I could have a little chat with you today. Oh, about overthrowing the Historian. Bwana? Hello?" Mihalik hung up. "He hung up," said Mihalik.

"Maybe you ought to take it a little easier, Frank," said Cheryl. "Everybody seems to be a little touchy about the Historian. They probably didn't like being lizards just as much as we didn't."

"Take it *easier!* I'll go over the son of a bitch's head! I'll go right to the King!"

"Oh, that's terrific: the King. Santa himself."

"You wait, Cheryl," said Mihalik excitedly. "You'll see some action."

"That's what I'm afraid of." Mihalik rushed out of the room; Cheryl shivered.

King Proximo was as little help as Bwana had been. The old monarch sat on his throne wearing his gold crown, holding his gold scepter, his fat pink face wreathed in a broad smile. "Frank, Frank!" he cried happily. "How wonderful to see you this glorious day! Were you a lizard just a little while ago? I was a lizard. It was marvelous! That Historian! And he has such a sense of humor, too! Ha ha."

"Your Majesty," said Mihalik as he knelt at Proximo's feet, "It's about the Historian that I wanted to talk to you."

"Excellent fellow, came highly recommended, does a great job and on a limited budget, too."

"He's planning to overthrow you *and* Queen Hesternia. He's planning to make himself the actual dictator of time."

"Ha ha," said King Proximo. "Always something new from that joker. Dictator of time, eh? Well, we can't have that; I'll have to speak to him. Perhaps he just doesn't feel appreciated. We must do something for him, declare a holiday in his honor or put his picture on a stamp or something."

Mihalik was feeling desperate. "He doesn't give a hoot in hell about anything like that! He wants it *all!*"

The King laughed. "Well, he can't have it all. *I* have it all."

"He'll take it away from you."

"He won't. I've been in the future, you know; and I've seen it. I rule all the way to the end. I mean, the beginning. *My* beginning, *your* end. You know what I mean. As a matter of fact, I don't think this Historian is due to last more than another one or two galactic revolutions."

"But if he can change things—"

"Hey, can he ever! Do you know what I looked like, oh, two or three thousand years ago? I looked like a Hogarth caricature of Richard III. It was either his idea of a joke or some kind of petty revenge for something, I forget. I spent decades like that; it wasn't any fun, either, let me tell you: limping around, dragging my leg, my back all hunched over, snarling at everybody, muttering to myself, drowning princes. Finally he relented and turned me into this." Proximo leaned forward and spoke in a soft voice. "Confidentially, this jolly old soul stuff is almost as bad. Ha ha." It was the most pitiful laughter Mihalik had ever heard.

"If he can change things—little things, big things—maybe he *can* change the future. My future, your past."

"How can he change my past?"

"*I* don't know, Your Majesty, I don't even understand the rules here.

How does he change the present? *Your* present, I mean. He manages that and, from my point of view, that would be more difficult than changing the future. Anybody can change the future—"

"You're wrong, there," said King Proximo. "The future always ends up to be this way. It's even more locked-in than simple predestination. There's no way around it, so you can't do anything about changing it."

"How do you know?"

Proximo's eyes opened wider. "Because the Historian told me so," he said, astonished. "Ha ha."

"See? He's setting his plan into motion. In a little while, if you exist at all, you and Hesternia will be doing guest appearances on talk shows and writing memoirs to pay your rent while Mr. Big-Shot Historian whips the whole universe around to his liking. And strictly off the record, he's not quite sane, you know."

"He's not?" The King began to look terrified at the edges of his cheerful smile.

"How could he be? He's—"

Just then, both Mihalik and King Proximo were changed into other forms. They could still think, but they couldn't move or speak. They had become large, sentient chocolate-covered caramels. They heard footsteps approaching. A few moments later, the Historian's voice penetrated the chocolate. "A little taste of home, Mr. Mihalik? Mad, am I?" he said in a low, even, crazy voice. "Plotting behind my back, are you? I hope this demonstrates the foolishness of even daring to try such a thing. I'll release you sooner or later, but I'll let you suffer so you won't be tempted to get in my way again. You should see how stupid you look. I should have made you into pralines, that would have been even sillier. When you're human again, you'll find that you won't savor the tastes of food or drink ever again: a permanent reminder from me. And I can do worse. I can make sex the most tedious thing in the world. I can—"

There was a loud thump, and the Historian fell to the floor, making another thump. "Frank?" called Cheryl. Mihalik couldn't answer; he was still a three-foot-square lump of chocolate-covered caramel. Ants were beginning to cross the glossy black floor of the throne room; Mihalik could hear their tiny footfalls. "Frank?" called Cheryl again. She was close to hysteria. "You've got to be here somewhere, I heard the Historian talking to you; but all I see are these two huge blocks of candy." She broke off a little of Mihalik's chocolate; it hurt him like a knife wound. "It's lousy chocolate, Frank. We had better stuff back in 1996. Oh, merciful heavens! Is that *you*, Frank?"

Mihalik tried to think of a way he could communicate as an inanimate cube of candy. Nothing came to mind.

"It must be you! And this must be King Proximo! I can tell by the crown and the scepter. All right, I'll force the Historian to change you back. Thank God he didn't turn you into . . . into. . . ." She couldn't bring herself to finish the sentence; despite herself, she was beginning to giggle.

A few minutes later the Historian came to his senses, firmly tied and gagged, with Cheryl sitting on his chest. "Do it," she said.

"Gaa gaa gaa," said the Historian. Cheryl removed the gold-threaded cloth from his mouth. "I can't do anything like this," he said. "I have to use my equipment. I'm a technician, not a magician, you know."

Cheryl gave him a penetrating stare; she had seen Mihalik and Dr. Waters do it, but this was one of her first. "Okay," she said, "but I'll be watching every move you make."

"Won't do you any good," said the Historian. "You won't know what I'm up to. I could switch us all to a universe where you don't exist and you'd be gone. Then I'd be unguarded and at complete liberty to achieve my goals." Cheryl knew that was true; it was some quandary, all right.

It seemed like a stalemate; actually it seemed that way because Cheryl preferred a stalemate. It was really total victory for the Historian, but Cheryl wasn't ready to admit that yet.

"Of course," said the Historian airily, "there wouldn't be much pleasure without some kind of opposition."

"Aha," said Cheryl, "your typical mad-scientist weakness."

"No," said the Historian, "my gallantry. Untie me."

"Why should I?"

"Because if you don't, the ants will cart your boyfriend over there to their hole in the ground, gram by gram."

Cheryl nodded and let loose the Historian's bonds. "The King and Mihalik will be people again very shortly," he said. "Then the war can start."

"Oh, good," said Cheryl unhappily. Mihalik couldn't talk, of course, but he heard everything that was said in the throne room. He was even unhappier than Cheryl.

The Historian walked arrogantly away, and Cheryl sat on the steps of the throne. She watched ants climb all over her dear Frank. Then about five minutes later, without a sound or a flicker of lightning, Mihalik and King Proximo returned to their former selves. "Uck," said the King, "there are ants all over me."

"We've got to get to work," said Mihalik forcefully. "We don't have much time."

"*You* don't have much time," Proximo reminded him. "I'm going to let him do whatever he feels like."

Standing to one side, Cheryl murmured Yip Harburg's lyrics to "If I Only Had the Nerve." She sighed, knowing it was hopeless. "Be a lion, not a mowess," she said.

"Nope, ha ha."

Mihalik stared at the happy old King. "All right," he said slowly, "I'll fight him alone if I have to."

"And I'll be with you, darling," said Cheryl. Mihalik gazed down into her lustrous eyes, and he was filled with a new and daring courage.

"And so will I," came a voice from the back of the huge hall. It was Bwana, bandaged and on crutches, but with a look of defiance on his face. Behind him were dozens of other men and women.

"You've done it, Frank," said Cheryl wonderingly. "Just like one of the Dr. Waterses said you would. You've founded the Temporary Underground."

"Watch my dust," said Mihalik tersely. He turned on his heel and strode manfully toward his new allies.

A Moral Dilemma, or Tough Luck, Cheryl

As many courageous and powerful leaders have learned to their dismay, it is unrewarding to battle an enemy who knows Everything and can even control the movements of the celestial spheres. How many people can name the guy who was trying to keep the walls together inside Jericho while Joshua was doing his bit outside? That was pretty much the position in which Mihalik found himself. The Historian wasn't God in actual fact, but the effective distinction was so small as to be, for all practical purposes, negligible. For example, the Historian couldn't create life, he couldn't make a man out of insensate clay; but he *could* transfer to a reality where such clay was just about to be animated spontaneously into a living man, thanks to some local quirk of natural science. It would seem to an unbiased spectator that the Historian had performed the miracle, and that was good enough.

The Temporary Underground, Mihalik's forces, numbered two hundred and nine, including himself and Cheryl. The other several thousand citizens of the city—the 1939 New York World's Fair, or wherever and whatever it was—preferred to huddle in their cellars and laugh the day away until the conflict was decided. The Historian had no allies: he didn't need any. He was barricaded in his suite with all his equipment and his clipboard. He was having a great time changing the universe every ten minutes or so, exercising his creativity, gleefully imagining the consternation he was causing the besieging army.

After the time he'd spent as a cube of chocolate-covered caramel, nothing disconcerted Mihalik; the other recruits in his Underground were of less cheer, however. They were scared out of their minds. First they were turned into plastic lawn flamingoes, then they were molecules of formaldehyde floating randomly in interstellar space, then they were dandelion puffs captured in blocks of Lucite, then they were keys on Barry Manilow's pianos, then they were unrepentant demons imprisoned in a vast sea of ice. Mihalik was the biggest demon, his huge limbs immobile in the gelid dungeon. He had kind of dug being a drifting molecule. He'd even had a vague urge to move on toward greater things, maybe an amino acid or something; but this helplessness and his growing frustration were driving him slowly buggy.

"Okay, wise guy," shouted someone from somewhere out of sight, "what do we do now?"

"We wait for our chance," said Cheryl.

"Right," said another voice sarcastically.

The Historian appeared suddenly, making his way carefully toward Mihalik, wrapped in a great black fur coat and hat. He had fleece-lined gloves on his hands and high black leather boots on his feet. His breath left little clouds in the hellish air. "Whoa," he said, almost slipping on the ice. "Mihalik? Want to discuss terms?"

Mihalik only clenched his teeth. "Nuts!" cried Cheryl.

"Over here!" yelled an unhappy rebel. "I'll do anything!" The Historian ignored everyone but Mihalik and Cheryl.

"Don't let him get to you, Frank," she urged. "He's just trying to use psychology."

"Psychology wouldn't touch him," said the Historian, smiling wickedly. "I've seen dead flounders with more on the ball than he has."

"All right," said Mihalik evenly, "go ahead and gloat. You're mighty and powerful and you've got us at a disadvantage. Now what?"

"You're 'disadvantaged' right up to your heroic armpits." The Historian shrugged. "So here's the deal: I want you to worship me."

"Okay," said Mihalik.

That startled the Historian. "You will?" he asked, suspecting some clever subterfuge.

"Sure," said Mihalik. He didn't even know what "subterfuge" meant.

"If I send you back to your universe, will you still worship me?"

"If you want."

"I can check, you know. I can whip you right back into this glacier if you try any funny stuff."

Mihalik tried shrugging, but he couldn't move a muscle. "I know when I'm licked," he said.

"Frank!" cried Cheryl. "What are you saying? You—"

"Shut up, Cheryl," said Mihalik. He'd never said that to her before.

"And I want everybody else in your universe to worship me, too," said the Historian. "You'll be my prophet."

"Sounds fine," said Mihalik. "What happens to me when I die?"

"Oh, you won't die. You'll ascend bodily into the 1939 World's Fair."

"How could anybody ask for more than that? You're on."

"Frank!" screamed Cheryl.

"Shut up, Cheryl," said the Historian. "Frank, you won't regret this. You'll have all sorts of special privileges, too; I'm very generous that way. I'll get you out of this ice now—just you. It will take only a couple of minutes."

"Take your time," said Mihalik, "I'm not busy." The Historian walked cautiously back across the frozen lake.

"You cruddy traitor!" yelled one of the rebels. All the other Underground members joined in shouting insults and curses; even Cheryl wept bitterly. It meant nothing to Mihalik; he was made of stern stuff.

A few moments later, just as promised, Mihalik was standing in the Historian's parlor; he was normal size and dressed in a fresh Agency uniform. Cheryl had not come with him. The Historian regarded him warily. "No tricks now," he said. "Remember what I can do to you. Remember what I can do to your girl friend."

"You don't have to rub it in," said Mihalik grumpily. "I'm a tough competitor and a fierce fighter, but I'm not an idiot. I can size up a lost cause when I see one."

"Good. Now, let's hear a little sample worshipping."

"Thank you, O Historian, for releasing me from the dreadful lake of ice."

The Historian frowned. "That was terrible, but I guess you'll get better with practice. Well, you know the rules—one golden calf or anything like that, and it's back to Popsicle City. Got it?"

"To hear is to obey."

"That's better." The Historian came toward Mihalik with a couple of sheets of paper in his hand. "I didn't bother with clay tablets," he said. "I made a kind of preliminary list of commandments here that I want you to take a look at. There are seventy-six of them so far. Now we'll be having a test on this material tomorrow, so I want you to—"

Mihalik took the pages with one hand and slipped his right foot behind the Historian's. He jabbed hard at the man's nose with the heel of his other hand and yanked the Historian's leg out from under him at the same time. The Historian hit the floor hard, and Mihalik dropped beside him instantly. "I have my fingers on this pressure point in your throat," Mihalik said in an ugly low tone. "I have my other hand on the opposite point. Now do you know what happens if I press real hard on both of them at the same time?" The Historian's eyes were wide with fear. "You go to sleep," said Mihalik. "Your brain gets no blood. If I press for a little while, you'll wake up feeling real bad. If I press too long, you won't wake up at all. Now we're ready to negotiate."

"Uh huh," said the Historian in a squeaky voice.

"I want Cheryl with me."

"Uh huh." His nose was broken and bloody, and he was struggling to breathe.

"I want you to send us to our correct universes."

"Uh huh."

"Do whatever you want with these fools here, but leave our universes alone from now on."

"Uh huh."

"How do I know I can trust you?"

The Historian just stared. They had come to the inescapable fine print in the contract: there was no way that Mihalik could keep the Historian from pulling some kind of trick once the Historian got his hands on his equipment again. "I may be mad, as you said," squeaked the Historian. "I may be ambitious and hungry for power and all of that, too; but I'm still an honorable man. We're all honorable men, Frank. Shakespeare said that."

Mihalik thought about that for a moment, but he didn't loosen his hold on the Historian's throat.

"Frank?" said another voice curiously.

Mihalik looked up. Standing in the doorway, wearing a white lab coat and looking bewildered, was Ray, good old Ray, the best backup man in the business. "Where you at, Ray?" said Mihalik. He took his fingers off the Historian's neck, clasped his hands together, and brought them down as hard as he could on the terrified man's larynx. The Historian gave a strangled scream, took a few difficult, rattling breaths, and died.

"You killed him, Frank."

"Had to, Ray. Did you come to take me home?"

"No, 'fraid not," said Ray, staring at the contorted corpse on the carpeted floor. "I came to tell you why you're stuck here. Why *we're* stuck here, now."

"Oh." Mihalik began to wonder if possibly he'd been a little premature in his dispatching of the Historian.

"We need energy, Frank, lots of it. We're marooned here because of something called 'temporal—' "

" '—inertia.' I know. Cheryl told me all about it before."

Ray looked around the room. "Where is she?"

Mihalik stood up and took a deep breath. "Frozen into an ocean of ice, but it's all right: she wasn't the real Cheryl, anyway."

"Oh, that's okay then, I suppose," said Ray. "Now, see, we need this huge amount of force from this side to unstick you, and then they'll be able to draw us right back to our world."

"We tried that a long time ago. It didn't work."

"You didn't use enough force," said Ray.

"How big a force are you talking about?" asked Mihalik.

Ray dug in a pocket and pulled out a scrap of paper. He handed it to Mihalik. "A whole hell of a lot," he said.

Mihalik read the note; it was written in the familiar scrawl of Dr. Waters: *Hi, Frank, how's the boy? Slight hitch—need your cooperation if we're ever going to see your foolish mug around here again, not to mention Cheryl and Ray. Vital that you subject yourselves to great force, a minimum of 5×10^{42} newtons. Ray will be briefed; so if anything happens to Ray, you're finished. Regards to all. See you soon unless you screw up. Your friend, Bertram A. Waters, Proj. Dir.*

Mihalik read the note through a second time. "It still doesn't mean anything to me," he said.

"I know," said Ray, "that's why he briefed me. See, the force we have to get hit with is really *huge*. You're not to worry, though, because almost everything has been taken care of. Or it should have been, a long time ago."

"Almost everything? And 5×10^{42} newtons? What in God's name is a newton?"

"Oh, a newton is equal to exactly one hundred thousand dynes. They're units of force. It takes one newton to accelerate one kilogram one meter per second per second."

"Uh huh. That would be a little tap on the wrist. Now the big number—"

"What *we* get pounded with, you mean."

"—is roughly how much force? Give it to me in terms I can understand."

Ray smiled. "That's easy, Frank. There's never been a force like that in the whole history of the world. Dr. Waters calculated that the only way we could shoot back home is if we stand under the moon when it crashes into the Earth."

"What?"

Ray patted the air soothingly. "Now, I know it sounds risky—"

"When the MOON crashes into the EARTH?"

"There's no other way, Frank. And Dr. Waters' calculations even leave a little room for error. See, the mass of the moon is about 7.35×10^{22}

kilograms, and its orbital velocity, on the average, is 1.33×10^{10} meters per second. You end up with a collision of a pretty hefty 6.5×10^{42} newtons, which as you can see is a safety factor of 1.5×10^{42} newtons, any way you look at it."

"*Safety factor!*" shrieked Mihalik. "With the moon falling down out of space onto our heads, you're talking about how nice that it's going to hit a little harder than you figured? We won't even be *jam*, Ray. We won't even be a damp stain. The whole world is going to feel it, buddy, and whoever happens to be hanging around underneath while the moon falls those last couple of miles, well, they'll be lucky to have two electrons to rub together when it's all over."

"This is all assuming that the people in the past—in the past from the viewpoint of here, in the future from our own time, I mean—took care of binding up the moon for us."

Mihalik laughed; he was actually delighted. He'd never heard such intense nonsense before, and he'd listened to a lot of it since that high noon in 1996 when he let Dr. Waters bathe him in that amber ray. This was the best nonsense yet. "Bind up the moon?" he asked. He felt a gentle curiosity; he hoped Ray had been briefed on that, too.

"Oh, sure," said his eager backup man. They were still standing around awkwardly over the dead body of the Historian. Mihalik gestured toward the armchairs, and they seated themselves. "See," Ray continued, "there's this thing called Roche's limit."

"Roche's limit. Okay."

"Now Roche's limit says that if a body is being pulled in toward another body, like the moon toward the Earth, at a certain distance depending on their relative masses and one thing and another, there will be these terrific tidal forces that will rip and tear at them and pull them apart and shred them down into puny little rocks and stones. That's what's going to happen to the moon, see? It will end up just rocks and stones in orbit around the Earth, like the rings around the outer planets. Roche's limit is where Old Luna goes blooie, doing you and me no good at all, except that these wonderful engineers who lived maybe seven hundred thousand years ago from here were supposed to wrap the moon up in something so that it would all hold together."

"Why would they do that?" asked Mihalik. "I think rings around the world would be less traumatic than the whole moon blamming into us broadside."

"They did it as a favor to Dr. Waters," said Ray.

"Oh," said Mihalik. "What did they use?"

"Well, see, I'm not sure they actually accomplished it because I left before Dr. Waters came back from the future to ask them to do it. I think he suggested Dutch tape."

"You mean duck tape, Ray."

"I don't know. Dr. Waters, *he's* the smart one. He figured in all the angles, pal, let me tell you. Did you know that the Earth has been slowing down on account of the pull of the moon? Ever since the beginning, I guess. And if the Earth slows down, the loss of angular momentum has to be taken up somewhere else in the system—by the moon, that is. So the moon speeds up a little and escapes a little farther away. Now this gets tricky but kind of neat the way it all works out and all: way far up in the future—where we have to go—a normal day will last more than thirty-six hours because the Earth will have slowed down so much. After a certain point, the moon will be far enough away that it won't be having as big an effect on the Earth, and the process will start to reverse; the Earth will reel the moon in like a gasping trout. That's when all the special effects start to go off: volcanoes, earthquakes, all that end-of-the-world stuff. The moon will be so close to the Earth, see, it will be whipping around in orbit in just two hours, instead of a month. It will be so close you could almost hit it with a slingshot. The Earth will regain momentum and start spinning faster and faster. Continents will fracture and sink, tidal waves will slosh over everything, it will be just awful. Right about then, that's when the moon hits Roche's limit. That's when the whole ball of wax hits the fan. You and I will be waiting around to see what happens; if we're lucky, the duck tape will hold and the moon will go blammo into our tired old world. If the moon shatters into fairy dust, well, we'll be the first and the last to know about it. How's *that* for something to look forward to, Frank? Did you have any idea when you volunteered to go back in time that you'd end up at the end of the world, waiting for the goddamn moon to come screaming down on your head like the Flyswatter of the Gods?"

Mihalik had listened to this somewhat overwrought speech with his eyes closed, fighting down nausea. "I just want to go home," he said. "I just want to wake up in the morning and be home. Maybe it's all a dream, Ray. Maybe—"

"We have work to do," said his faithful companion. "We have to get ourselves to the last days of the world as we know it."

Mihalik opened his eyes. The dead body of the Historian was right where it had been; the World's Fair and the everlasting fields of flowers were still out beyond the boarded-up windows; Frank heard the tocking of little stones hitting the wood, just as the Historian had claimed. At this moment, Mihalik regretted his violence. He didn't want to go with Ray to the end of the world; he'd rather take his chances with Cheryl in the lake of ice, slaves of an insane despot.

It was too late, though. It was too late. Mihalik had acted, he had made his choice, and now he had to see it through to the conclusion. His gaze fell on a framed quotation by the Historian's desk (so like the framed quotations Dr. Waters always tacked up everywhere): "Can a man kill time without doing injury to eternity?" It was attributed to somebody named Thoreau. Whoever he had been, he'd hit the nail right on the head.

The image of a hammer pounding a nail made Mihalik wince—*he* was going to be the nail, and the hammer was going to be the hurtling moon of destruction.

. . . and Your Little Dog, Too!

They left the Agency Building and wandered out into the Fair. Mihalik forgot for a moment that Ray had not actually seen the Fair before, so he pointed out a few of the more interesting sights. "I know what those are," said Ray, bouncy as a child, hurrying toward the thematic white sphere and pyramid. "The Pylon and the Terrasphere."

"The Trylon and Perisphere," Mihalik corrected.

Ray turned suddenly. "Frank," he said, "I know you're a hero, a better hero than I could ever hope to be, though we've had all the same training and I'm younger and stronger than you. I have to remind you, though, that I did much better on my English College Boards. I know what a 'pylon' is, and even 'terrasphere' makes slightly redundant sense, but there just aren't any such words as 'trylon' and 'perisphere.' "

Mihalik smiled. "Ray, one thing you're going to have to get used to about the past and the future: nobody ever does anything for a good reason. History only pretends that they did."

Ray blinked his big solemn eyes and nodded. "Where are all the people, Frank? The Historian's defeated, the battle's over. Where *is* everybody?" Ray turned and looked first down one avenue, then down another. "Come out, come out, wherever you are, and meet the young hero who fell from a star."

Mihalik grunted and grabbed Ray's arm. "Why the hell did you say that?" he asked.

Ray looked puzzled. "I don't know. Why? Did I say something wrong?"

"I just didn't expect you to show up here quoting *The Wizard of Oz,* too, just like all the unreal people in the unreal universes."

"Did I make a quote? I didn't realize it."

"And haven't you noticed? You haven't once made a reference to candy. When you said the Earth was going to reel in the moon, you could have said 'like taking a candy cane from a baby' or 'like gobbling down a boxful of pecan turtles.' You didn't, though."

Ray shrugged. "Does all that mean something?"

"Yes, but it's beyond human reason to comprehend."

"Maybe Dr. Waters will know," said Ray. "So why are all the people still hiding?"

Mihalik scratched his scalp. "Maybe they're afraid of *me* now. Maybe they think I'll be just another Historian."

"The Dorothy Syndrome, Frank," said Ray, his expression awed as a philosophical notion took form in his mind. "Dorothy's house landed on the Witch, right? Hooray, hooray, Dorothy's a heroine. Now, what if the situation had been slightly different: her house lands on the Witch *and* a Munchkin; is she still a heroine? Sure, of course—getting rid of the Wicked Witch is worth the life of one poor Munchkin. Okay, take a third case: her house flattens the Witch and *two* Munchkins. Is she a heroine now? How about four Munchkins? Eight? At some point the Munchkins are going to say, 'Hey, forget it, we'd rather just live with the Witch. You stay in Kansas and stop crunching our citizens into the dirt.' "

"Ding-dong, the Witch is dead!" recited Mihalik thoughtfully. *"And so is Fred! And Paula and Jake and Monroe and Alma and Larry and Laureen and Estevan and Arly and Sol and—"*

"Exactly, Frank. We'd better find out where you—where *we* stand pretty fast. We might be in a lot of trouble."

"You mean, these people might not allow us to go to the far future and get pulverized by the moon."

Ray looked disappointed. "You're having some doubts, aren't you, Frank?"

Mihalik shook his head. "No, I'm really starting to enjoy all this. It's like a combination of a come-as-you-are party and Amateur Night on the executioner's block."

"First we still have to find the people who live here."

Mihalik made an impatient gesture. "They can just go fry ice, Ray, for all I care. We don't need 'em." The mention of ice caused him a sudden, unexpected, and deep stab of remorse. He remembered Cheryl, trapped for eternity. Her suffering was Mihalik's responsibility. He should have had the Historian rescue all the rebels before Mihalik did anything terminal to the only person who knew how to trade off the universes.

They walked through the eerily deserted Fair. It was all new to Ray, as exciting and fresh as when Mihalik had first seen it—how long ago? It was impossible to tell. He realized that if everything went according to

Dr. Waters' plans—and Mihalik was now willing to be swept along by them, though he didn't have all the confidence in the world—they'd return to 1996, each only the tiniest tick of a clock, less than a picosecond, after their separate departures. To the observers, they wouldn't even have vanished; they'd only have been magically transformed in appearance. Mihalik would never know how long his wanderings had lasted. He was truly beginning to feel like the Odysseus of Time, all right; he was longing for home and unsure how he was going to get there or what he'd find on his arrival.

"How are we going to do this?" asked Mihalik as they watched flags of all nations snapping in the warm breeze. How few of those flags or the nations they represented still existed in Mihalik's own troubled time! Yet that grimy, penniless, weary world called to him, his own Ithaca singing in his yearning blood.

"Do you remember where you arrived? When you first came to the World's Fair?" asked Ray.

"Uh huh. The Hall of Industry and Metals."

"Because that's the site where Dr. Waters would eventually build his chronoport. We're supposed to look there; Dr. Waters was almost positive the equipment would still be there. It was supposed to be guarded all through history, the millions of years between 1996 and here, because we'd need to use it now; otherwise, vast and unpredictable cataclysms might result from the ensuing paradoxes. For eons, that building was the holiest place on earth."

"Chronoport?"

Ray looked embarrassed. "Dr. Waters is trying out different names. He'll probably end up with 'time machine,' but right now he thinks it sounds too prosaic."

"The hall is over there a little way," said Mihalik. He wondered if the ancient machine would still be there and, if so, if it could yet be made to function. "Say," he said, "I just thought of something. If we're going to use his wonderful chronoport to zip up to the farther future, why can't we just use it to go directly home?"

"Because this isn't the real future, Frank. I'm surprised you even had to ask. When we witness the collision of the Earth and moon, we won't be in the real future, either; but the energy of that collision *can* throw us into our own reality. Dr. Waters will do the rest. In the real future, by the way, nobody's going to strap the moon up in duck tape. That's silly, Frank."

"I thought it sounded silly, but it's getting hard to tell, lately. After you've been a cube of chocolate-covered caramel. . . ." He let his voice trail off. "So if the moon doesn't get wrapped—"

"Don't even worry about it. The whole process I described would take hundreds of billions of years. The sun won't last that long, anyway; both the Earth and moon will be destroyed when the sun becomes a red giant before its own death. The moon's never going to crash into the Earth; not in the real universe, at least."

"Oh, good," said Mihalik, amazed that he even gave a damn.

The Hall of Industry and Metals was as empty and quiet as the rest of the exhibits. Mihalik led Ray to the dark storeroom where he had spent so much of the early part of his adventure. "Right in here," he said, opening the door.

There it was, the chronoport, surrounded by velvet ropes and plaques and statues and unguessably old vessels of ceramic or gold that had once contained flowers or offerings of other kinds. The room had served as a shrine for a vast quantity of time. Maybe the people who had pilgrimaged here had no idea what the apparatus was, why it was being guarded, and what would eventually be done with it. It may have been the greatest mystery in the long story of mankind, more puzzling than the fate of the *Mary Celeste* or the disappearance of the Lost Colony of Painesville.

"Gosh," said Ray, examining the heaps of treasures and the curious and indecipherable artifacts.

"Let's just go," said Mihalik.

"I want to fill the pockets of my lab coat—"

"Listen," said Mihalik, "when we left the 1939 World's Fair, Cheryl and I had a souvenir Heinz pickle pin for you. When we ended up in what we thought was home, the pin had disappeared. Maybe the application of force moves something across time only if it's not in its right reality to begin with. I don't think you'll be able to take any of this with you."

"You really thought to get me a souvenir? That was swell, Frank. I wish I had that pin. Anyway, let me try." Mihalik watched sulkily as Ray scooped up emeralds—here in the metaphoric Emerald City, what else would they be?—and stuffed his pockets to bulging. "Okay," he said. He went to check the meters and readouts. "Everything seems in order here. They've kept it all in perfect condition. I don't see so much as a smudge or a fingerprint, and it all smells like lemon-refreshed ammonia, too. They must have cleaned it off just this morning."

Mihalik was paying no attention. He went to a space enclosed by a low railing of incorruptible gold. He stepped over and saw two X's set into the floor with hundreds of small emeralds. That was where he and Ray would have to stand. . . .

Two X's. Did that mean that the past had informed the future (or *vice versa,* or both) that Cheryl would not make the journey with them under any circumstances? That Cheryl had been destined from the beginning to be left behind? Mihalik chewed his lip; okay, if that *had* always been Cheryl's fate, why did he still feel guilty?

"Hit your mark, Frank," said Ray.

Mihalik went to his X and found a note waiting for him on the floor, held in place with a large, loose emerald. He bent and picked up the note, letting the precious stone roll aside. The message was mankind's first comprehensible communication from intelligent beings from interstellar space.

The Note, Followed by a Contest for the Reader

"What's that you got, Frank?" asked Ray, as he completed his calibration and pre-push check-out of the chronoport.

"A note."

"That's strange. Anything interesting?"

Mihalik read it:

Dear Frank:

You don't know us, but we're intelligent beings from interstellar space. We call ourselves the nuhp. We visited your world not many years after you made your historic journey through time. We knew nothing of time travel, but we were taught its secrets by your Dr. Waters. He told us that you'd planned to leave a note in the time capsule at the Fair, but that you hadn't actually accomplished it. No matter, it was the thought that counted. We would have found the time capsule and read your note, and it would have been a plea for help. Consider your plea heard. So your argument with Cheryl about the effect of leaving the note is still inconclusive: you are achieving the desired effect without performing the seemingly required cause.

Have no fear; your journey to the far future will go off without a hitch, the careening moon will do its job, and you and your pal, Ray, will return safely to your present. We hope you don't mind us giving away the ending.

There are a few things you must tell Dr. Waters when you see him next, because he will not know these things and he *must* know them in order to make certain decisions involving the continued existence of the entire universe. You can see that we nuhp are concerned that everything go smoothly.

First: we have deciphered most of the messages from Sirius. Evidently they are nothing to worry about. As you know, they are the same series of signals repeated every 11.4 seconds. The first part of the message makes sense, but it soon dissolves into gibberish. The message reads:

> YOU MAY ALREADY HAVE WON MXBLENR FTYP D
> WAZN'WS'L VRBOK

Second: when we visited your world, we gave your people the necessary knowledge to make interstellar travel possible. Since then, we have made great mathematical discoveries that allow virtually instantaneous transportation from any point in the universe to any other point. See diagram and accompanying mathematical proof. Now you have the freedom of space as well as time. You are as gods. So are we. It's better than the insurance racket.

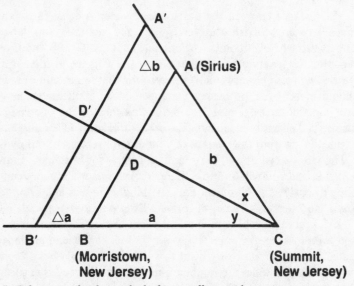

Fig. 1: Schematic of nuhp method of interstellar rapid transit.

Discussion: we have drawn a triangle ABC at whose vertices are Sirius, the bright star that follows the constellation of Orion around; the town of Morristown, New Jersey; and the town of Summit, New Jersey. These points are chosen merely for illustration. Point A can be any cosmic locus at all; points B and C can also be any convenient points. It will be shown that the closer points B and C are, the less time it will take to travel to the selected point A.

Now make D the midpoint of AB. It is assumed that, for practical purposes, all points on the Earth's surface are equidistant from the cosmic locus; therefore, AB and AC are equal. Then: $\dfrac{AD}{\sin x} = \dfrac{AC}{\sin CDA}$ and $\dfrac{BD}{\sin y} = \dfrac{BC}{\sin CDB}$. Bearing in mind that AD = BD, we arrive at the equation: $\dfrac{\sin y}{\sin x} = \dfrac{b}{a}$.

And then we displace line AB to the position A′B′, so that $\Delta a = B′B = \Delta b = A′A$. We take logarithms of both sides of $\dfrac{\sin y}{\sin x} = \dfrac{b}{a}$; the result is log b − log a = log sin y − log sin x. We differentiate, remembering that x and y are constant: $\dfrac{\Delta b}{b} - \dfrac{\Delta a}{a} = 0$, or $\dfrac{k}{b} - \dfrac{k}{a} = 0$. Therefore, b = a; that is, AC = BC.

The distance between the Earth and any star is equal to the distance between Morristown, New Jersey, and Summit, New Jersey, or between whatever points we designate as B and C. If B and C are separated by a very small distance, then the distance to the cosmic locus A will also be very small, and crossing that minor gulf of space should present few problems. We applaud our mathematicians on bringing the farthest, most mysterious reaches of the universe as nearby and as easily reached as the corner forgstore. (We nuhp have withheld forg from the humans of your era, for reasons of our own.)

Human beings must learn and encompass all things, Frank Mihalik, and you will find that there are yet greater and more ennobling discoveries to be made. For one thing, *blue* seas and *brown* or *green* land masses? Come on, Frank. Even our four-year-olds can pick out more tasteful combinations when they dress themselves. If you want to keep the oceans blue, why not make the land an understated yellow? If you really want to add a few bold slashes of color (we nuhp are an older race and have moved quite beyond that sort of thing), why not make the rivers a vibrant crimson?

But lose the brown, Frank. Really. You should hear what some of the other residents of our galaxy say about the way Earth looks from space. Brown and blue, it's unbelievable. . . .

Third: it's crucial that Dr. Waters learn about the four basic units out of which the entire universe is built. No, not earth, air, fire, and water. You know how atomic particles are made up of even smaller particles, how quarks are made of fantods, which in turn are made of even more ephemeral kleinstens, which consist of the vast variety of urs in different combinations. It seems to go on forever, Frank, *but it doesn't.* There *is* a bottom line, a group of ultimately small units that are not particles, waves, or wavicles, either. We don't have enough time to explain exactly what form they take; they're just constructs in one sense, mathematical-physical-philosophical notions; yet they can be detected and demonstrated. Indeed, their only quality—as they seem immune from the effects of the four universal forces—seems to be pure existence.

"Gee," said Ray, reading over Mihalik's shoulder, "they're letting you in on the fundamental hidden knowledge of the ages."

"Right," said Mihalik scornfully, "just in time for me to get mashed into thin pink gruel by the moon."

"Imagine knowing the secrets of the universe!" said Ray.

"Aw, hell." Mihalik continued reading:

What, we hear you asking, is matter made of, then? The answer seems to be: something else. These four units are chronons, animons, gravitons, and Stoff (a human word in approximation of an idiomatic nuhp term). Chronons, as you've learned, are the basic material of time. Dr. Waters will have perfected his knowledge of chronons by the time you return to your own reality. Gravitons are theoretical units of gravity, according to human science. Nuhp physicists isolated them many tens of thousands of years ago. Animons are the essential basic unit of "spirit" or whatever you want to call the animating force of living things. Stoff is the immaterial quality that when combined in sufficient quantities becomes "charge," "spin," "the weak force," and certain other properties of tangible matter. It's all a lovely unified field, just as your Dr. Einstein predicted.

The important thing to remember is that everything in the universe consists of these four units; also, that they are always found in groups of three, never more or less, and never more than one of each type in any triad. If you put one chronon and one graviton and one bit of Stoff together, you get life. That is the essential difference between a living animal and a corpse, the presence of this triad in sufficient quantity. A bit of Stoff, a chronon, and an animon gives you mind or consciousness. A bit of Stoff, an animon, and a graviton equal space. And a chronon, an animon, and a graviton create time.

"You need a chronon, an animon, and a graviton to build time?" asked Ray. "I thought time was just a flow of chronons."

"Evidently not," said Mihalik. "Just the way gravity isn't just a flow of gravitons."

"And time and space are actually composed of these things?"

"These immaterial things. Yes, that's what they're saying."

Ray's face screwed up comically as he tried to get a grip on the concepts. "Yes, but I thought space was, you know, the place where there wasn't anything."

"Well, we're wrong about that, apparently. Let me finish the note."

Now we must give you the most essential information of all. With a working knowledge of the four fundamental units of reality, Dr. Waters will be able to build the defenses against the direst threat to life and liberty the galaxy has ever known. It is of the utmost importance that you warn him, Frank, that he has very little time. All life on Earth and on countless other worlds is in his hands. This threat, more terrifying than anything your writers of fiction could imagine, is far more than we nuhp, purveyors of peace and understanding, can hope to battle. Dr. Waters must be your champion and ours, as well. Tell him to expect the following early warnings:

The words were at the bottom of the page. There were no more pages. "Oh, great," groaned Ray.

"What do we do now?" asked Mihalik.

"We take Dr. Waters this stuff and hope that he can make sense of it. We hope that he can recognize the early warnings without having to be told about them by these nuhp jerks. You think they would have left such an important message in a safer place. I wonder where the last page is."

"Did you see it over by the control panels?"

Ray shook his head. "The place is clean as a whistle, Frank."

They searched the rest of the room, among the pots and caskets and other junk that had collected in the shrine during the long millenniums. They began throwing the various treasures around carelessly, tearing the place apart to find the nuhp's final revelation. It was hopeless; after a couple of hours, Mihalik and Ray were forced to admit that the page was nowhere in the room. "We're just going to have to have faith in Dr. Waters," said Mihalik. "He'll have to do the best he can without all the data he was supposed to get."

"He's never failed us yet," said Ray hopefully. Mihalik wondered how true that sentiment was.

"Are we ready?" asked Mihalik.

"You stand on your X, I'll stand on mine. I can set the machine for a twenty-second delay. Then things will start to happen very fast."

Mihalik took a deep breath and let it out. "Fire away," he said. Ray made a final adjustment and flipped a few toggle switches; then he hurried to his place on the stage beside Mihalik. There was a flicker of amber light, a sizzle, a snap, and a moderate clap of thunder.

SON OF
HAVE YOU BEEN PAYING ATTENTION?

In 1978, in my Doubleday novel *Death in Florence,* I included a surprise quiz on page 145 that I called HAVE YOU BEEN PAYING ATTENTION? I asked ten questions about the course of the novel up to that point, and offered autographed copies of my next Doubleday book, *Dirty Tricks,* to the first ten people who sent me correct answers. It was, I thought, an absurdist thing to do in the middle of an absurdist novel; besides, I liked hearing from the readers, whether they had the right answers or not. Most authors get very little feedback from their audience.

Well, guess what! Here's another contest, and for the first ten people who send correct answers, I will award autographed copies of the forthcoming companion novel, to be published by Doubleday about a year after the present book appears. That sequel of sorts, *The Bird of Time,* is set some hundred years after the events of *The Nick of Time* and relates the story of the Captain Hartstein who appeared briefly here in Book Five. The winners' names will be printed in *The Bird of Time,* too.

Sound exciting? You betcha. And all you have to do is spot the fallacy in the nuhp's solution to instantaneous interstellar travel. There is one small mathematical error cleverly disguised in the "proof" of their discovery. An elementary knowledge of calculus is required, but any high school or college-level math teacher ought to be able to help find the error. All the rest of the proof is mathematically rigorous, and the fallacy is so subtle that it may be easily overlooked, so be on your toes! The contest ends six months after publication of *The Nick of Time.* As before, no purchase is necessary; but go ahead: buy the book anyway. Start a George Alec Effinger collection. Be the first on your block to own all of my titles! Get them now, before they either become collector's items or are shredded back into pulp.

Send your entries to:

> *The Nick of Time* Mystery Fallacy
> Box 15183
> New Orleans, LA 70175

Void where prohibited by law, but maybe we could negotiate something anyway. I'm really a nice guy once you get to know me.

Book Six

Plus Ça Change,
Plus C'est la Même Chose

The Hall of Industry and Metals disappeared, left far behind in the past. The meadows of flowers disappeared, too. Mihalik had a quick glimpse of dimly lighted rocky landscape, and then he was rolling and tumbling down the side of a steep gorge. The air was filled with grotesque thunder, a steady, bone-rattling, grinding growl that was punctuated frequently by even louder detonations. The stony ground tore at Mihalik's clothing and lacerated his skin, and he needed desperately to slow his slide down the barren rock face. He tried to catch onto a narrow ledge but his momentum carried him over it, and he succeeded only in scraping his chest raw and bloody. He dug in his feet and spread his arms as wide as he could, but it didn't help; he surrendered and fell the rest of the way to the bottom of the narrow fissure, hitting his head on one boulder, injuring a shoulder on another. When he reached the bottom, he lay face down on the dry cracked earth, too dazed and too full of pain to move. He gasped for breath. It was difficult to fill his lungs: first, because he felt as if he'd cracked a rib or two, and second, because the air didn't seem to be thick enough to breathe. He took shuddering, heaving inhalations, trying to ignore the pain. The roaring of the hurricane, the rocking and shaking of the quaking ground, the rattle of the loose rocks as they pelted and plunged down on top of him all made him withdraw even further into himself. He put his arms around his head for protection, closed his eyes, and tried to catch his breath.

"Frank?" It was Ray, calling in a feeble voice from nearby.

Mihalik didn't want to move, he didn't want to look for his friend. Mihalik was no coward, but he was in no hurry to resume being a hero, either. "Ray," he called, "you all right?"

"That was some ride, Frank. I hurt all over."

"Can you move? Anything broken?"

"I'm never going to be the same again, Frank, but I don't think I broke any bones. I wonder how I look without skin, though."

"Probably like I do, a couple hundred pounds of ground round." Mihalik took a deep breath, held it, then let it out slowly. He was preparing to roll over and stand up, an act that took as much raw nerve as anything he'd ever had to do in his life. He rolled over, all right; but he didn't get up. He was stopped by the moon, which was growing rapidly in the near-black sky. It filled almost the whole of the heavens, eclipsing the sun and everything else.

"It shouldn't be long now, Frank," said Ray weakly. "We had only a few seconds to spare."

Mihalik's wide eyes stared at the terrible sight above him. He lay on his back, paralyzed, unable to speak, unable to cry out. The moon was so close he could see the strips of silver duct tape that bound it together. There wasn't enough time even to seek a shallow hole, any sort of insufficient hiding place. . . .

"Frank—"

"Ray—"

How do you even try to describe the catastrophic violence and terror and unbearable tumultuousness of the collision of two planetary bodies? Mihalik would never be able even to make an attempt. He saw only that brief glimpse and then it happened and then he and Ray were gone, lassoed by mathematics out of harm's way *au nick du temps.* Later, when he had regained his grip on sanity, when he had recovered and rested and was able to think of that instant without panic, he began to wish that he *could* have witnessed more. It was surely the most staggering display ever enacted on this particular stage. Still that single moment when he saw the moon hanging overhead, only a few miles away and zeroing in on him, stayed burned into his nightmares for the rest of his life. It wasn't something that one could come to terms with, not even with the best psychoanalysis and pharmacology money could buy.

And in his real home, in his real 1996, Frank Mihalik couldn't afford much of either.

On his back, propped up a little on his elbows, his face bloody and filthy and twisted with fear and pain, his silver and blue Agency uniform all but torn into tatters, as pathetic a sight as could be imagined, he lay on the transmission stage. The silence was flecked with the sound of clicking: it was from the cameras that had gone off when the photographers had snapped Mihalik's picture just before he'd disappeared. A bell had begun to toll the noon hour just as Mihalik had been sent into the past, so long ago, and the ringing note still sounded through the stillness. To the others an inconceivably short time had passed. There hadn't been time for the blink of an eye. There hadn't been enough time for the human brain to register the transition—first there had been Frank Mihalik, proud and solemn and dressed in his one-piece green coverall, sitting on a folding chair—and then there was . . . this pitiful wreck of a man, staring wildly as if he'd beheld the very end of the world itself.

His first thoughts were of Ray, who was nowhere to be seen. Mihalik was alone on the transmission stage. "Ray?" he called, startled by the hoarse, almost inhuman quality of his voice.

"I'm here, Frank," came Ray's familiar, hearty voice from somewhere in the crowd. How could that be?

Dr. Waters was the first to reach the transmission stage. "Don't move, Frank," he said. "We'll have a doctor examine you right here. You may have broken bones or internal bleeding. Do you need anything for the pain?"

"No," croaked Mihalik. "Ray?"

"This Ray hasn't gone back to get you yet," said Dr. Waters. "It will be days before he leaves. Don't worry; he was rescued the same time you were, but he will go back to the time he came from. You'll be there when he goes, and when he gets back."

"Good," said Mihalik. He was exhausted. "Note."

"You mean the one from the nuhp?" asked Dr. Waters.

Mihalik nodded, bewildered. How could Dr. Waters know about the message from the extraterrestrials now, only a few objective seconds after their handshake prior to Mihalik's departure? Dr. Waters hadn't known about it then.

"In the trillionth of a second while you were gone," said Dr. Waters, "I went into the future. I was actually *taken* into the future, to learn all that I needed to know to rescue you. I was returned just about the time you reappeared. We're both time-travel veterans now, my boy." His dark magnetic eyes glowed with a strange intensity. He absently stroked his carefully trimmed mustache. Already Dr. Waters was turning over in his mind the results of this experiment, designing further tests, making newer theories, planning greater conquests. Suddenly he seemed to shiver, and he returned his attention to Mihalik. "That's all for later, Frank, after you've been attended to. We have plenty of time to talk. Plenty of time." His eyes glittered: *I Have Seen the Future.*

"Yes, sir," said Mihalik.

"Cheryl's here," said Dr. Waters, raising one eyebrow. He backed away.

Cheryl ran to the edge of the stage and took one of Mihalik's bloody hands. She kissed his trembling fingers. "Frank!" she said, sobbing.

Mihalik looked at her with a powerful mixture of tenderness and anger. He struggled to understand his feelings, but they were too confused, too conflicting, too inappropriate. "Cheryl," he murmured.

"I told you to be careful," she said, in a gentle voice.

He was not amused. "You didn't come back, did you?" he said. "You didn't come back to try to save me. The other Cheryl did, but you didn't. You stayed here. You never even—"

"Frank," she said, aghast, "you've been gone only a split second. There hasn't been time to do anything. If you needed help, I would gladly have volunteered. Maybe in a few days, if someone needs to make the trip, I'll go. I don't understand these time-paradox things. I don't see why someone will have to go in a few days if you're back now, safe and sound."

"Someone will have to go," said Mihalik, feeling an odd bitterness, "and it will be Ray, not you."

"What are you doing, Frank?" said Cheryl, frightened. "Why are you treating me this way?"

"I don't know," he said. There was the knowledge that this Cheryl, *his* Cheryl, had risked nothing, had never left her safe niche in time. All his adventures, his pain, and the risks he'd faced, he'd shared with another Cheryl, a Cheryl from another universe who was lost forever. It meant that his feelings for this Cheryl were now different, but it seemed that never in a million years would he know in what ways they were different. He sensed his old feelings beneath an overlay of guilt and betrayal and faithlessness; he might never sort them out. They sat like a cluster of black jujubes at the center of his heart.

"Don't you still love me?" she asked. "What happened back there? What did you mean, 'the other Cheryl'?"

"We're going to have to do a lot of talking, honey," said Mihalik. "I have a lot of healing to do, inside and out."

She nodded, letting his hand go. She sat on the edge of the transmission stage, watching him fearfully.

Ray pushed his way forward. "You were supposed to watch your ass, buddy," he said. He looked concerned.

Mihalik forced a smile. "While I was busy watching my ass, something hit me on the head."

"What?"

"Say, that's right, you don't even know about it yet. Well, Ray, all I can say is thanks. You pulled me out of the damnedest mess you can imagine. I'll never be able to repay you for it."

"Well, hell, Frank, we're pals and all, and we're in this project together, and I'm sure that if it was the other way around—"

Mihalik raised a hand to cut him off; they were both a little uncomfortable. "Just thanks. Even more now, when I think that you'll do it knowing that you'll come back just as bad off as I am."

"I will?" Ray turned just a touch paler. "Well, damn it, what are friends for? You can't have all the glory, anyhow."

Mihalik laughed; it hurt. "You can have as much as you want, Ray." He looked from Ray to Cheryl and back, wondering about friendship and love, wondering how much of what he felt toward her was the result of his final estimation of himself: the inadequacy, the failure, and the shame.

"You're wearing different clothes, Frank," said Ray.

"Uh huh. Picked them up in the future."

"The future? We sent you into the past."

"Right. I went into the past first, but I ended up in the future. That's where you'll have to come get me."

Ray shook his head. "I don't understand. How long were you gone?"

Mihalik shrugged. "There's no way to tell. A couple of years altogether, I think."

"A couple of years?" Both Ray and Cheryl were astonished. "Then you *must* have had some time of it."

"I guess I did," said Mihalik. A lot of his adventures were already beginning to seem unreal to him; later on, he probably wouldn't be able to sort out what had really happened from what he had dreamed about it.

Cheryl moistened a handkerchief with her mouth and wiped away some of the dirt on his face. "You've got lines on your face, Frank. Where you didn't have them before."

"Laugh lines," he said.

"They make you look a little more, oh, distinguished. They suit you."

"Then it was all worth it, I guess," said Mihalik, feeling sullen again.

"Will I spend that long in the future, too?" asked Ray.

"No," said Mihalik, "you were only there a few hours."

"Just long enough to get as torn up as you."

"Sorry, pal. It all happened right at the finish."

Ray sighed. "I can't say I'm rarin' to go, but—"

"Ray, you're going to have a box seat for the most spectacular event you've ever seen. This one quick, awful look will stay with you as long as you live, I promise."

Ray didn't look too heartened by that, either. "Then don't tell me about it," he said. "I don't want you to spoil it for me."

"Dr. Waters will fill you in before you go. You'll know what's going to happen; but believe me, it more than lives up to your expectations."

"Okay," said Ray, "now you've got my curiosity aroused. Now I don't mind getting my knees scraped a little."

"That's enough," said a doctor in a green overall, carrying a black bag, "let me through." Ray stood aside, and the doctor began a quick examination of Mihalik.

"I think I'm okay," said Mihalik.

"Compared to what?" said the doctor. "Let me make the decision, all right? Nothing seems fatally messed up; you don't seem to have left anything important behind you, but we're going to put you into the hospital for a few days just to make sure."

"Hey, I'm—"

"You knew you'd be quarantined. It was part of the plan." Two men rolled a gurney up to the transmission stage and carefully lifted Mihalik onto it. Cheryl, Ray, and Dr. Waters followed the doctor to the waiting ambulance. Mihalik tried to look back at them, but the movement was too painful. He was grateful for the interruption; he didn't feel like more conversation, more pretending that he was still brave and untarnished and ready to do the whole thing over again. Before they even raised him into the ambulance, he was asleep.

You're out of the woods, you're out of the dark, you're out of the night

"Huh?" said Mihalik, waking suddenly from a terrifying dream of being pursued.

"Just need to get your blood pressure, Mr. Mihalik," a nurse said softly. She wrapped his arm and squeezed the bulb. "You cried out in your sleep."

"I hope I'm not disturbing anybody."

The nurse smiled. "There isn't anybody else on this whole floor. You've got it all to yourself. We have *you* all to ourselves. We're proud to have you as a patient, Mr. Mihalik."

"Thanks, I guess, but—"

"Dr. Waters told us you'd be modest; he also gave us an idea of what you went through. You're on mild sedation—your physician thought it would be a good idea for a little while. You were treated for severe bruises and lacerations and we have you on an IV; but other than that, you seem to have come through everything just fine."

"Great." Mihalik stretched out his legs; the pain wasn't gone—he knew it was still there, somewhere—but it was hiding. The clean sheets and the comfortable pillows felt wonderful. The peace, the soothing quiet, the likelihood that he had at last come home did more for his state of mind than any medication.

"We won't be able to feed you as well as you dined in the places you've been," said the nurse. "You'll have to adapt to our standard of living again."

"You know," he said, smiling, "it will be a pleasure. I *am* hungry. What time is it?"

"About two in the afternoon. Wednesday. You've slept the clock around. Would you like some lunch?"

Mihalik nodded. "What do you have?"

"Anything you want," said the nurse.

"I want a box of Raisinets and a Vernor's," he said.

The nurse unwrapped his arm, made a notation on a chart beside his bed, and nodded. "We'll have that in to you in a couple of minutes. Need something for the pain?"

"Not just yet."

"All right, Mr. Mihalik, you just lie still. You've done your part; now it's our turn."

That was all right by him. He just stared up at the ceiling for a while not noticing the time pass, until they brought his lunch in on a tray. He wolfed the Raisinets and washed them down with the ginger ale. Then he clicked on the holovision set and watched daytime shows for a while. Just before dinnertime, the telephone rang. He picked it up. "Hello?" he said.

"Mr. Mihalik, the Man from Mars would like to speak to you. Please hold the line for a moment."

Mihalik felt a thrill of excitement. He hadn't expected this kind of reception. "Mr. Mihalik?" came the familiar voice.

"Yes, sir."

"I hear you've had quite an adventure."

"Yes, sir."

"I want you to know that we're all proud of you. It's people like yourself who remind us what this world is all about, why we have to keep fighting to restore it to its former greatness."

"Yes indeed, sir."

"And it's people like yourself who are making the contributions that will go a long way toward bringing about that end. You're an American, aren't you, Mr. Mihalik?"

"Born and raised, sir."

"Well, you know, so am I. I know I'm supposed to speak for the world as a whole, but I just can't help being proud that it was an American who conquered time. I'd like to invite you to the White House, where your President and I would like to congratulate you in a formal ceremony. You'll receive the highest civilian award."

Mihalik couldn't speak for a moment. He was a hero, all right, he knew that; but he never thought of himself as anyone special. "I don't know what to say, sir. It's a tremendous honor."

"You bet your sweet ass it is. We'll make arrangements another time, after you've been released from the hospital. On behalf of the starving, miserable, homeless, squalid, filthy people of the world, thank you for your courage. And say hello to Dr. Waters for me."

"I will, sir."

"Goodbye." There was a click. Mihalik set the phone down. He was going to the White House, on Fifth Avenue, to get his reward—a never-ending free supply of Three Musketeers bars for him and all his progeny unto the end of time. It was too much. Mihalik wept.

The thought of the candy reminded him of Athos, Porthos, and Aramis; of Madame de Romiers; of the other Cheryl, who had fought beside him shoulder to shoulder, against the enemies of their beloved Queen Anne. . . . Mihalik wept some more.

Not long after, a soft knock came at the door. Dr. Waters and Cheryl came in. He took the chair beside Mihalik, and she sat at the foot of the bed. "How are you doing?" asked Dr. Waters.

"Fine," said Mihalik. "Got a call from the Man from Mars. He said to say hello to you."

"Oh, Frank," said Cheryl, "that's wonderful."

"I have to go to some reception or something." He looked anxious about the notoriety.

"I'll be there with you, Frank," said Dr. Waters. "Are you all recovered?"

Mihalik paused a moment before answering. "You know," he said at last, "this sure feels like home. It looks like home. It *ought* to be home. Yet I can't shake the feeling that maybe it *isn't* home. That maybe I'm in just another wrong universe, only it's going to take longer than usual for me to find out. I might not learn the truth for twenty or thirty years. Then, all of a sudden, something bizarre will pop up. I feel like I'm going to walk around for the rest of my life, waiting for the wrong thing to tap me on the shoulder."

Dr. Waters nodded thoughtfully. "You've earned a little time to work out your doubts, son," he said. "I don't really know what I or anyone else can do to prove that this is your true reality."

"I don't, either," said Mihalik sadly. "And what about the future? Is there only one? Is it inescapable?"

Dr. Waters shook his head. "That was just another lie of a false universe."

Mihalik nodded; that was good news. "I thought I was going crazy sometimes."

"You mean when you started hurting people at the Fair? Back in 1939?" asked Dr. Waters.

"How did you know about that?"

Dr. Waters smiled. "I know your whole story. Don't forget, I've been in the future. I've been filled in on everything."

Mihalik frowned. "Yes, when I started hurting people. I thought, what difference does it make? Then when I was in the future, and people didn't get well at midnight any longer, I still had that feeling: what difference does it make? These aren't real universes, these aren't real people. At least, that's what I told myself. I never really believed it, though, and now I'm carrying around a lot of guilt for some of the things I did."

"You mean the other Cheryl," said Dr. Waters. "In the ice."

"Yes," said Mihalik. "I can't stop thinking about her."

"What did you do to her, Frank?" asked Cheryl. This other Cheryl was like an extension of her. She wanted to know what had happened.

Dr. Waters waved a hand at her, and she was quiet again. "It's all right, Frank," he said. "You didn't abandon her to eternity. You forget about the nature of infinity. In one of the infinite universes there will be someone—me, a Historian, Cheryl, you yourself—who will find a way to cross to *her* universe and set her free."

"But—"

"There *has* to be, Frank. In an infinite number of realities, it isn't just *anything* that will occur; *everything* will occur. Including the rescue of the other Cheryl. You have nothing to feel bad about."

"But that means," said Mihalik, threading his way through the concepts, "that means that everything always has to work out for the best, because if it didn't, someone from another universe would arrive to fix it."

"I suppose so."

"So we're all living in the best of all possible worlds," said Cheryl.

"Every world is the best of all possible worlds," said Dr. Waters.

"How can that be?" asked Mihalik.

Dr. Waters took out his expensive French cigarettes and lit one. "I'll show you the math, Frank," he said, exhaling smoke, "and you can see if it makes any sense to you."

"I'll have to take your word for it, then. Does that mean that we were really helpless? That there was no way we could have gotten ourselves home to our own universe?"

"It seems that way," said Dr. Waters. "You couldn't have gotten back here any more than an ice cube can become water again just by wishing. It takes energy. Truth and illusion, George; you don't know the difference."

"What? Who's George? I'm Frank, remember?"

"It was a line from an Albee play," said Cheryl helpfully.

Dr. Waters nodded. "And the next line is, 'No; but we must carry on as though we did.' "

"Is that profound?" asked Mihalik.

"Sure is," said Cheryl.

Mihalik thought some more. He felt the dark stain on his spirit begin to vanish, leaving him with contentment and hope he hadn't felt in many months. He reached out and took Cheryl's hand. "You still have my favorite Mounds in the whole world," he said.

She smiled, though a tear slipped from one eye. "And you'll always be my Almond Joy," she said.

"Good," said Dr. Waters, "I wanted to get you two reconciled again. Now I want to discuss a little proposition with you, Frank. Something I learned about in the future."

Mihalik felt odd misgivings. His heart felt suddenly as cold as a frozen Snickers.

Dr. Waters went on. "Scientists are supposed to be untainted by thoughts of reward; but if, after all the work is done, there *are* financial benefits, what's wrong with collecting them?"

"Nothing, I guess," said Mihalik warily. He saw one or another Dr. Waterses, sitting behind a big desk high in a tall skyscraper, wielding uncheckable power.

"Well, listen. It occurred to me that very soon, when we have all the bugs worked out, there might be a tremendous potential for commercial exploitation."

"What do you mean?"

"I mean tourism, Frank."

Mihalik relaxed. Dr. Waters *wasn't* plotting to rule the world. And he was right; Mihalik had never considered how lucrative an industry might spring up from their efforts. "Tourism?"

"Trips into the past," said Dr. Waters with enthusiasm. It was obvious that he'd thought about this a great deal, that he had all the details worked out. "Just think of it: wouldn't you like to travel around, see the sights of history, leave our shabby little present for a couple of weeks every year?"

"Sure," said Mihalik, "but the past—"

"I know. Like I said, we'll work out the bugs; then you and I can go into business together. The Mihalik-Waters Trans-temporal Travel Agency. How does that sound?"

Mihalik liked the idea. A hero's life is a short and glorious one; but there were always younger, faster kid heroes coming along. Mihalik, truth to tell, didn't have many more good years left in him. It was time to start casting around for a good long-term investment. "Sounds good to me," he said.

"Fine, my boy," said Dr. Waters, smiling, putting out his hand. "We'll shake on it here. You rest up, and when you're ready we'll talk about the Agency some more."

Mihalik stared. "What did you say?" he asked in a strangled voice.

"The Agency. We're founding the Agency."

Mihalik lay back on his pillows and closed his eyes. He massaged his throbbing temples. "Uh huh," he said. "And I guess I have to get to work on a letterhead for the Temporary Underground, too."

"What's that, Frank?" asked Cheryl.

He'd forgotten that she didn't know about any of this. He just waved a tired hand.

"You'll find out," said Dr. Waters gleefully. To Mihalik, it seemed like the man couldn't wait to get started.

About the Author

GEORGE ALEC EFFINGER'S first novel, *What Entropy Means to Me*, was nominated for the Nebula Award. Since then, he has published many more novels, including *The Wolves of Memory, Death in Florence*, and *Heroics*, while maintaining his reputation as one of the finest short story writers in the science fiction field. His short fiction has been collected in *Mixed Feelings, Irrational Numbers, Dirty Tricks*, and *Idle Pleasures. The Bird of Time*, the sequel to *The Nick of Time*, will be published by Doubleday in 1986. He lives in New Orleans, Louisiana.